Yanagi

Yanagi

The Secret Underwater Trade
Between Germany & Japan 1942–1945

by
Mark Felton

Pen & Sword
MARITIME

First published in Great Britain in 2005 by
Pen & Sword Maritime
an imprint of
Pen & Sword Books Ltd
47 Church Street
Barnsley
South Yorkshire
S70 2AS

ISBN 1 84415 167 0

A CIP catalogue record for this book is
available from the British Library.

Typeset by Kirsten Barber,
Leeds, West Yorkshire

Printed and bound in England by
CPI UK

For a complete list of Pen & Sword titles please contact
PEN & SWORD BOOKS LIMITED
47 Church Street, Barnsley, South Yorkshire, S70 2AS, England
E-mail: enquiries@pen-and-sword.co.uk
Website: www.pen-and-sword.co.uk

To Fang Fang,

forever in my heart

Contents

Acknowledgements

The author would gratefully like to acknowledge the contributions and kind assistance of the following individuals and organizations without which this project could not have been completed. First, I would like to express my thanks to Brigadier Henry Wilson and all the staff at Pen & Sword Books for their patience, assistance and encouragement concerning my project, and for publishing the end result; many thanks to my editor, Kirsten Barber, for all her hard work and assistance in bringing this project to fruition; also to Jon Wilkinson for the jacket design.

I was assisted by a number of U-boat veterans throughout the research for this book, and I would like to thank Carl Evans for introducing me to Karl Kaiser, formerly of *U-181*; many thanks to Heinz Sandmuller, formerly of *U-35* and *U-234* for generously taking time to answer my questions, and to Arthur Baudzus, formerly of *U-859*, and author of a novel of the same name, for contacting me and assisting me in understanding life aboard a Far East-bound U-boat.

A great debt of thanks to Ted Agar for kindly giving me permission to reproduce photographs from his collection; many thanks to Paul Tidwell, who discovered the wreck of the Japanese submarine *I-52* in the Atlantic, for pointing me in some interesting research directions and answering my questions; many thanks also to Ken Dunn, Hubertus Weggelaar, Ed Dalder, Hans Mair, Fernando Almeida, Howard Cock, Mike Yared, J.T. McDaniel, and the superb *Uboat.net*, the finest website and database available on the subject; to Benjamin Felton for knowing instantly what I was talking about concerning U-boats, for the use of his excellent and growing U-boat book library and for introducing me to *U-534* in Birkenhead where the seeds of this project first began to germinate; to Alex Crawford for filling in the blanks regarding the air battle over *I-29*; and to Ben Mercer for kindly providing my author photograph.

I would like to thank the staff at the following institutions for their kind assistance: the National Archives at Kew; the Albert Sloman Library at the University of Essex; the Federal German Navy (*Bundesmarine*); and the British Library in London.

Finally I would like to thank my wife, Fang Fang, for her love, support and belief in me throughout this project; for all her practical and emotional support; for occasionally acting as an unpaid research assistant and sounding board, and for her infinite patience and encouragement.

Introduction

The best way to gain even a cursory insight into the lives and conditions of service of the men of the U-boat arm of the Second World War German Navy is to spend an afternoon roaming around one of the preserved vessels to be found around the world. Although hardly any examples remain of the 1,171 U-boats of all types commissioned into the German Navy between 1935 and 1945, a little effort and travel can transport one back to the world of the 'Iron Coffins': a world of fetid air, bad food, and the constant tension of imminent attack. For those who want to experience for a fleeting moment the claustrophobic reality of life beneath the waves, U-boats have been preserved in Chicago and at the U-boat Memorial at Laboe in Germany. These boats are pristine museum pieces that have been altered to accommodate modern tourists. For a truly eerie experiment in time-travel, a visit to the hulk of *U-534* in Birkenhead, near Liverpool, provides the uninitiated with an opportunity to experience the stark reality of service aboard a U-boat, and is testimony to the agonized deaths of hundreds of these machines at the hands of Allied air and sea power.

U-534, a Type IXC40 sunk in the Kattegat off Denmark in May 1945 and raised in 1996, is of the same general type and configuration as many of the U-boats discussed throughout this book, a workhorse of long-range hunting and transportation for the German Navy during the Second World War because of its large fuel capacity and extended range. Although *U-534* has no immediate connection with the German operation of U-boats and transport links with the Indian Ocean and Far East, the configuration of the boat none the less recommends it to all as a memorial to courage, tenacity and desperation on the part of the men who crewed these tools of war. To stand in the forward torpedo room of *U-534*, with its insides ravaged by fifty years of contact with salt water, one can visualize the bunks that would have been slung next to the torpedoes suspended in their racks, the busy toing and froing of sixty plus teenagers and men, the smell of unwashed bodies and food on the turn, stumbling through each compartment filled to capacity with boxes and crates of every description – everything permeated by grease, and the smell and taste of engine oil and lubricants. Now imagine, if you will, remaining confined within this steel tube for nearly 200 days, with no relief from the constant fear of attack from above and the unpleasant possibility of death by drowning or worse. It would often take some 200 days of living on one's nerves and a rudimentary diet, never seeing the sun or having the luxury of a wash in fresh water, before a U-boat would reach the steamy tropics, perhaps at Penang in Malaya or Surabaya in Java, completing incredible combat patrols whose purpose was both the interdiction of Allied commerce, and the delivery of secret military equipment and personnel to the Japanese. On arrival in the Far East the Germans could expect a brief respite from immediate death, the chance to repair the battered submarine, overhaul the diesel engines and batteries, and load up all available spaces with a cargo of raw materials bought off the Japanese, essential to the Nazi war effort back home.

For many of the men, the Indian Ocean was also to offer a happy killing ground for U-boats already driven from their traditional hunting grounds in the North Atlantic and North Sea by advances in Allied anti-submarine technology and convoy escorting prowess. Many U-boat skippers, often highly decorated individuals who had made their names in the Battle of the Atlantic, and who, more often than not, proudly wore the insignia of the Knights Cross (Nazi Germany's premier award for courageous service) around their necks, found another chance to prove their skills in a strategic backwater most of us do not associate with the U-boat war. The Japanese, for their part, although to use their submarine fleet very differently from the Germans, also prowled the Indian Ocean, and came as far as the North Atlantic to trade with Nazi Germany.

The traditional hunting of convoys and unescorted merchant ships was conducted alongside the requirements of both Germany and Japan for raw materials, manufactured products, and new and advanced technology, and as Allied air and sea power grew to become irresistible and all-powerful, such a trade between the two nations, code-named the *Yanagi* trade by the Japanese, could not be performed openly by surface merchant ships attempting to run British and American naval blockades. Nor could such a trade be conducted overland, certainly not after the entry of the Soviet Union into the war in 1941. The *Yanagi* trade was forced beneath the waves and was borne primarily on the shoulders of the German U-boat service. Submarines which had not been designed to cope with the added pressures of carrying cargo, but that retained some fighting potential were pressed into service, alongside obsolescent Italian submarines, in order to keep the strategically important *Yanagi* trade alive until the German surrender in May 1945.

The Germans established a network of bases and repair facilities throughout Asia aimed at supplying the requirements of an assortment of submarines. Some of these submarines, such as the long-range Type IX U-cruisers, were engaged in anti-commerce interdiction, while others ran supplies from Europe to Asia and back again, or worked locally transporting spare parts and goods between the network of German and Japanese naval facilities that existed throughout the region. Many of these U-boats were sunk en route to or returning from the Far East, and all boats, regardless of type or purpose, carried *Yanagi* trade goods and technical or diplomatic personnel, who used the U-boats as a form of underwater taxi to shuttle between distant parts of the globe.

The Japanese, although only to dispatch an occasional submarine to Europe, were to lose men and vessels as well, but the bulk of both surface blockade-running operations conducted until 1944 and the submarine-borne trade of 1942–45 was carried out by the Germans, who suffered the greatest losses in terms of men and *matériel*. Both the Third Reich and Imperial Japan, though not maintaining the closest of relationships as allies and having an innate distrust of the other and markedly different war aims, none the less received thousands of tons each of valuable *Yanagi* goods. The Germans prioritized the kinds of raw materials unavailable to them in Europe, and the Japanese benefited from high technology weaponry and other items that kept Germany at the forefront of military technology developments until their surrender. When the war in Europe was over, the Imperial Japanese Navy wasted no time in snatching those U-boats and former Italian submarines lying in ports within their control, and interning their former allies in prison camps, forcing many defeated German crewmen to instruct Japanese submariners on the operation of their former vessels.

Standing in the rusty and silent forward torpedo room or at the chart table in the control room of the Type IXC40 *U-534* is as close as most of us can come to comprehending the enormous effort expended by the Germans on their U-boat offensives, and the closest we can get to understanding the conditions on a boat motoring its way slowly to the Far East in 1944 or 1945. Perhaps the greatest tribute to the hardy Far East U-boat adventurers is the fact that often after spending some 200 days cramped inside a constantly moving steel tube, they would endure a return trip, with some commanders and boats making several forays to the Japanese sphere of operations. But, for most of the boats and crewmen featured in this book, there was to be no happy respite from war. For a significant total, both German and Japanese, the memorial to this interesting facet of the story of the Second World War is the rusting hulks their bones still occupy on the seabed, stretched out through a catalogue of sunken submarines from the North Atlantic to the Strait of Malacca.

This book is by no means the definitive work on this fascinating subject. Rather, it is a survey of the entire German and Japanese cooperative effort at sea during the Second World War. Considerations of space make it impossible to tell the stories of the many U-boats and Japanese submarines that appear on these pages in exhaustive detail. Each story is one of human struggle, endurance and sometimes tragedy, and each would be worthy of lengthy individual service histories. But placed within the context of German–Japanese naval cooperation, each has a story to tell as part of the geo-political, economic and military account of two very different allies attempting to achieve a means of supplying each other's material requirements by the unlikely employment of submarines for the task. This was the secret *Yanagi* trade.

Chapter 1

Laying the Foundations: Submarine Developments in Germany and Japan Between the Wars

The Re-emergence of the U-Boat

The seeds of the massive German U-boat campaign against Allied merchant shipping during the Second World War had been laid at the signing of the Treaty of Versailles on 28 June 1919, the moment Germany was brought to account for the slaughter and destruction of the First World War, and the moment the Allied nations that had defeated her divided up the spoils of war among themselves. Because the U-boat service of the Imperial Navy had been so successful during the First World War, sinking 5,000 Allied ships and taking the lives of around 15,000 people for the loss of 5,000 U-boatmen,[1] the newly reformed German Navy (*Reichsmarine*) of the Weimar Republic was expressly forbidden from designing, constructing or operating submarines of any description. U-boats that were then under construction when the First World War came to an end in 1918 were ordered to be destroyed, and the boats that had been surrendered to the Allies on ceasing hostilities were ordered to be distributed, for the purpose of study, among the navies of the victorious powers: Great Britain, the United States, France, Italy and Japan. Although these navies did subject the former Imperial boats to intensive testing and study, for some inexplicable reason the Allies failed to commandeer the documentary records and archives of the German submarine construction companies, and these were quietly taken over by the *Reichsmarine*.

The new German Navy continued the research and development of underwater technology, thinly disguising their illegal operations under a new naval section with the deliberately misleading title of 'The Torpedo and Mine Inspectorate', based at Kiel. Although Germany could not actually physically construct submarines, her submarine designers and experts became a valuable commercial resource in their own right. The Allied nations could not stop these technical personnel, who were all private citizens, from going abroad to work. Consequently, design work was sold to Japan and cooperative contracts were made with shipyards in Argentina, Italy and Sweden. All of these intrigues were hidden behind a dummy firm named NV Ingenieurskauntor voor Scheepsbouw or IvS, which was set up at The Hague in the Netherlands in 1922. The commander in chief of the *Reichsmarine*, *Admiral* Behnke, provided IvS with defence funding, and this enabled the company to manufacture two modified First World War Type UBIII U-boats for Turkey. Many of the engineers employed by IvS were drawn from Krupp, the large German armaments firm. Heading the IvS board of directors was Dr Hans Techel, formerly head of construction at Germaniawerft, while the post of technical director was filled by a former U-boat skipper, *Korvettenkapitän* Ulrich Blum. As well as fulfilling contracts for Turkey, during 1925 negotiations were ongoing with Spain regarding the construction of several new submarines. The German negotiating team was headed by *Korvettenkapitän* Wilhelm Canaris who was later to head the wartime German military intelligence organization, the *Abwehr*. Canaris recommended that the *Reichsmarine* create a liaison office, under the misleading title of *Ausbildung* or Training, with construction contracts negotiated and administered from within the navy and the building work undertaken outside Germany by IvS. The *Reichsmarine* adopted this system, placing *Admiral* Spindler in charge of the new submarine office. When both completed Turkish boats were launched in 1927, IvS personnel gained practical experience testing the craft and of course this was invaluable secret training for future U-boat operations.[2]

In 1928 the Germans became bolder in their violations of the Treaty of Versailles, quietly establishing a new cover firm in Berlin, Ingeieurbüro für Wirtschaft und Technik GmbH (Igewit). In the meantime, Spindler had begun to create the nucleus of a U-boat training programme for German Navy crews, essential if a new generation of officers and men were to operate the secretly planned boats of a proposed reformed U-boat service. In 1927 theoretical lectures on U-boats had been introduced into the curriculum of officer cadets at the German Naval Academy at Mürwik on the Baltic. Emphasis was placed on learning the tactics and equipment of the First World War, and in developing ideas about where to take

U-boat operations in the post-war environment. A full training programme for senior officer cadets was begun at Kiel in 1929. Spindler's replacement at the secret U-boat section was *Admiral* Schottky, and he quickly realized that theoretical exercises were all well and good, but the students also required practical training on actual submarines. Unfortunately, the construction of elaborate simulators was vetoed on the grounds of cost by the navy, so instead, in 1930, Schottky organized thinly disguised 'tourist' trips made up of students, engineers and retired and serving naval officers, and dispatched them to Finland to receive training on the two boats recently completed for the Finnish Navy (*Vetehinen* and *Vesihiisi*). Construction also continued on the *E1* for the Spanish Navy, but following her completion and launch in 1931 the submarine was damaged. A German testing team, under *Kapitänleutnant* A.D. Brantigam, gained extensive practical experience on the boat at Cadiz, which was the design basis for the later Type 1A U-boat. Brantigam himself had recently returned from Japan, where he had been employed by the Imperial Japanese Navy in the integration of German technology into the development of new submarines.

As early as 1932, during a new programme of German naval modernization, the *Reichsmarine* proposed to construct a fleet of sixteen medium-sized U-boats, and in 1933 established the *Unterseebootsabwehrschüle* (Anti-Submarine Defence School) at Kiel in northern Germany under the command of *Kapitänleutnant* Slevogt. Once again, the establishment's title was deliberately misleading – it was a U-boat crew-training establishment in all but name. Concurrently, submarine designers and engineers continued fulfilling foreign contracts.

A total of five U-boats had been completed by May 1933 for the Finnish Navy, and the *Reichsmarine* actually managed to delay the delivery of the final boat, which was in a similar configuration to the later Type II U-boat, until 1936, thereby allowing intakes from the Anti-Submarine Defence School at Kiel some actual training time on a submarine. This was of course only possible with the tacit collusion of the Finnish Navy, who did not pressure Germany to deliver the final boat too excessively. By November 1934 the component frames of twelve U-boats had been constructed in the Ruhr industrial heartland of Germany. Based on designs provided by IvS, the *Reichsmarine* secretly transferred the frames to the warehouses of shipyards Germaniawerft and Deutschewerke in Kiel in January 1935. The boats' diesel and electric propulsion units and torpedo tubes were secretly manufactured elsewhere in Germany and followed the frames to Kiel shortly afterwards.

Germany began construction of a new fleet of U-boats for the *Reichsmarine* in 1935, after Hitler had given his approval to the scheme. This followed Hitler's announcement on 16 March when he had repudiated the provisions of the Treaty of Versailles, reintroduced conscription in the armed forces, announced the existence of the *Luftwaffe*, and of a programme of naval rearmament.[3] Because the Germans had already secretly been constructing all the necessary components to assemble U-boats prior to Hitler's announcement, Germaniawerft was able to successfully launch the first official U-boat since 1918 on 15 June 1935.[4] A Type IIA coastal submarine designated *U-1*, she was placed under the command of *Kapitänleutnant* Klaus Ewerth. The covert U-boat training establishments were dispensed with and replaced by the *Unterseebootesschülflotille* (U-boat School Flotilla), with an attached technical training unit consisting of six brand-new Type IIA U-boats (*U-1* to *U-6*). At this time the title of the navy was altered from *Reichsmarine* (State Navy) to *Kriegsmarine* (War Navy), indicating clearly the direction of German naval rearmament.

Although Hitler had, following his March announcement of a rearmaments programme for Germany, chosen to ignore the restrictions of the Treaty of Versailles, he was nevertheless keen to remain on good terms with the greatest naval power on earth – Great Britain. The Royal Navy was enormous, with a massive system of bases and fuelling stations spread around the globe. But Hitler also realized that in spite of Britain's military strength, the British government had no intention of committing the country to another war with Germany over violations of a treaty many in Britain thought to have been unnecessarily restrictive. On 18 June 1935 the Anglo-German Naval Treaty was signed, restricting the German Navy to 35 per cent of the strength of the Royal Navy, but permitting Germany to construct submarines for the first time.[5]

It may be noted that Germaniawerft had launched *U-1* on 15 June, during negotiations between Britain and Germany, and it was clear to the British that the Germans were going to construct submarines with or without British approval. On 22 July 1935 the *Kriegsmarine* High Command met with the Defence Minister, *Generalleutnant* Werner von Blomberg, to discuss their proposal to begin construction of a fleet of forty-eight new U-boats, with anticipated completion of the building programme by October 1939. This was duly accepted, with the addition of a forty-ninth projected boat in 1938. The production of U-boats had continued in secret prior to this agreement, allowing the *Kriegsmarine* to swiftly establish its first overt submarine combat unit on 27 September 1935, the 1st U-boat Flotilla '*Weddingen*' at Kiel, under the command of *Fregattenkapitän* Karl Dönitz, a former First World War U-boat skipper.[6]

The personality and energy of Dönitz was to dominate the U-boat Arm from its rebirth as an offensive tool in September 1935 until its surrender in May 1945. Dönitz was born on 16 September 1891 and entered the Imperial German Navy as an officer cadet in 1910. In 1914, and the outbreak of the First World War, Dönitz was serving as a *Leutnant zür See* aboard the light cruiser *Breslau*. The *Breslau*, along with another German warship, was actually at sea, deep in the Mediterranean when war broke out. The two ships sought refuge from the might of the Royal Navy's Mediterranean fleet at Constantinople in Turkey. Turkey, as an ally of Germany, requested the use of the two light cruisers and their crews to bolster her own navy, and Dönitz found himself part of a foreign naval service. This did not particularly suit the young Dönitz, who requested and received permission to return to Germany in 1916 to enter the navy's U-boat War Academy. He was promoted to *Oberleutnant zür See*, and after graduation was appointed as First Watch Officer aboard *U-39*, commanded by the U-boat ace *Kapitänleutnant* Walter Forstmann, based at the port of Pola on the Austro-Hungarian Adriatic coast. Having proved himself on the *U-39*, Dönitz was given his first command on 1 March 1918 – the Type UCII minelayer submarine *UC-25*. In August 1918 he was transferred to command the larger Type UBIII *U-68*, operating out of Pola again. In October 1918 he had been made a prisoner of war in Malta after British escorts sank his boat during an attack on a convoy. Dönitz stayed in the navy after being released from British captivity, joining the *Reichsmarine* of the Weimar Republic. Hitler appointed him *Führer der Unterseeboote* (Leader of U-boats) in 1936, and *Befehlshaber der Unterseeboote* (Commander in Chief of the U-boat service) in 1939.

By September 1938, a year before the outbreak of the Second World War, the *Kriegsmarine* had been furnished with thirty-nine new U-boats, with a further thirty-three then under construction. As if all this were insufficient, in the summer of 1938 German shipyards received contracts to construct a further twenty-five vessels. Planning was also developed for another twenty-six with six more projected in the near future, giving Germany a total late 1939 submarine fleet of 129 vessels. This equalled the tonnage of the Royal Navy's own submarine service – just one of many disturbing developments that stirred the Admiralty in Whitehall. The *Kriegsmarine*, by now under the command of *Grössadmiral* Erich Raeder, constructed submarines under the 'Z Plan', formally adopted on 31 December 1938, and which saw an incremental increase in the strength of Germany's U-boat arm as the years progressed. Accordingly, it was expected that the peacetime navy would possess 162 U-boats by 1943, 230 by 1945 and 247 by 1948. When war came in September 1939, the U-boat service was not quite as well prepared and equipped as might have been expected. Dönitz had available fifty-five U-boats that were combat ready, too few to wage a methodical war of attrition on British merchant ships, which Dönitz had already identified as the best use of his boats. The quality of the available U-boats was also not ideal, being limited to the Type IA and Type IIA coastal boats, with a shortage of the ocean-going Types VII and IX. It was with these limited available forces that Dönitz was able to commence a vigorous and aggressive campaign against Allied commerce, during which the British were driven close to having their supply lifelines severed. No less an authority than Winston Churchill was to comment later that the only thing which really worried him during the Second World War was the U-boat threat.

Japan's Submarine Force

Japan, as an ally of Britain and the United States during the First World War, benefited technologically from the German surrender in 1918. Seven former U-boats (all subsequently scrapped) were transferred to the Imperial Japanese Navy in 1919,[7] and sent to the giant Yokosuka Naval Base, located south of Tokyo. Schemes for designing and constructing their own submarines were under way at this time, and the Japanese intended to integrate excellent German design work and build this into their own submarine programme, with the assistance of former U-boat officers such as Brantigam, and other designers and technicians. By the summer of 1919, German specialists had already begun to arrive in Japan, and with some alarm American intelligence 'claimed that by 1920 "over 800 submarine building specialists, etc. have gone to Japan." Engineers and ex-U-boat officers were most sought after, commanding the highest salaries.'[8] These German experts forming the main body of the submarine warfare 'brain-drain' from Germany were employed almost exclusively by the Kawasaki Company.

The Japanese decided to develop a submarine force based upon three basic types of boat. The first, the *Junsen* Type, was developed from features taken directly from the U-boats they had been awarded in 1918, also incorporating design elements of the British K-class submarine of the First World War. Eighteen of this class of submarine were constructed for the Royal Navy beginning in 1916. Each vessel displaced 1,883 tons surfaced, was 338 feet in length, and was capable of 23 knots surfaced or 9 knots submerged. The K-class was powered on the surface by steam turbines instead of the more usual diesel engines. This gave the class the required speed to keep pace with the fleet, and they were designed primarily to interdict surface warships. The Japanese interest in the construction of fleet submarines demonstrates their notion that the submarine was a tool to be employed almost exclusively as an underwater 'cruiser', and not a vessel for dedicated commerce raiding. For the Royal Navy the K-class proved to be a disaster. The vessels required around five minutes to submerge, handled terribly, and were so prone to accidents that the British lost five during peacetime. Their torpedoes would also prove to be practically useless against their intended targets – massively armoured warships of the period.

The Japanese were, and remain, exceptionally good at taking Western-invented products and improving on them to produce a far superior end product. This process was applied to the First World War technology at their disposal, allowing the Japanese to turn out modern submarines that would play an important role in the coming war. The Japanese were to design and construct a multitude of submarine types, far more diverse than the Germans, though not as technically advanced. From the British K-class the Japanese developed two individual submarines, KD1 and KD2 (*Kaidai*) prototypes that would eventually lead to the development of the *Kaidai* Type fleet submarine built between 1924 and 1939. Thirty-three boats of this type were constructed in seven successive variants, operating as fleet submarines. The British L-class submarine would form the design template for the L-3 Type, three being built from 1921 onwards, though they would be relegated to training after 1941. Nine examples of the L-4 Type, which was basically the British L-class with stronger torpedo armament, were built between 1922 and 1926.

The *Junsen* Type boats were primarily reconnaissance submarines. They were designed to operate independently, basically to replace cruisers in the role of fleet reconnaissance. To this end, they were designed to accommodate a floatplane to extend their scouting potential, which was stored on board inside a waterproof hangar located next to the conning tower. The *Junsen* Type was double hulled, an amalgamated design of the German U-cruiser submarines of 1917, and the *Kaidai* Type prototype submarines of the early 1920s. Three successive series of *Junsen* Type submarines were constructed between 1929 and 1938. Problems with the type included bad submerged handling because of the large hull, which measured 320 feet by a little over 30 feet in width, and a very slow crash-dive speed. Of the eight boats constructed, all were lost during the war.

The Japanese developed a fleet, or long-range submarine type, the *Kaidai*, whose design came out of the *Junsen*, and the earlier *Kaidai* prototype boats. The *Kaidai* boats were larger to allow for improved cooperation with surface ships of the battle fleet, and for anti-commerce actions along likely enemy sea routes. *Kaidai* Type submarines were designed to operate as part of a flotilla, and their larger displacement would enable them to operate with the main fleet.

The Type-A was another cruiser submarine design, derived from the *Junsen 3* Type of 1934. Four were constructed, each being 2,919 tons surfaced, a little over 373 feet in length, having a crew of 114 and a range of 16,000 miles at 16 knots surfaced.

Another type of Japanese submarine, a medium type known as the KT (*Kai-toku-chu*) Type, had been developed from much earlier Schneider-Laubeuf French boats of 1917. Because of their slow speed and age the four boats of this class were relegated to training before the war.

More modern types entered service shortly before the war. These were double-hulled coastal types ordered under the 1940 and 1941 building programme, designated the *Kaisho* Type. They were designed for coastal patrols in home waters, and in the defence of naval bases. Eighteen examples were built, and although perfectly designed for anti-commerce work, all were destroyed in fleet actions, the Japanese never deploying them to their full potential. The

Japanese were very keen, along with the development of surface aircraft carriers, to utilize fully the potential for aircraft carried aboard submarines. Accordingly the I-13 class and I-400 class submarine aircraft carriers were designed and built. The I-400 class submarines were enormous for the time; in fact at 400 feet in length and 5,223 tons displacement they were the largest submarines in the world. Each boat carried three floatplanes modified into bombers, and the submarines' primary mission was to attack the west coast of the United States, and the strategically important Panama Canal.

When Japan opened hostilities against the United States in December 1941 the Imperial Japanese Navy possessed forty-one cruiser and fleet-type submarines, but twenty of these boats were obsolete. Another twenty boats derived from all three classes were under construction in Japan.

All Japanese submarines came under the control of the 6th Fleet, which had an additional three surface cruisers that served as flag ships. Following rapid Japanese advances at the beginning of the Second World War, the 6th fleet was based at Kwajalein in the Marshall Islands.[9]

Notes

1. Miller, D., *U-Boats: History, Development and Equipment 1914–1945*, Conway Maritime Press, London, 2000, p. 14.
2. *Ibid.*, pp. 16–17.
3. Mollo, A., *The Armed Forces of World War II*, MacDonald & Co. (Publishers) Ltd, London, 1981, pp. 2–15.
4. Miller, D., *U-Boats: History, Development and Equipment 1914–1945*, Conway Maritime Press, London, 2000, pp. 20–1.
5. Mollo, A., *The Armed Forces of World War II*, MacDonald & Co. (Publishers) Ltd, London, 1981, p. 13.
6. For an excellent account of Dönitz's First World War activities see: Stern, R., *Battle Beneath the Waves: U-Boats at War*, Cassell & Co., Chapter 5, UB68.
7. Miller, D., *U-Boats: History, Development and Equipment 1914–1945*, Conway Maritime Press, London, 2000, p. 14.
8. Boyd, C. & Yoshida, A., *The Japanese Submarine Force and World War II*, Naval Institute Press, Shrewsbury, 1996, p. 14.
9. Mollo, A., *The Armed Forces of World War II*, MacDonald & Co. (Publishers) Ltd, London, 1981, p. 261.

Chapter 2

Campaign Beneath the Waves: U-Boat and Japanese Submarine Operations 1939–1942

The German U-Boat Campaign in the West 1939–1942

The German establishment of U-boat bases in the Far East, and U-boat operations in the Indian Ocean and Pacific, only occurred as a result of the *Kriegsmarine*'s failure to achieve victory in the Battle of the Atlantic. However, at the beginning of the war in 1939 Germany placed great faith in a combined strategy of *Blitzkrieg* on land, and a comprehensive U-boat offensive aimed at strangling Britain's supply lines to the rest of the world. While remarkably successful in the first strategy, allowing for the complete German domination of Western Europe by 1940, the second strategy was to produce for Germany very mixed results, eventually forcing Dönitz to look elsewhere from 1943 onwards in the campaign to destroy the Allied merchant lifelines.

When Britain declared war on Germany, following the German invasion of Poland on 3 September 1939, Dönitz had already positioned thirty-nine of his operational U-boats at strategic points in the Eastern Atlantic and North Sea. These U-boats managed to account for around one hundred ships that were in the process of making for safe ports, but many more were left to pass unharmed because U-boat skippers were strictly adhering to operational orders that categorized the types of ships which were considered valid and legal targets at this early stage of the war. U-boats were permitted to attack without warning warships, troop transports, armed merchant vessels of the belligerent powers, other vessels which were accompanied by warships or were travelling in convoys, and any ships identified as conducting warlike activities, or carrying weapons or other war supplies. On the very day that war commenced between Germany and Britain, *U-30*, commanded by

Kapitänleutnant Fritz-Julius Lemp, torpedoed and sank the liner *Athenia* (13,581 tons). Lemp argued that he believed the vessel was an armed merchant ship, as she was zig-zagging, which was against regulations for innocent merchantmen to do, but this oversight cost the lives of 112 civilians. The period that followed was for the U-boat service a 'happy time', when some skippers made for themselves incredible reputations and the U-boat ace was born again. One such man was *Kapitänleutnant* Günther Prien, who in a show of amazing seamanship and nerve, managed to infiltrate *U-47* into the Royal Navy's base at Scapa Flow in the Orkney Islands during the night of 14 October 1939 and sank the Royal Sovereign-class battleship HMS *Royal Oak* (25,750 tons), killing 883 men. Incredible though his feat was, unrestricted interdiction of British merchant ships (the real purpose of the U-boat fleet) was not permitted until November 1940, Hitler harbouring hopes of a peace with Britain instead of a continuation of the war in the West. Even though some restrictions were maintained over the validity of certain types of target, and considering the fact that the U-boats were beset with untold torpedo failures, Dönitz's boats managed to sink over 250 ships, equating to approximately 855,000 tons, between September 1939 and February 1940.

The fall of France in June 1940 provided the Germans with a series of new naval bases on the Atlantic coast, and the *Kriegsmarine* was incredibly quick in securing these facilities. The first fighting boat to arrive was Lemp's *U-30*, which put into Lorient on 7 July to restock its supply of torpedoes. The capture of Lorient, Brest, La Pallice, St Nazaire, La Rochelle and Bordeaux was strategically advantageous to Germany for the simple reason that prior to the fall of France, U-boats based at Kiel and Wilhelmshaven in Germany had been forced to negotiate a well-defended stretch of water off Scotland in order to traverse the British Isles and hunt, the English Channel having been abandoned as a transit route or hunting ground following the loss of several U-boats. The new French bases also enabled U-boats to remain on station for longer periods of time, because of the shortened distance to refuel, rearm and revictual.

The period between June and October 1940 was known in the U-boat service as the 'happy time', when U-boats systematically butchered poorly defended convoys, accounting for an incredible 282 ships (1,490,000 tons). The loss to the *Kriegsmarine* was only seven

U-boats, indicating the poor state of British anti-submarine defences. However, the British were to score a notable victory on 7 May 1941 when they successfully forced Lemp, now in command of *U-110*, to the surface. The crew abandoned the slowly foundering U-boat. This gave a Royal Navy boarding party enough time to retrieve the U-boat's top secret code books, confidential papers, and most prized of all, an Enigma machine which had been left ready to send a coded message. The machine and associated materials were passed to Bletchley Park, the British code decryption centre, where Enigma was eventually cracked.

The breaking of the Enigma code by the British was to severely hamper the later ability of the U-boats to take an effective part in the war, and also enabled the British and the Americans to hamper both the surface and sub-surface *Yanagi* trade between the Germans and the Japanese. The British also perfected and improved upon the monitoring of U-boat wireless traffic in a bid to provide the Admiralty with up-to-date information on U-boat dispositions. When combined with Enigma, this enabled the Allies to re-route convoys away from hunting U-boats.

As British anti-submarine defences stiffened during 1941, the United States, which had maintained active neutrality though provided the Royal Navy with convoy escort vessels through the Lend-Lease programme, found herself attacked elsewhere. On 7 December 1941 the Imperial Japanese Navy launched a devastating 'surprise' attack on the United States Pacific Fleet stationed at Pearl Harbor in Hawaii. This 'Day of Infamy' was to herald a second 'happy time' for the U-boats, as Dönitz dispatched long-range Type VIICs and Type IXCs to begin hunting off the east coasts of the United States and Canada. The United States inadvertently aided Dönitz's plan by refusing to introduce convoys until the slaughter had begun, and, so secure was mainland United States in its belief of invulnerability to air attack that no blackout precautions were established on the east coast. This meant that ships plying the coast were conveniently silhouetted against the brightly lit towns and cities, aiding U-boat skippers enormously in launching their attacks. Dönitz dispatched two groups of U-boats to American and Canadian waters to wreak havoc as part of Operation *Paukenschlag* (Drumbeat): a small group of Type IXCs who would patrol off the eastern seaboard of the United States, and *Gruppe Zeithen*, consisting of seven smaller Type VIIC U-boats, positioned off Newfoundland. Positioned in the

Atlantic were Type XIV U-tankers, a type known as a *Milchküh* (Milkcow), whose job was to supply particularly the Type VIIs, which were not designed to operate so far from their bases. It was to be a foretaste of the elaborate refuelling net necessary for U-boats to operate successfully in the Indian Ocean after 1943. The operation was an unmitigated success from the German point of view, and the second 'happy time' certainly lived up to its name. The U-boats of Operation Drumbeat sank 567 ships, equating to almost 3 million tons, between January and June 1942, the Germans only losing twenty-one submarines.

It was inevitable that the United States and the Royal Canadian Navy would eventually get their acts together, but Dönitz was to prove a wily and slippery opponent. Once the campaign against the North American eastern seaboard began to turn more in the Allies' favour, Dönitz ordered operations to be transferred into the largely undefended Caribbean Sea and the interdiction of the oil industry. U-boats boldly shelled oil installations in the Gulf of Mexico and sank tankers off the Dutch colonies of Aruba and Curacao, and the British islands of Trinidad and Tobago. U-boat operations in the Western Atlantic, the Caribbean and the Gulf of Mexico were aided greatly when the Germans routinely changed the Enigma code from 'Hydra' to 'Triton' in February 1942. Ten months would elapse before the British successfully penetrated 'Triton'.

Dönitz now deployed the Wolf Pack tactic in the Atlantic, which saw groups of U-boats operating together to interdict a single convoy and hopefully achieve the maximum amount of damage. The German Signal Intelligence Service, *B-Dienst,* worked closely with the U-boats in the hunting down of convoys to attack, enabling Dönitz to form the packs at sea and send them in to attack particular convoys. This was the beginning of the Battle of the Atlantic proper, the great duel between the Allies and Germany over the survival of transatlantic trade, and ultimately of Britain's ability to fight the war. Although Wolf Pack tactics were initially reasonably successful, getting under way from September 1941, overall U-boat losses rose to over forty by the end of 1942. The Germans had managed to sink a further 1,800,000 tons of Allied shipping.

As the Allies rapidly improved their methods for detecting U-boats through better radar and radio direction finding equipment, coupled with the breaking of the Enigma naval code and the use of Ultra intelligence decrypts of intercepted German radio traffic, the writing was on the wall for a *Kriegsmarine* victory in the Battle of the Atlantic. Ultra enabled the Allies to pinpoint the positions of U-boats and intercept the *Milchküh* tanker submarines, which coupled with much stronger and more efficient convoy escorts meant higher U-boat losses for fewer gains. The Germans required better U-boats with which to turn the tide against the technological superiority of Allied anti-submarine countermeasures.

Dönitz was forced to look elsewhere, to the South Atlantic and Indian Ocean, to continue his U-boat offensive. As 1942 drew to a close, the Germans were in danger of having their U-boats swept from the Atlantic, and early to mid-1943 was to see the strategic situation deteriorate further as the mid-Atlantic 'Gap', a huge area of ocean out of the range of Allied aircraft patrols, was closed with the arrival of American escort carriers. The 'Gap' was where Dönitz had concentrated his Wolf Packs to attack convoys bereft of air cover half way across the Atlantic. It was during this period of uncertainty that Dönitz began to seriously consider overtures made by the equally overstretched Japanese concerning basing some German U-boats in the Far East. The Indian Ocean certainly appeared to be a backwater regarding convoy protection and Allied warship activity, and it was an important transit area for Allied supply convoys. The scene was set for another German 'happy time' in the tropics, far from the war in Europe.

The Japanese Submarine Campaign in the Far East 1941–1942

Japanese submarines actually opened hostilities against the United States. On the night of 6 December 1941, twelve Japanese submarines quietly took position in an arc south-east and south-west of Pearl Harbor, Hawaii. Five other submarines moved stealthily towards the US Pacific Fleet's anchorage, each carrying a two-man midget submarine secured to the casing. The task of the midgets was to penetrate the harbour defences and attack the fleet while the larger I-Class submarines lay in wait for any American surface craft that steamed close to the islands. They would also report weather conditions to the Imperial Fleet, which was preparing to launch its carrier aircraft against the base, and, somewhat unrealistically, recover any downed Japanese pilots lost during the air attack.

None of the five midget submarines returned from their missions, all being sunk either outside of Pearl Harbor or just inside by

American patrol craft. The first was sunk by the destroyer USS *Ward* on the morning of 7 December just outside the harbour buoys by a depth charge attack, the first fighting between Japanese and US forces in the Second World War.

The Japanese submarine force was smaller than the German U-boat fleet and it was intended primarily not for attacking enemy merchant shipping, but for destroying Allied warships and supporting operations by Japanese ground forces throughout the Pacific. The Japanese submarine force was well-equipped, well-trained and superbly led, but the force played only a minor role in the Pacific War, its biggest success prior to the end of 1942 being the torpedoing of the aircraft carrier USS *Saratoga* 500 miles west of Pearl Harbor in January, one of the carriers the Japanese had failed to destroy on 7 December 1941. The *Saratoga* survived to fight again. This attack reinforced the Japanese strategy of using submarines primarily as vessels to attack warships, and for reconnaissance. Imperial General Headquarters never moved to redirecting its submarine force to dedicated commerce raiding, even though the Japanese sent their submarines far and wide. For example, on the day the Imperial Fleet attacked Pearl Harbor, the *I-16* was off the western coast of the United States, not interdicting commerce, but scouting. She did sink a single American merchant ship that same day, but this was incidental to her primary mission.

As related, many of the larger Japanese I-boats were fitted with an aircraft, the Yokosuka E14Y1 reconnaissance floatplane, housed in a waterproof hangar on deck. This enabled the Japanese to return to Pearl Harbor to assess the damage to Battleship Row, and to launch reconnaissance flights over the west coast of the United States, Alaska and the Aleutian Islands, as well as two air raids on Oregon (see Appendix I). In March 1942 submarines off the Frigate Shoals refuelled Japanese floatplane bombers that attempted to bomb Pearl Harbor for a second time.

Japanese submarines were surprised by Allied improvements in radar and radio direction finding techniques, which were beginning to take a toll of U-boats in the Atlantic. Japanese submarines were ill-equipped to detect Allied countermeasures, and, as will be seen, the boats employed on the long journeys to occupied France, bringing trade goods to the Germans, were routinely equipped with the latest *Kriegsmarine* radar detectors to help them survive Allied anti-submarine measures in the Bay of Biscay. In the same way that the British had broken the German naval Enigma code, so the Americans, centred on the Naval Combat Intelligence Unit at Pearl Harbor, broke Japanese naval codes, enabling them to ascertain the whereabouts of Japanese surface and submarine assets.

The Japanese continued to score some submarine successes even though the naval war in the Pacific was beginning to turn against them, following the invasion of Guadalcanal in 1942. On 13 November the *I-26* sank the cruiser USS *Juneau*, killing most of her crew, but Imperial General Headquarters directed that submarines were to be used in evacuating the Solomon Islands instead of launching a coordinated campaign against Allied commerce, which certainly in the earlier stages of the war in the Pacific could have resulted in the isolation of Australia. The US Navy used its Pacific submarine force to blockade Japan, sinking most of the Japanese merchant fleet by 1945 and cutting the nation off from critical supplies.

By late 1942 large numbers of Japanese submarines were running supplies to the garrisons defending New Guinea – such was to be the fate of a large part of this potent fighting force for the remainder of the war, used up as a glorified taxi and supply service, or in their traditional role as fleet scouts unable to cope with encounters with Allied anti-submarine forces.

German–Japanese Naval Cooperation: Diplomacy and Communications

In September 1940, Germany, Italy and Japan had signed the document known as the Tripartite Pact. This pact between the three countries created the Axis partnership in which the nations were supposed to broadly cooperate together in a war and respect one another's territorial gains. Following the Japanese attack on the United States Pacific Fleet on 7 December 1941, Germany and Italy declared war on the United States, even though neither the Germans nor the Italians were obligated to do so under the terms of the Tripartite Pact with Japan.

The navies of Japan, Germany and Italy had no common grand strategy, even though all elements of the Axis partnership were fighting for the defeat of the Allied nations, with the exception of Japan whose war was primarily with the United States, Great Britain, and the British Empire and Dominions, and did not include the Soviet Union until 1945. The Soviet Union remained at peace with Japan until August 1945, which was the result of the Red Army's success in resisting a strong Japanese border incursion into Mongolia during the spring and summer of 1939. The Japanese had no intention of aping Hitler and fighting a war on two fronts. As the international situation developed, with conflict likely for both nations elsewhere, Japan and the Soviet Union were anxious to avoid further fighting and so concluded the Japan–Soviet Non-Aggression Pact in April 1941. Shigenori Togo, the Japanese Foreign Minister, in an address to the *Diet* (Japan's parliament) in November 1941 stated:

> The Japanese-Soviet neutrality pact, concluded in April this year, is also intended to secure safety in the north ... Although hostilities subsequently broke out between Germany and the Soviet Union, our government have steadfastly maintained this policy of preserving security in the north.[1]

As mentioned, Germany declared war on the United States immediately following Japan's attack on Pearl Harbor, but Japan had not attacked the Soviet Union in support of Operation *Barbarossa*, the German invasion of Russia, which had begun on 22 June 1941.

An agreement was initialled between Germany and Japan regarding proposed *Yanagi* trade exchanges on 8 November 1942, however this agreement was not formally ratified until 2 March 1944, by which time the exchange system was already well developed between the two countries. As for relations between Japan and the Soviets, Stalin honoured the terms of the Non-Aggression Pact until August 1945, just weeks before the ultimate surrender of Imperial Japan, when Red Army forces routed the under-strength units of the Japanese Kwangtung Army occupying northern China.

Turning to their new allies in the West, the Japanese followed the Tripartite Pact by signing the German–Japanese Military Agreement in Berlin on 18 January 1942. However, many historians who have analysed German–Japanese diplomatic and military cooperation during the Second World War have criticized much of the appearance of cooperation as window dressing. In reality, the efforts of the Germans and the Japanese to even establish a cooperative effort with clearly defined goals amounted to remarkably little. The Tripartite Pact provided for the establishment of technical commissions designed to implement strategic plans, but they met only for the sake of form, and military talks had not been staged by the time of Japan's attack on Pearl Harbor. The joint commissions had virtually no influence over the course or aims of the German–Japanese alliance, this role being usurped by the German Foreign Minister, Joachim von Ribbentrop, and the Japanese Ambassador to Berlin, General Hiroshi Oshima. These two men could not agree on the direction the alliance should follow and their views also diverged from those of their leaders. For example, even though Japan had been defeated by the Red Army at the Battle of Halhin Gol in Mongolia between May and September 1939, and had subsequently negotiated a non-aggression treaty in 1941 with Stalin, Oshima advocated a joint German–Japanese offensive against the Soviet Union. Both the Imperial Japanese Navy, who looked to the Pacific as the arena of future conflict, and the Imperial Household Agency who advised Emperor Hirohito, opposed such a plan. Ribbentrop went even further, advocating an alliance of Germany, Japan *and* the Soviet Union against Great Britain, running completely contrary to the core values and war aims of Hitler and the Nazi government, which was the defeat of 'Jewish Bolshevism' in the East.

Such was the poor state of diplomatic relations between Germany and Japan that neither side told the other very much about their military strategy and operations. Liaison conferences were held in Germany between 18 October and 5 November 1941, but the first the Germans were to hear of the Japanese attack on Pearl Harbor on 7 December was, incredibly, on the radio – reported by the BBC! The Germans had also left the Japanese largely in the dark concerning Operation *Barbarossa*, the invasion of the Soviet Union, which began in June 1941. This is borne out in US Army G-2 intelligence reports of the time, the American Ambassador to Tokyo reporting in a telegram to the State Department in Washington DC on 27 July 1941 that:

> Former Foreign Minister Matsuoka informed the Turkish Ambassador that he had cabled Ribbentrop 48 hours in advance of the Nazi attack on the Soviet asking if there were any truth in reports of such an attack and Ribbentrop replied with a categorical denial.[2]

This reflected the other level of the German–Japanese alliance – a level of distrust between the two nations, and a reflection of the distrust between Europeans and Asians at this time. The Americans, immediately prior to the unexpected Japanese assault on Hawaii, had been monitoring relations between the Germans and the Japanese, particularly on German attitudes towards the Japanese as a nation, and as a people. Brigadier General Sherman Miles, Acting Assistant Chief of Staff of the US Army's G-2 Intelligence Department, wrote to the Army Chief of Staff on 30 July 1941 recording some startling observations. Miles noted that the American Ambassador in Tokyo had, on 23 July, pointed 'to a trend in Japanese public and private opinion indicating that Japan is no longer a happy partner in the Tripartite Agreement'.[3] The Ambassador also stated that:

> if the Germans run true to form they would sooner or later overshoot their mark in Japan, and that the proud and sensitive Japanese people would eventually realize the fundamental contempt and scarcely concealed arrogance of the Germans for the Yellow Race.[4]

The reports of the US State Department and G-2 also contain some sinister utterances on the part of German diplomats, which perhaps shed some light on the very difficult relationship the Germans and Japanese maintained throughout the Second World War. For example, the United States Minister to the Thai Royal Court reported to the Secretary of State on 26 July 1941 stating that the Prime Minister of Thailand:

> had informed him [the American Minister] that Lt. Col. Scholl, German Military Attaché, had called and warned him [the Prime Minister] against 'going too far' with Japan, 'because', said the German Attaché 'you cannot trust Japan.' The German Attaché stated further that 'Germany will settle with Japan after she has won the war in Europe.'[5]

The closer relationship between Thailand and Japan was probably a reference to the recent purchase by Thailand of modern Japanese bomber aircraft as part of a modernization of the Royal Thai Air Force. This particular snippet of information was considered by America so important to the desired aim of shattering the German–Japanese alliance that G-2 recommended that it should have been placed in the hands of the Japanese Ambassador to Washington DC.

23

Apart from talking on a diplomatic level, the navies of Germany and Japan needed to be able to communicate securely with each other if joint operations were to proceed successfully. It would be a futile and costly exercise to dispatch surface blockade-running ships loaded down with expensive cargoes, through waters teeming with both friendly and hostile warships and submarines. The likelihood of the Japanese sinking merchantmen or later U-boats engaged in the *Yanagi* trade, and Japanese submarines travelling to Europe being accidentally destroyed by the Germans, would have been likely had no steps been taken to clearly identify the vessels concerned, their destinations, routes and speeds. To achieve this desired aim, a joint communication plan was signed between the *Kriegsmarine* and the Imperial Japanese Navy in Berlin on 11 September 1942. The agreement grew out of the 18 January 1942 German–Japanese Military Agreement.

Even the relatively simple exercise of designing and implementing a joint communications framework that would facilitate useful trade exchanges between the two nations was to stretch the boundaries of cooperation. According to Weierud,[6] the agreement provided a detailed framework on how both navies could communicate with each other, and what means should be utilized to facilitate such communications. The agreement, as signed between *Vizeadmiral* Erhard Maertens, Director of the Naval Communication Service, and Rear Admiral Tadao Yokoi, Japanese Naval Attaché in Berlin, would lead to the encryption of naval communications traffic between the two navies through the German T-Enigma machine. The Germans christened the system TIRPITZ, the Japanese modifying this name to TIRUPITSU, which was easier for the oriental tongue to pronounce. From the beginning, both the Germans and the Japanese feared, with good reason as it turned out, that the naval Enigma code was compromised. Aside from the fear of Allied penetration of Enigma was the problem of actually constructing and delivering the necessary machines to enable communication between the two allies in the first place. The Imperial Japanese Navy had placed an order with the Germans for 800 T-Enigma machines, but never received the required amount.[7] There were delays in the design and delivery of the machines, and because of the naval blockade in place against the Reich and the Allied bombing campaign, the Germans experienced difficulties in procuring an adequate supply of materials to ensure that construction met demand. In the meantime two manual systems were invented for use in German–Japanese naval communications, receiving the code-names SUMATRA and TOGO.

The T-Enigma system, properly the 'Japanese–German Joint Use Code No. 3', was the only system that was ever actually used. According to Weierud, some twenty messages were sent by Japanese submarines on arrival off the coast of France between March and August 1944. The Japanese submarine *I-30*, for example, departed from Lorient in occupied France on 22 August 1942 with fifty T-Enigma machines aboard, only to be sunk outbound from Singapore (discussed in more detail later). Only sixteen of the machines had been offloaded in Singapore previous to the disaster. It has also subsequently appeared clear that Germany was not in a position to manufacture sufficient numbers of T-Enigma machines to facilitate the completion of secure German–Japanese naval communications, and Weierud notes that on 18 May 1943 Tokyo informed Berlin that they had cancelled the purchase of manufacturing rights for the Enigma-type cipher machine, most probably the T-Enigma. Germany and Japan immediately began talks concerning a new machine that would be more secure; especially as considerable signals traffic was expected over the system, the Japanese Naval Attaché settling for an order of 400 new A-Enigma machines. The *Yanagi* submarines were subsequently employed transporting the new A-Enigma machines to Japan as part of their cargoes. The Japanese submarine *I-29*, which arrived back in Japan on 16 April 1944 from a successful *Yanagi* trade run to Bordeaux in occupied France (discussed in detail later), carried ten of the new machines.

Strangely enough, production of the older T-Enigma machines had been continued by Germany and they were still being prepared for shipment to Japan during the summer of 1944. According to Hamer, Sullivan and Weierud,[8] several of these top secret machines were captured in a warehouse near the German U-boat base at Lorient during the Allies' advance from Normandy in August 1944, with probably around a total of seventy examples of these machines falling into Allied hands.

The Japanese left it too late in the war to move to encrypting communications traffic using cipher machines, and regardless of the 1942 joint communications agreement, Germany suffered profound difficulties in actually manufacturing and delivering the machines for them to facilitate effective secret communications between the two navies, which would have been of inestimable value in the shipment of *Yanagi* trade goods by submarine between Europe and the Far East.

Communications was to prove just one aspect of a succession of problems encountered by the Germans and the Japanese in attempting to coordinate their military efforts, and was to highlight part of the problem that the Germans and the Japanese were simply not natural allies, each remaining wary of the other's plans and technology, and often not particularly keen on sharing ideas or communicating with each other. Relations between these erstwhile allies were to remain tense throughout the course of the war. From surviving documentation the Japanese appear to have felt that the Germans were always trying to dominate the relationship, 'that Japan is being treated as a satellite, if not as a dependent',[9] not helping the alliance of two massive war machines bent on dominating their respective spheres of influence.

Notes

1. 'Japanese Foreign Minister Togo Shigenori's Address to the Imperial Diet', 17 November 1941, *New York Times*.
2. Miles to Chief of Staff, 30 July 1941, Exhibits of the Joint Committee, PHA, Pt. 14, Exhibit No. 33 Military Intelligence Estimates Prepared by G-2, War Department, Washington DC.
3. *Ibid.*, Miles to Chief of Staff, 30 July 1941.
4. *Ibid.*, Miles to Chief of Staff, 30 July 1941.
5. US Minister Thailand to Secretary of State, 26 July 1941, Exhibits of the Joint Committee, PHA, Pt. 14, Exhibit No. 33 Military Intelligence Estimates Prepared by G-2, War Department, Washington DC.
6. Weierud, F., 'TIRPITZ and the Japanese–German Naval War Communication Agreement', *Cryptology*, Volume 20, No. 3, Summer 1999.
7. *Ibid.*
8. Hamer, D., Sullivan, G. & Weierud, F., 'Enigma Variations: An Extended Family of Machines', *Cryptology*, Volume 22, No. 3, July 1998.
9. US Ambassador Tokyo to Secretary of State, Washington DC, 23 July 1941, Exhibits of the Joint Committee, PHA, Pt. 14, Exhibit No. 33 Military Intelligence Estimates Prepared by G-2, War Department, Washington DC.

Chapter 3

German Raiders, the *Yanagi* Trade and the Blockade-Runners

German Auxiliary Cruiser Operations in the Indian Ocean and the Far East

German mercantile raiders, also designated auxiliary cruisers because of their armament, operated throughout the Indian Ocean, South Atlantic and Far East during the Second World War. The eleven converted merchantmen deployed as raiders by the *Kriegsmarine*[1] netted a large tally of Allied ships, and posed a very considerable threat until they themselves were ultimately hunted down and destroyed. Tactically, the operations of each raider depended upon the personality of the respective captain, and had a direct bearing upon the survivability of each ship as Allied anti-surface forces grew in strength and technological aids as the war progressed.

One of the most notable raiders was the *Michel*, under the command of Knights Cross holder *Korvettenkapitän* Helmut von Rückteschell (formerly commander of the raider *Widder*). The vessel was originally constructed as a freighter, built by Danziger Werft in 1939, and operated by the Gydnia-American Shipping Line as the *Bielsko*. Seized in Danzig at the outbreak of war, she was renamed the *Michel* and taken into auxiliary service with the German Navy. The 10,900 ton ship was converted to carry two Arado Ar 196A-3 spotter floatplanes and was fitted with six 5.9in guns and a single 4.1in gun, as well as a secondary armament consisting of four 37mm and four 20mm anti-aircraft guns. She also mounted six torpedo tubes, making for a formidable vessel crewed by 400 men.

The *Michel*'s first cruise was an unmitigated success and she was the eighth such raider to leave Germany. Departing from Kiel on 9 March 1942, on 19 April she sank her first ship, the British tanker

Patella (7,468 tons), and destroyed another tanker, the American *Connecticut* (8,684 tons) on 22 April. On May Day, after chasing, engaging and failing to sink the *Menelaus* (which ended up being the only merchant ship to survive an encounter with a German merchant raider during the war, perhaps indicating the effectiveness of this form of merchant ship attrition and the professionalism of the raiders' skippers), an embarrassed von Rückteschell decided in future only to attack Allied shipping at night. The technique he developed was to approach his prey from the darkest part of the horizon, and with gun crews standing by at 'Action Stations', have a star shell sent up to illuminate the target. The gunners would then blast the unfortunate merchantman out of the water, although on several occasions the merchant vessel would immediately surrender to allow the crew time to take to the boats. On board the *Michel* was a small, high-powered motor launch named the *Esau*, an early version of what has subsequently developed into the RIB (Rigid Inflatable Boat). It was used to stalk prey ahead of the main vessel. It was armed with torpedoes, so could attack merchant ships independently of the 'mother ship', and could also be armed with depth charges, providing the *Michel* with a formidable anti-submarine escort.

The *Michel's* cruise through the South Atlantic was considerably more successful than most U-boats would ever manage. On 20 May von Rückteschell sank the 4,245-ton Norwegian freighter *Kattegat*, and in June sank two more freighters, the American *George Clymer* (7,176 tons) on 7 June, and the British *Lylepark* (5,186 tons) on 11 June. July proved to be even more fruitful hunting. On the 15th the *Michel* sank the 8,006-ton British passenger ship *Gloucester Castle* and the next day bagged the 7,893-ton American tanker *William F. Humphrey*. On the 17th the 7,984-ton Norwegian tanker *Aramis* was sent to the bottom. Because of the size and space aboard the *Michel* many of the merchant crews from the sinking of these vessels were rescued and made prisoners of war aboard the raider. On 14 August the *Michel* sank the 5,874-ton British freighter *Arabistan* and on 10 September the 7,241-ton British merchantman *Empire Dawn*. The next day witnessed the destruction of another American freighter, the *American Leader* (6,778) tons. The British vessel *Reynolds* (5,113 tons) was dispatched to the deep on 2 November, and just prior to entering the Indian Ocean the *Michel* caught and sank her thirteenth ship of the cruise, the 5,882-ton American freighter *Sawokla*, on 29 November.

Steaming into the Indian Ocean the *Michel* encountered the Greek freighter *Eugenie Livanos* (4,816 tons) on 8 December, and sank her. Christmas 1942 gave way to the fourth year of the war and the *Michel* sank the 7,040-ton British freighter *Empire March* on 2 January 1943. She then steamed back into the South Atlantic to prepare for the journey home. At this stage, von Rückteschell was awarded the Oakleaves to his Knights Cross. In need of fuel and provisions, and carrying a large group of prisoners, the *Michel* needed to head to France, but German Navy command realized that because of increased and more effective Allied air and sea activity against German surface vessels and U-boats throughout the North Atlantic and the Bay of Biscay, it was unlikely that the *Michel* would actually survive a return passage. Accordingly, the *Michel* was ordered to Japan for refuelling and supplies, a decision that would have struck cold fear and dread into the hearts of the British, American, Norwegian and Greek prisoners on board the raider. The *Michel* made her way to Malaya, first dropping anchor at Tandjoengpriok, where the Japanese had laid on a welcome for the crew. The unfortunate civilian prisoners of war were handed over to the Japanese authorities when the ship arrived at Singapore (then renamed Shonan by the Japanese occupying forces), before arriving at Kobe, Japan, on 2 March. The raider was to spend two months refitting and resting at Kobe and Yokohama, but the exertions of command had proved too much for von Rückteschell, who left the ship too exhausted to continue. *Korvettenkapitän* Günther Gumprich, formerly the commander of the raider *Thor*, replaced him.

The *Michel* eased herself out of a bustling Yokohama harbour on 1 May 1943 to begin her second raiding cruise into the Indian Ocean. Off the west coast of Australia, Gumprich encountered and sank the 7,715-ton Norwegian freighter *Hoegh Silberman* on 15 June, and two days later claimed another Norwegian, the 9,940-ton tanker *Ferncastle*. From this position the *Michel* steamed into the Pacific Ocean to hunt, encountering nothing for virtually three months. On 11 September the *Michel* was near Easter Island, and preparing to return to Japan for further supplies, when she found and sank her final victim, the 9,977-ton Norwegian tanker *India*. The next vessel she encountered was no lumbering freighter, and when the *Michel* was only 100 miles off the coast of Japan the American submarine

USS *Tarpon* torpedoed her. Struck by three torpedoes, she sank, taking Gumprich and around 200 crew with her. Subsequently, Berlin complained to Tokyo that an insufficient effort was made by the Japanese authorities to locate and rescue the 200 men who had survived the sinking. Approximately half of these men eventually made it to shore, with the rest succumbing to exhaustion, wounds or the ever-present sharks. However, ships like the *Michel* demonstrated the huge damage just a few raiders could wreak upon Allied merchant shipping, and how widely such craft could operate. It also demonstrates that German–Japanese naval cooperation could be extremely effective in keeping vessels such as the raiders operational and potent far from their bases in Europe, enabling the *Kriegsmarine* to maintain a global reach, if on a limited scale.

Blockade-Running Between the Germans and Japanese 1941–1944

Germany and Japan maintained not only a military alliance throughout the Second World War, which saw their respective forces operating many thousands of miles apart, but also a trade in weapons technology and raw materials. They termed this the *Yanagi* trade, and believed it to be vital to the maintenance of the respective fighting forces of the two countries.

Both Germany and Japan lacked some of the raw materials or technology that each believed would ultimately have contributed to overcoming the massive Allied forces arrayed against them, and so each was determined to carry on this secret trade even in the face of increasing odds and setbacks, and, as outlined previously, even though there was a marked lack of trust between the two nations.

Japan was desperate to obtain new weapons technology from Nazi Germany, which was consistently producing weapons that were often technologically superior to anything being fielded by the Allied nations, and which Japan was incapable of producing organically. In turn, Germany required certain raw materials that were unavailable to the war effort in Europe and were extremely difficult to obtain owing to the dominance of the world's oceans by the Royal Navy and US Navy, effectively blockading German ports to this kind of international trade. The Germans also required medicines and pharmaceuticals produced in the Far East, particularly drugs such as quinine and opium. Japan's large new Asian empire, the so-called East Asia Co-prosperity Sphere, could theoretically supply everything the Germans required. Germany was particularly short of rubber, and 58 per cent of the world's rubber came from the British colony of Malaya, then under Japanese occupation.[2] The Germans also had requirements for specialist metals such as bismuth, selenium and caesium. The Japanese in return had requirements for mercury, optical glass and specialized steels, because they themselves lacked the technology and ability to produce these products domestically at that stage. Both Axis partners were also interested in sharing plans, handbooks and working examples of their latest military inventions and developments, though this was by no means a totally open trade, with both sides, particularly the Japanese, maintaining a natural suspicion towards their erstwhile allies.

Although only Germany was at war with the Soviet Union at this time, Japan could not send the required raw materials and medicines to Europe overland, the usual route being via Siberia, because Japan had signed a non-aggression pact with Stalin through which the Japanese were keen to maintain good relations. Two alternatives were left open to Germany and Japan, both involving dangerous sea voyages lasting months. First, surface blockade-runners began travelling between Europe and the Far East, with other merchantmen sailing from the Far East to German occupied ports in France. This trade was exclusively the domain of the Germans. This constituted the main *Yanagi* trade operations between the two countries. The second possibility only arose after the virtual failure of surface blockade-running operations, and this was the transportation of more limited *Yanagi* cargoes by submarine. In these operations both the *Kriegsmarine* and the Imperial Japanese Navy participated.

The ships utilized by Germany in the surface blockade-running programme were almost entirely of German registry, consisting of vessels already commissioned into the merchant marine or vessels taken as prizes from the occupied countries of Europe. A few Italian vessels were also pressed into service, but these ships were operated under strict German control. The Japanese possessed a considerably smaller merchant fleet than Germany and, as mentioned, none of her ships was assigned to blockade-running to Europe during the war. The Germans also had one other source of raw materials coming from the Far East – Vichy France. Prior to the outbreak of hostilities in the Far East, a few Vichy French surface blockade-runners managed to evade Allied patrols in the Atlantic, principally by travelling via the Pacific and Atlantic Oceans. An example, noted by British intelligence, added a further dimension to combating the blockade-runners supplying Germany:

> The Vichy ship 'FRANCIOS L.D.' [*sic*] arrived at Casablanca on the 30th October, 1941, with 5,700 tons of rubber from Indo-China, after an unbroken voyage, it is believed, around Cape Horn.[3]

By 1942 the Japanese had control of the strategically important Sunda Strait, which connected the Indian Ocean to the Far East and thereby greatly shortened the long sea voyage from Europe, enabling ships to make the journey via the Indian Ocean without having to be refuelled en route. Arriving in the Far East ahead of the blockade-runners were German commercial representatives whose job it was to negotiate the purchase and shipment of materials from the new Japanese empire in South-East Asia to German-occupied France. However, cooperation between the Germans and the Japanese did not initially run smoothly. In September 1942 the German Commercial Attaché in Tokyo complained to the Japanese authorities that because Japan was so slow in actually concluding a pact with Germany concerning strategically vital rubber, it would mean that German *Yanagi* blockade-runners would face long delays before being loaded. Another complaint was that the Japanese would not allow Germans anywhere near the loading of *Yanagi* cargo at Singapore, and although the Japanese had offered to refuel the German ships, this appeared to be nothing but idle talk. Finally, the Germans had dispatched tankers to the Far East to collect a huge quantity of coconut oil, but after the ships' arrival the Japanese had proposed to substitute the cargo for copra instead.

Japan was also highly sceptical about the likely success that ships could expect in attempting to break the Allied blockade. On 21 August 1942 the German Naval Attaché in Tokyo, *Admiral* Paul Wennecker, received a secret message from Imperial General Headquarters, which stated:

> According to the interpretation of Admiral Nomura,[4] the Japanese Navy considers that the naval blockade runner traffic is much too unfavorable. Clarification of this issue is to be effected. Excerpts from cruise reports of incoming ships can be given to the Japanese Navy as explanation of the slight traffic in the Oceans.[5]

Although the Japanese were apparently not overwhelmingly confident regarding the projected success of the *Yanagi* programme, they none the less made energetic efforts to secure for their war machine considerable quantities of manufactured materials from the Germans. For example, in September 1942 Japan requested that Germany send them one million tons of steel, and a similarly huge consignment of aluminium. The Germans were also requested to supply more ships to the Japanese merchant fleet, though the Japanese had no intention of using these ships on the periodic *Yanagi* runs between the Far East and Europe. As regards the request for merchant ships, the Germans replied that they themselves did not possess any surplus of vessels to sell to Japan, and were hard-pressed providing an adequate supply train to the German troops then fighting in North Africa under Rommel. Germany also truthfully pointed out that the increased Allied aerial campaign being directed against the Reich meant that much of the steel produced by Germany was to be redirected into aircraft production for the *Luftwaffe* (the German Air Force 1936–45). The Germans could claim that Japan was not practically supporting the *Yanagi* trade as all the ships involved in transporting cargo to and from the Far East were German. The Germans had already sold four of the twelve ships actually in the Far East to Japan, and seven of the remainder had been leased by charter.

Allied assessments of the purpose and benefits of a trade relationship between Nazi Germany and Imperial Japan concluded positive outcomes. The British noted in May 1942 that: 'The present war needs of Japan and German Europe are in important respects complimentary.'[6] British intelligence identified that Germany's main deficiencies were rubber, wolfram, tin, hemp, hides and vegetable oils. The lift capacity of just thirteen ships, equating to approximately 100,000 tons, 'would cover essential needs of the first three and make a valuable contribution towards the others'.[7] Later reports suggest that Germany 'planned to import between June 1942 and June 1943 enough rubber, tin, tungsten ... and vegetable oils not only to meet fully her current needs but also to build up stocks'.[8] In July 1943 the British reported in detail regarding the important need for Japan to continue with the *Yanagi* trade:

In order to increase her productive capacity and improve the technical quality of her weapons, Japan must import from Germany heavy machinery (especially rolling mills for her iron and steel industries, and machine tools); finished and semi-finished materials such as mercury, special steels, optical glass, etc., special components, such as ball-bearings, fuel injection pumps, etc., and modern German equipment, aircraft, guns, R.D.F. [Radio Direction Finding] etc. *It is vital to take all steps to prevent her from doing so.*[9]

More ominously for the Allies, Japan's requirements for many of the items previously outlined 'require even less carrying space'[10] than the quantities of raw materials requested by the Germans. An intelligence summary prepared for Prime Minister Winston Churchill in May 1942 warned that 'The successful passage of a few ships would have benefits to the Japanese war effort out of all proportion to the size of the cargoes carried.'[11] Clearly, the interdiction of the *Yanagi* trade would have to be a top priority for the Allies. If the Allies could destroy the cargo material that the Japanese had already purchased, and which lay in French ports, this material 'cannot be replaced for several months'.[12] The ships would have to be sunk before they arrived in the Far East.

American intelligence estimated that by the beginning of the winter of 1942–43 at least twenty-six ships 'were distributed between Europe and the Far East which were serviceable as blockade runners. Beginning in November, and during the following weeks, fourteen of them set sail of which ten were sunk.'[13] The Allies conducted extensive aerial photo-reconnaissance missions over the German-occupied French Atlantic ports, allowing them to construct a fairly detailed picture of the movements and locations of the *Yanagi* blockade-running vessels. The first ships to be identified in the 1942–43 season outward bound through the Bay of Biscay were located by aircraft on 6 and 7 November 1942. The *Anneliese Essberger* was subsequently scuttled on 21 November to avoid her capture by American forces, but the *Karin* managed to run the blockade and continued on to the Far East. The *Cortellazzo* departed from Bordeaux on 29 November, followed by the *Germania* on 11 December. The former vessel was intercepted and sunk by British destroyers 500 miles off Cape Finisterre on 1 December, and a Royal Navy sloop intercepted the *Germania* on 15 December, the blockade-runner scuttling herself to avoid capture. Such losses in ships, men and *Yanagi* cargo were clearly unacceptable to Germany, and led to the Naval High Command ordering the cessation of all *Yanagi* sailings during

December 1942 and January 1943. The Germans informed Japanese representatives in Europe that the *Yanagi* trade was to be suspended in the light of such heavy shipping losses, the Japanese Naval Attaché in Rome informing Tokyo on 22 December that, 'Certain things have arisen making it necessary to cut out the return *Yanagi* shipments for a while.'[14] The Americans subsequently became aware, through intercepted radio transmissions, that the Germans planned to resume *Yanagi* sailings from the middle of February 1943, and were planning to transport approximately 75,000 tons of Japanese purchased *Yanagi* cargo from France to the Far East.

Allied interdiction continued to prove devastating to the Germans, who lost transports returning from the Far East in January and February 1943. These losses, which amounted to two ships, in turn caused another cancellation of operations. By March the Japanese had successfully applied enough diplomatic pressure for a limited resumption of the *Yanagi* trade to be considered by Germany. Four ships, the *Portland*, *Osorno*, *Alsterufer* and *Himalaya* were detailed to transport 20,000 tons of *Yanagi* cargo to the Far East, but the results demonstrated to both parties the massive challenge faced by ships attempting to run the Allied blockade.

The Germans and the Japanese were well aware of how precarious a supply line the *Yanagi* operation was rapidly becoming, and the Japanese Naval Attaché in Berlin requested that the Germans provide increased protection for the vessels, including the provision of U-boats to operate as escorts. The *Portland*, although she did rendezvous with the Type IXC U-boat *U-174* (*Oberleutnant zür See* Wolfgang Grandefeld), was subsequently sunk later into her voyage, and the *Himalaya* was forced to turn back. Only the *Osorno* and the *Alsterufer* made it to the Far East intact. As these ships attempted the difficult passage to the Orient, seven German *Yanagi* ships, packed with vital raw materials destined for the Nazi war machine, departed for Europe from the Far East. At the end of September 1942, under the cover of winter weather, the first westbound *Yanagi* ship, the *Rhakotis*, departed Yokohama and steamed to Singapore to collect the valuable trade cargo for the Germans. On 15 October the *Rhakotis* began loading tin, rubber, zinc ore, lard, tea, quinine bark, coconut oil, and 50,000 yen in pearls. By 5 November, with loading of the cargo complete, she cast off from Singapore's busy anchorage and headed towards Batavia (now Jakarta, Indonesia). On 1 January 1943, well into the final leg of her journey to France, she was intercepted by the Royal Navy's HMS *Scylla* and sent to the bottom with scuttling charges before the ship could be boarded. Only a single ship, the *Pietro Orseolo*, reached France, the rest all being sunk.

Yanagi was becoming an expensive and largely fruitless programme. At this point a proposal was mooted by Germany about the feasibility of using submarines to break the Allied blockade and transport the *Yanagi* cargo, although both sides realized that employing submarines as cargo vessels would have meant both a diminution of their fighting potential and a vast reduction in the cargo tonnage that could be physically transported.

Yanagi operations were curtailed again throughout the winter of 1943–44 from Europe to the Orient. Although five German ships attempted to sail home from the Far East, four of them were sunk en route, and the fifth, the *Osorno*, managed to limp into the Gironde estuary half wrecked from RAF air attacks, her captain forced to beach the ship to save the cargo.

The Germans were also concerned lest one of their U-boats sank a blockade-runner by mistake, and to avoid any likelihood of such an occurrence they defined a clear route the *Yanagi* ships should use when sailing into and out of occupied France. The route, known as 'Lane A', was a 200-mile wide strip of ocean running from the coast of France to approximately 30W, and then southwards to 05S. The route was divided into four sections, and if the *Kriegsmarine* signalled to U-boats at sea that one of these sections was closed, it indicated that a blockade-running vessel was en route, and submarines should avoid hunting within that section of the lane until otherwise informed by U-boat Control. The problem was that because the Allies had so successfully penetrated German naval communications, they could use this Ultra intelligence to roughly approximate the position of individual blockade-running vessels. They then had the option of whether to intercept and destroy them. Although the Allies were obviously concerned not to reveal to the Germans that they had infiltrated Enigma by sinking every blockade-runner and U-boat they learnt the position of, Ultra intercepts nevertheless allowed the Allies to track most of the movements of blockade-runners very effectively. An example of the total Allied infiltration of Enigma is the case of the *Hohenfriedburg*, which had departed from Batavia for France in December 1942, heavily loaded with *Yanagi* cargo from the Japanese. On 13 February 1943, U-boat

Control sent a message to U-boats at sea forbidding attacks on surface merchantmen travelling alone in the southern sector of 'Lane A'. From the decryption of this order, Allied intelligence knew that a Europe-bound *Yanagi* ship was expected, as the southern-most sector of the route was closed first. The message also ordered that all attacks were to be suspended up to and including 26 February, which gave the Allies important indications of exactly where the blockade-runner would be on that date. The message also identified the ship as the *Hohenfriedburg*, call sign 'LIYG'. The Allies knew that this was the former *Herborg*, armed with one 75mm gun, and four 20mm anti-aircraft guns, and backed up with four machine guns. Further decrypts indicated that the *Hohenfriedburg* must have been carrying an especially valuable cargo, as U-boat Control ordered no less than four U-boats to rendezvous with the freighter, and escort her into port. The U-boats were unsuccessful in their mission, as an Enigma message decrypted on 26 February from the Type VIIC *U-264* (*Kapitänleutnant* Hartwig Looks) indicated: 'Object-to-be-protected was sunk by heavy cruiser, LONDON class ... I have complete crew on board. Am starting return.'[15]

The Germans did make mistakes, and the example of the fate of the freighter *Doggerbank* indicates that the 'Lane A' system was not foolproof. During Christmas 1942, the *Doggerbank* loaded up with around 3,200 tons of rubber in Saigon, French Indochina (now Ho Chi Minh City, Vietnam). According to a single survivor rescued from the sea on 29 March 1943, the blockade-runner had been sunk on 3 March by an unidentified submarine at approximately 31N 37W. It is assumed that a U-boat accidentally sank the *Doggerbank*, code-named '*U-905*' by the Germans. What seems to have caused this unfortunate encounter was the strictly enforced radio silence being observed by the *Doggerbank* while in transit in an effort to avoid detection by the Allies, and the fact that the ship was travelling at a higher speed than that anticipated by the *Kriegsmarine*. After the *Hohenfriedburg* had passed through 'Lane A', the ban on U-boats attacking single ships north of the line 15N had been lifted by U-boat Control until 1 March. On 1 March 'Lane A' was closed once more for twenty days between 05S and 15N, and from 15N to 30N between 5 and 26 March. On 15 March, U-boats were advised that the sections of 'Lane A' where it was anticipated the *Doggerbank* would be passing were off-limits for attacks on single ships, with the *Kriegsmarine* remaining ignorant of the *Doggerbank*'s sinking on

3 March. The increased safety derived from maintaining radio silence and increasing speed to complete the hazardous journey to Europe more rapidly had placed the *Doggerbank* into a 'hot' zone of 'Lane A' in which the U-boats present had not been ordered to avoid attacking freighters travelling alone. The *Doggerbank* had been sunk simply because she was fatally ahead of schedule. The *Yanagi* ship *Karin* stuck to the correct time and speed schedules, but was nevertheless forced to scuttle herself when she was sighted in 'Lane A' by the USS *Eberle* on 10 March, which was directed into position by Ultra decrypts. This amounted to a massively disappointing series of surface blockade-running failures for the Germans and the Japanese. The Germans did, however, determine to change the route of 'Lane A' in an attempt to save further *Yanagi* ships from interception by Allied warships. The route was extended to follow a northerly course into the German port of Stettin via the north of Iceland and the Denmark Strait. *U-191* (*Kapitänleutnant* Helmut Fiehn), a Type IXC40, was dispatched by U-boat Control to conduct a reconnaissance of the ice boundary in the Denmark Strait, and report its accessibility to the blockade-runners.

The new section of 'Lane A' was to prove no more propitious for the *Yanagi* ships than the run into France had been. The *Regensburg* had departed for the Far East in the autumn of 1942, but had been torpedoed and damaged by the American submarine USS *Searaven* in the Sunda Strait on 13 October. The Japanese had patched her up and she had then made her way towards Europe without further incident. Because of a concern regarding ice on the new route into Stettin, *U-161* was dispatched to rendezvous with the *Regensburg* on 20 March 1943. The U-boat, which actually met the freighter on 24 March, relayed the latest ice reports to the captain, who then proceeded to the Denmark Strait. The Allies once again managed to intercept a *Yanagi* vessel, and the *Regensburg* scuttled herself after being spotted by the British cruiser HMS *Glasgow* on 30 March. Once more a valuable ship and her cargo failed to make their destination.

The approach to Europe of the sixth *Yanagi* vessel of the season remained unknown to the Allies because they had received no previous communications naming the use of the ex-Norwegian merchantman *Irene* as a blockade-runner. The Allies only became aware of another blockade-runner through the interception of U-boat signals. The Allies were only able to intercept and read radio messages sent *from* U-boats to Control, which enabled them to obtain a fix on the boats from the captain reporting his position.

On 30 March the Allies discovered the existence of the *Irene* when they decrypted the signals traffic of *Oberleutnant zür See* Wolfgang Grandefeld, commanding *U-174*, ordering him to remain at the rendezvous site he had been sent to some days previously, and to expect the *Karin* and the *Irene*. Grandefeld was to pass to the blockade-runners' captains, new charts and orders concerning taking the new northern route into Germany. The Germans, however, following the disastrous attempt to re-route the *Regensburg* into the Denmark Strait, subsequently decided against a similar passage for the *Irene* and directed her instead into western France. On 9 April U-boat Control directed four U-boats to form a close escort for the *Irene*, advising that the U-boats should remain surfaced as much as possible so that their anti-aircraft armament could be employed to protect the freighter from the inevitable Allied aerial activity in the Bay of Biscay. The Germans took further measures to ensure the intact delivery of the *Yanagi* cargo, advising that the *Luftwaffe* would dispatch long-range fighter-bomber escorts, and the *Kriegsmarine* would send destroyers to meet the little flotilla. Unfortunately the Germans soon realized that the dispatch of destroyers would have probably resulted in their loss, so this part of the protective umbrella was dispensed with. All of these precautions were to no avail as on 10 April HMS *Adventure*, which was searching for the outbound blockade-runner *Himalaya*, happened upon the *Irene*, with the inevitable consequence that the *Irene* was forced to scuttle herself.

Thereafter, Allied intelligence was informed through its decryptions that the Germans had reopened the entire length of 'Lane A' to U-boat operations, indicating the end of blockade-running activity for the time being. Only a single ship, the *Pietro Orseolo*, had successfully reached France intact, and a desultory record of six out of seven incoming blockade-runners having been sunk raised serious questions as to whether the *Yanagi* system was actually worth all the effort, and whether an alternative transportation method could be found to decrease these massive losses. Some ships had been fully loaded in the Far East ready to attempt the return to Europe, or were on their way, when the Germans received news of the sinking of the *Hohenfriedburg*. They immediately cancelled the sailings of two blockade-runners sitting in Batavia harbour, and ordered three others that had departed the Far East prior to 10 April to turn back.

An example of the serious situation faced by surface blockade-runners is perfectly demonstrated by the story of the German merchant ship *Ramses*. The *Ramses* was constructed in 1926, displaced 7,983 tons and had a maximum speed of only 12 knots. She departed from Hamburg on the 1 July 1939 and arrived in Shanghai on the 25 August. Unfortunately, the opening of hostilities in Europe in September 1939 effectively trapped the *Ramses* in Japanese-occupied Shanghai, and she remained in port until the 29 March 1941, when she sailed to Kobe in Japan. Arriving in Darien in the Dutch East Indies in May, she was loaded with rubber and soya beans, and then left to sail to Valparaiso. The Japanese, however, ordered her to sail back to Japan, and she made for the port of Yokohama. She duly arrived on 30 July and her original cargo was offloaded. German armed merchant raiders had sunk many Allied merchantmen in the Far East since the opening of the war, and the *Ramses* was designated a floating prisoner of war camp in Yokohama harbour, the prisoners consisting of Allied merchant navy crews from these early German naval successes, who had unfortunately been captured by raiders such as the *Michel* and been handed over to the Japanese for internment when raiders refuelled and supplied in Japanese ports.

In 1942 the *Ramses* was released from prison duty, and loaded with a large *Yanagi* cargo consisting of 4,200 tons of whale oil, 700 tons of fish oil, 700 tons of lard, 50 tons of coconut oil and 300 tons of tea. She departed from Japan on 10 October 1942 and sailed to Kobe and Balikpapen in Borneo, where she offloaded a mixed cargo weighing around 1,000 tons, and then headed for Batavia. As mentioned previously, German industry desperately required rubber, and the *Yanagi* blockade-runners carried large cargoes of this material as a priority item. The *Ramses* accordingly took on board 4,000 tons of rubber at Batavia, as well as 1,500 cases of the drug quinine. She then sailed for Bordeaux in German-occupied France.

The crew of the *Ramses* was a mixture of German merchant marine and *Kriegsmarine* officers and men. The ship's defensive armament, consisting of two 20mm anti-aircraft guns and four machine guns, was crewed by a regular naval contingent, consisting of a lieutenant, two petty officers and fifteen ratings. In order to break through the Allied blockade, a plan had been formulated for blockade-running vessels, such as the *Ramses*, in which they were to pass from one German merchant raider to another, in this way

40

negotiating Allied air and sea searches in the Indian Ocean. The rapid destruction of the raiders themselves soon put paid to this plan. Having negotiated the Cape of Good Hope, the surface blockade-runner would theoretically pass from U-boat to U-boat as protection from Allied attack in the Atlantic, using 'Lane A'. But, as shown by the experience of other blockade-runners such as the *Regensburg*, cooperation between U-boats and freighters was extremely difficult to achieve, and U-boats could do little to protect the ships once they had rendezvoused without putting the U-boat in grave danger of destruction. Once within range of land-based aircraft, the *Luftwaffe* was supposed to provide Focke-Wulf Fw-200 *Condor* bombers to fly close protection missions over the merchantman until they arrived safely in port. The Focke-Wulf Fw-200 *Condor* was the *Luftwaffe*'s long-range maritime patrol aircraft. Despite small numbers, the *Condor* achieved a very respectable record for attacking Allied commerce on the high seas, and for searching out convoys for U-boat attack. They would fly great patrol loops over the eastern Atlantic. The *Condor* was an adaptation of a four-engine commercial airliner, and they were also used as emergency transport aircraft, notably during the final stage of the Battle of Stalingrad in January 1943. To improve morale on board the blockade-runners, all crews had been promised a new Blockade Running Medal by the *Kriegsmarine*, should they reach France.

In the case of the *Ramses*, she was never to see Europe again. The Australian light cruiser HMAS *Adelaide* was based at Fremantle in Western Australia, and her task was to provide escort to merchant shipping negotiating the twin German and Japanese submarine threat in the Indian Ocean. On 23 November 1942 the *Adelaide* departed from Australia to escort three merchant ships that were loaded with oil drilling equipment bound for Abadan, an island situated on the south-western corner of Iran. She sailed in company with the Royal Netherlands Navy light cruiser *Heemskerch*. On 25 November, a tanker, the *Goldmouth*, joined the small convoy and the Australian corvettes HMAS *Cessnock* and HMAS *Toowoomba* also joined up to further stiffen the convoy defences. At 2.16 pm on 28 November the *Adelaide*'s masthead lookout reported smoke on the horizon off the starboard bow, and over the course of the following two minutes the top of the *Ramses*' superstructure became visible. At 2.18 pm Captain Esdaile ordered a change of course, and the *Adelaide* began to close on the as yet unidentified ship. Four minutes later the

German lookouts on board the *Ramses* spotted the Australian warship bearing down on them, and the *Ramses* immediately altered course away from the *Adelaide* emitting a distress signal, which included a false ship's name as identification. As officers attempted to discover the true identity of the German ship following a glance through shipping publications carried on board the *Adelaide*, at 2.50 pm the captain ordered 'Action Stations!' and the cruiser's main armament was brought to bear upon the mysterious ship. At 3.19 pm the *Adelaide* picked up another distress call originating from the unknown vessel, and by 3.28 pm the *Adelaide* was close enough to enable the Navigating Officer, Lieutenant J.W. Penney, to positively identify the ship as the German *Ramses*, which was known to be armed. In the back of Captain Esdaile's mind was the fate of the cruiser HMAS *Sydney*, which had been sunk by the German merchant raider *Kormoran* in November 1941 when Captain Burnett approached the armed merchantman. The *Sydney*'s entire complement of 635 officers and men was lost in the sinking. The *Sydney* had been struck by a torpedo during the exchange of gunfire with the German raider and had eventually sunk, although another theory suggests that one of the light cruisers' magazines exploded after the battle, resulting in the loss of the ship and her entire ship's company. The loss of HMAS *Sydney* is still being hotly debated.

Aboard the *Ramses*, frantic efforts were under way to scuttle the ship before the Australians arrived, or opened fire. At 3.36 pm two port side boats were lowered, taking off a majority of the crew, the fuses of the Japanese scuttling charges fitted in Yokohama for just such an eventuality slowly burning down in the guts of the ship. At 3.44 pm there was a loud explosion originating in the stern of the ship, and dense black smoke began to billow over the vessel, whipped by the wind into a black shroud to cover the destruction of another precious *Yanagi* blockade-runner. The *Heemskerch* had joined the *Adelaide*, and both cruisers opened fire from a range of 12,000 yards directly into the cloud of smoke from which only the *Ramses*' masts and the top of her funnel were visible. Not all of the *Ramses*' crew had taken to the boats, and the captain, the *Kriegsmarine* gunnery officer and the wireless officer were still fumbling around attempting to complete the scuttling plan in the bowels of the ship. *Adelaide* scored several hits on the sinking *Ramses*, which hastened the German officers' work of sending her to the bottom. At 3.52 pm she slid beneath the waves and the *Adelaide* set about rescuing the survivors as the *Heemskerch* returned to the convoy. Seventy-eight Germans were taken prisoner, along with ten seamen from the Norwegian Merchant Marine, who had been held as prisoners of war aboard the *Ramses* since the merchant raider had sunk their ship. The two other survivors were a pig and a dog! An officer aboard the *Adelaide* recalled:

> My most vivid memory of this action was the sight of some of our seamen who suddenly stopped hauling in German survivors, to rescue both the pig and the dog before them, indicating their priority in this rescue mission.

The dog's days were unfortunately numbered when, on arrival back at Fremantle, Australian quarantine officers had the animal destroyed to ensure that no canine diseases were brought into the country.

A final phase of *Yanagi* transports sailing from the Far East to Europe was planned for the winter of 1943–44, working in conjunction with the underwater delivery of supplies that had begun in 1942 on a very limited basis. The Germans had several ships sitting in ports in the Far East, including those vessels whose journeys home had been cancelled following the loss of the *Hohenfriedburg*, and those ships that had been ordered to turn back if they had departed from the Far East prior to 10 April 1943. The Germans undoubtedly were not prepared to allow these ships, with their massive cargo capacity, to simply remain idle in Japanese-occupied Asia, and therefore they planned one last *Yanagi* run under the cover of winter.

On 5 October 1943 the Allies intercepted intelligence indicating that two German ships, the *Alsterufer* and either the *Burgenland* or the *Weserland*, were en route to Singapore for loading, and that the *Osorno* was sailing to Bangkok in Japanese-occupied, though nominally neutral, Thailand. Further intelligence obtained by 17 October indicated that the *Rio Grande* had also recently arrived in Singapore and was being prepared for a run to Europe. In fact, according to Allied intelligence, they believed that the *Rio Grande* would be the first of the *Yanagi* vessels to depart for Europe, and would therefore be the first to be dealt with. In reality, the *Rio Grande* was the final German ship to enter 'Lane A', her captain having loitered south of the lane for four weeks before finally plucking up the courage to attempt the run to Europe. In the meantime, the *Osorno* and the *Alsterufer* had ploughed on through the heavy winter seas ahead of the *Rio Grande*.

Past experience had proved that U-boat communications traffic was the most reliable source for obtaining intelligence on the location and movements of the blockade-runners. It was realized that when a blockade-runner was expected, warnings to U-boats in the area were transmitted over the airwaves and the U-boats would respond. Using Ultra, Allied intelligence tracked communications to the Type IXD2 *U-849* under *Kapitänleutnant* Heinz-Otto Schültze, which was then entering the South Atlantic on the way to the Indian Ocean. On 15 November, the presence of blockade-running vessels around Schültze's position was confirmed in a message forbidding *U-849* from attacking lone merchantmen within a specified section of 'Lane A'. By early December, intercepts of German signals ordering closures of sections of 'Lane A' indicated that at least one blockade-runner was using the lane, and was probably just north of the equator. However, because blockade-runners were observing strict radio silence, the Allies could do little more than attempt to plot their position by dead reckoning, and rely upon the *Yanagi* freighter being spotted by a surface ship or aircraft. The *Osorno* was extremely lucky, and according to her report, she successfully passed a British armed merchant ship while in the South Atlantic, and evaded an attack by a Liberator thus:

> *Osorno* deceived enemy planes by the following behaviour: In spite of being ordered to stop, she continued to go. She set the distinguishing signal for a disguised ship, (raised) English flag on gaff, English cockade on hatch 1. She answered challenge with incomprehensible Morse signal. Extra crew were under cover, officer signaling on bridge.[16]

Evading Allied searches had cost the *Osorno* valuable time, and the closing of sections of 'Lane A' to U-boat operations indicated to the Allies this fact. On 22 December, the outer Biscay area was closed to U-boats, which indicated that the *Osorno* was going to make port shortly. U-boats in the area were sent the following message:

> Our blockade runner *Osorno* homeward bound today ... ship presumably disguised. In the event of meeting her, send report

immediately after getting out of sight. Cover name *U-1534* ...
Count on deceptive courses of all kinds. Attention is urgently
called to prohibition of attacks on unescorted independents ...
It is your duty to keep [presence of runner] absolutely secret
even from crews.[17]

The *Osorno* was extremely lucky, managing to avoid direct attack
from American aircraft aboard the carrier USS *Card* on 23 December,
the carrier being unable to pursue the blockade-runner because she
was running low on fuel. But, on entering the Gironde estuary, as
noted earlier, she was severely damaged by British aircraft on
Christmas Day 1943. Despite this, the *Yanagi* cargo was successfully
delivered intact to the Germans, a noted success for her skipper,
Captain Hellman, who was subsequently awarded the Knights Cross
for this extraordinary achievement.

The *Alsterufer* had disappeared from the Allies careful watch, and
once again the extensive penetration of U-boat communications was
to prove her undoing. The Germans had closed the final section of
'Lane A', the Bay of Biscay, to U-boats on 22 December. On
Christmas Day, the many U-boats then in the outer Biscay Bay were
informed that the *Alsterufer* was expected within the section by the
next day, and were to keep watch for her and report her progress to
U-boat Control. *U-305* subsequently spotted the *Alsterufer*, and
reported her as the *Osorno*, helpfully plotting her position, course
and speed. This information was promptly decoded and read by the
Allies within one hour. U-boat Control told *U-305* that the *Osorno*
had already arrived in port and suggested that they had located the
Alsterufer instead. The Allies also rapidly appraised this identification and preparations were made to sink the *Alsterufer* as she
approached port. The Germans dispatched eleven destroyers in an
attempt to shield the freighter from the expected Allied aerial assault,
but were unsuccessful. After the *Alsterufer* was sunk, Allied aircraft
turned on the escorts, resulting in three German destroyers being
sunk. The commander and thirty-three crewmen of the *T-25* were
picked up by *U-505*, with the remainder rescued by a neutral Irish
merchantman and two Spanish destroyers. These crewmen were
interned in the Republic of Ireland and Spain respectively for the
duration of the war.

The voyages of the *Weserland* and the *Burgenland* were considerably
less dramatic, for the Allies were able to neatly plot their positions as

they neared Europe and send forces to destroy them. Both ships appeared where they were predicted to emerge, straight into the lap of American hunter-killer forces. The *Weserland* was attacked and sunk by USS *Somers* on 3 January 1944, and the *Burgenland* was identified by American aircraft, then sunk by USS *Omaha* and USS *Jouett* shortly afterwards.

Sitting in various Biscay ports were eight cargo ships considered capable of making a new run to the Far East with around 50,000 tons of *Yanagi* cargo for the Japanese between them, and arrangements were made during spring 1943 between Germany and Japan to attempt to break the blockade with these ships during the winter of 1943–44.

On 20 November, Japanese Ambassador Oshima had visited Bordeaux from Berlin and had witnessed the loading of two blockade-runners, the *Dresden* and the *Tannenfels*, with a large consignment of steel, aluminium and formic acid. The Germans had decided to reduce the amount of cargo to be taken to Japan to 42,000 tons. This would enable the anti-aircraft armament on board the freighters to be stiffened up in the hope that with proper escort arrangements, the ships would be able to fight their way out of the Bay of Biscay. Constant Allied aerial photo-reconnaissance missions over the Biscay ports indicated to them that a further round of blockade-running from France to Japan could be anticipated during the winter. One of the ships earmarked as a *Yanagi* transport, the *Kulmerland*, was damaged by Allied bombing in September and had to be withdrawn from the coming operation. The loss of the *Kulmerland* reduced the tonnage of cargo that could be transported east to around 35,000 tons, although the Japanese Ambassador, Oshima, became fixated upon the incorrect figure of 32,000 tons. This created problems for the Japanese in deciding which of their purchases should be given priority out of their total stored material weighing collectively 50,000 tons. Oshima reported to Tokyo that aside from the problem of actually deciding what to transport, they should be aware that there was, in his opinion, a very slim chance that any of the remaining seven blockade-runners would actually survive the passage through the Bay of Biscay, let alone reach the Far East intact. As an example of his realistic attitude, Oshima recommended that the captains of these ships should be decorated by the Japanese *prior* to beginning their missions!

Meanwhile, the number of ships involved in the operation continued to decrease, reinforcing Oshima's pessimism. Early in November, the

Dresden struck a mine while negotiating the Gironde estuary, and was withdrawn. Then, during an Allied air raid on Bordeaux, an unidentified ship was struck by aerial torpedoes, and wrecked. The Japanese were left with only five ships, with a maximum lift of 29,000 tons. On 25 November, Allied intelligence became aware that five ships, the *Else Essberger*, the *Himalaya*, the *Fusijama*, the *Pietro Orseolo* and the *Tannenfels* were preparing to leave port. The *Pietro Orseolo* was bombed and put out of commission on 18 December, further reducing the effectiveness of the *Yanagi* run, to the point that on 19 January 1944 all sailings were cancelled. In great secrecy, the valuable cargoes were offloaded, and returned to storage.

Surface merchantmen continued to make relatively easy targets for Allied naval and air forces, and by January 1944 the losses alarmed Hitler – surface blockade-running had become virtual suicide cruises, with only around 50 per cent of ships reaching their destinations. Hitler ordered surface blockade-running halted in January 1944. There was, however, an alternative to surface ship attrition – underwater cargo delivery. This process had already begun in 1942 and was to provide both the Germans and the Japanese with a solution to continuing the important *Yanagi* trade. In January 1944 Ambassador Oshima contacted Tokyo to report the effective end of surface blockade-running, noting that since submarines were unable to deliver much of the heavy equipment purchased by the Japanese, the best that could now be hoped for was an exchange of patent rights between the two countries, and the licensed manufacture in Japan of the latest German military technology. This paperwork could be transported by submarine.

Germany had begun to make arrangements should the trade in raw materials, whether by surface or submarine vessels, from Japan and the Far East have been drastically reduced or curtailed entirely. Oshima reported his conversation with Albert Speer, the German Armaments Minister, in August 1944, to the Ministry of Foreign Affairs in Tokyo, commenting that 'Germany would be able to continue an abundant production of munitions within the area [as at August 1944]'.[18] Furthermore, the Germans had managed by this stage of the war to achieve a sufficiency of copper, manganese and molybdenum, the Japanese noting that sufficiency in copper was being met by 'having cartridge cases sent back from the front',[19] which seems remarkably inefficient! Germany held sufficient stocks of chrome, including obtaining limited supplies from the Balkans and

Turkey, for two years, 'but this supply, along with tungsten and nickel, would be seriously affected should the supply be cut off altogether'.[20] Germany was producing approximately 700,000 tons of aluminium each year, and Speer informed Oshima that he was using increased quantities, along with increased employment of wood, in aircraft production. Germany would manage to increase aircraft production while at the same time being less reliant on the importation of raw materials from the Far East. In the same way, the increased production of synthetic oil, backed by mineral oil from Romania, enabled Germany to continue the prosecution of the war. Oshima was struck by Speer's upbeat appraisal of the state of German industry and production capacity when the Reich was losing territory in both western Europe and on the Eastern Front, and being subjected to a massive Allied aerial bombing campaign which was rapidly reducing Germany to a bombed out ruin. Speer may have been overcompensating – desperately attempting to reassure Japan concerning the ability of its ally to continue the struggle (and the supply of technologically superior weapons), and downplaying the necessity of raw materials imported from the Japanese to bolster Japanese confidence in Germany. Such a strategy, if it was Speer's intention to convey such, backfired over rubber imports. As Oshima noted:

> With regard to rubber, in the past raw rubber had been considered absolutely essential for airplane tyres [sic], but success had recently been attained in making synthetic rubber of exactly the capability as raw rubber.[21]

Oshima added that, 'This may be said to be merely a puerile idea which came into his [Speer's] mind.'

Speer contended, 'they [the Germans] could manage even without any raw rubber at all'.[22]

Raw rubber, as well as many of the ores mentioned previously, regardless of Speer's boasts, would remain priority items aboard German U-boats engaged in the *Yanagi* trade until May 1945.

Notes

1. *Orion, Atlantis, Widder, Thor, Pinguin, Stier, Komet, Kormoran, Michel, Coronel* and *Hansa*.

2. Warren, A., *Singapore 1942: Britain's Greatest Defeat*, Hambledon and London, 2002, p. 9.
3. The National Archives (TNA): Public Record Office (PRO) ADM1/14955.
4. Admiral Kichisaburo Nomura was Japanese Ambassador to the United States from 1939 to July 1942, when he was repatriated. He subsequently served as Ambassador at Large and joined the Privy Council advising Emperor Hirohito in 1945.
5. Diplogerma 0427/21 August 1942, *Ultra in the Atlantic: U-Boat Operations*, SRH-008, National Security Agency, Washington DC, 1945, p. 185.
6. The National Archives (TNA): Public Record Office (PRO) ADM1/14955 9 May 1942.
7. *Ibid.*, TNA: PRO ADM1/14955 9 May 1942
8. The National Archives (TNA): Public Record Office (PRO) ADM1/14955 30 July 1943.
9. *Ibid.*, TNA: PRO ADM1/14955 30 July 1943.
10. The National Archives (TNA): Public Record Office (PRO) ADM1/14955 9 May 1942.
11. *Ibid.*, TNA: PRO ADM1/14955 9 May 1942.
12. *Ibid.*, TNA: PRO ADM1/14955 9 May 1942.
13. Diplogerma 0427/21 August 1942, *Ultra in the Atlantic: U-Boat Operations*, SRH-008, National Security Agency, Washington DC, 1945, p. 186.
14. *Ibid.*, Japanese Diplomatic No. 60230, 22 December 1942, p. 188.
15. *Ibid.*, 2110/26 February 1943, p. 194.
16 *Ibid.*, 2003/7 December 1943, p. 200.
17. *Ibid.*, 1239/22 December, pp. 200–1.
18. The National Archives (TNA): Public Record Office (PRO) HW1/3177 Japanese Ambassador, Berlin, Reports on German Supplies of Raw Materials: 12 August 1944.
19. *Ibid.*, TNA: PRO HW1/3177 Japanese Ambassador, Berlin, Reports on German Supplies of Raw Materials: 12 August 1944.
20. *Ibid.*, TNA: PRO HW1/3177 Japanese Ambassador, Berlin, Reports on German Supplies of Raw Materials: 12 August 1944.
21. *Ibid.*, TNA: PRO HW1/3177 Japanese Ambassador, Berlin, Reports on German Supplies of Raw Materials: 12 August 1944.
22. *Ibid.*, TNA: PRO HW1/3177 Japanese Ambassador, Berlin, Reports on German Supplies of Raw Materials: 12 August 1944.

Chapter 4

The Early *Yanagi* Submarine Missions

The Epic Journeys of the *I-30* and the *I-8*

On 4 April 1942 the Imperial Japanese Navy submarine *I-30* (New *Junsen* 2 Type)[1] left Japan for the Indian Ocean. Completed at the Kure naval yard and commissioned on 28 February 1942, the submarine was considerably larger than any German U-boat of the period, at 350 feet in length and 2,584-tons displacement, with a range of 14,000 nautical miles at 16 knots. In fact, this class of submarine was so large that the Japanese had been able to mount an aircraft catapult on board, with a watertight hangar located forward of the conning tower containing a Yokosuka E14Y1 reconnaissance floatplane. The aircraft was very superficially similar in appearance to the famous Mitsubishi A6M *Zero* fighter, although the Yokosuka was a smaller, very manoeuvrable, two-seater floatplane. The aircraft had been officially adopted for use on Japanese submarines towards the end of 1940, and had a maximum airspeed of 190 knots.[2] Although they mostly flew their reconnaissance missions unarmed, they could be fitted with a 7.7mm machine-gun, operated by the rear observer. These aircraft were extremely useful to the Japanese submarine force, providing the boats with an effective reconnaissance screen over a greatly extended range. One was even used to bomb mainland America in 1942, carrying two small incendiary devices on its symbolic two sorties over the country (see Appendix I).

The *I-30* was well armed, with six torpedo tubes located in the bow and eleven reloads in the bow compartment, as well as a 5.5in deck gun mounted aft of the conning tower. The submarine's crew numbered 110 men, including the pilot and rear-gunner of the 'Glen' floatplane (as the aircraft was code-named by the Allies).

On 27 March the *Kriegsmarine* formally requested, through diplomatic representations, that the Imperial Japanese Navy should begin anti-convoy operations in the Indian Ocean. The Japanese agreed to the request on 8 April, and withdrew a submarine force, including the *I-30*, from their base at Kwajalein in the tropical Marshall Islands. The *I-30* departed from Kure, Japan, for Penang in Malaya on 11 April, and was assigned to Captain Noboru Ishizaki's 8th Submarine Flotilla, which included the *I-10*, *I-16*, *I-18* and *I-20*, as well as two submarine support ships, or auxiliary cruisers, the *Aikoku Maru* and the *Hokoku Maru*. On 22 April the *I-30* left Penang in company with the *Aikoku Maru*, and headed for the coast of East Africa to reconnoitre possible targets for the navy. After spending some time running up the east coast of Africa, including launching the Yokosuka floatplane carried aboard on missions to reconnoitre Aden, Djibouti, Zanzibar and Dar-es-Salaam, once east of Madagascar the *I-30* detached herself from the submarine group and began her *Yanagi* mission.

The rest of the flotilla began operations against Allied shipping. Japanese midget submarines carried aboard the *I-16*, *I-18* and *I-20* were launched in an attempt to interdict the Allied invasion of Vichy French Madagascar. Force 121 conducted Operation Ironclad, the British amphibious invasion of the Vichy French colony of Madagascar on 5 May 1942. Allied intelligence were aware that the Imperial Japanese Navy was interested in basing a submarine force on the island, which, if the collaborationist Vichy government had consented to allow, would have meant that Japan could interdict Allied convoys and shipping in the western Indian Ocean and South African coast. A force of assault ships landed the British 29 Infantry Brigade (Independent), 17 Infantry Brigade Group and 13 Infantry Brigade, supported by Royal Marines and Fleet Air Arm aircraft from the carriers HMS *Illustrious* and HMS *Indomitable*. Naval gunfire support was provided by the battleship HMS *Ramillies* and the heavy cruiser HMS *Devonshire*. During the morning of 5 May the British had run head-on into Vichy French defences, and although they had tanks ashore, getting artillery landed proved difficult. The next day, the British delivered a frontal assault against the French defending the town of Antsirane, on the route to the capital Diego Suarez. The French forces surrendered on 7 May. The operation cost the British 105 killed and 283 wounded, with Vichy French casualties amounting to approximately 150 killed and 500 wounded. Other

French units located on the coast and inland continued to resist, necessitating the British to enact Operation Slimline Jane. The original invasion force had withdrawn and 22 East African Brigade Group, South African 7 Armoured Brigade and Northern Rhodesian 27 Infantry Brigade conducted the operation. All French resistance on Madagascar ended with a complete surrender on 6 November 1942. Thereafter, the Japanese had lost any chance of basing forces in the western Indian Ocean.

Each Japanese Type A midget submarine was a potent weapon of war, 78.5 feet in length and weighing 46 tons. The two-man crew consisted of a junior officer and an enlisted man. Armed with two 18in torpedoes, each midget could muster 19 knots submerged, with the potential for 100 miles running on the surface at a conservative 2 knots. In Diego Suarez harbour on 29 May there was a collection of Allied warships and supply vessels riding at anchor. HMS *Karanja*, *Genista*, *Thyme*, *Duncan* and *Active*, all convoy escorts, were berthed alongside a hospital ship, the *Atlantis*, the merchantman *Llandaff Castle* and an ammunition ship that was waiting patiently to be unloaded. During the afternoon an unidentified aircraft passed over the harbour, dropped a flare, and then disappeared. It was presumed that the strange visitor was an enemy reconnaissance spotter, either Japanese or Vichy French (who at this stage were still in control of the southern half of Madagascar) and immediate precautions were taken to change the dispositions of the major warships in the harbour. HMS *Ramillies*, an old Royal Sovereign-class battleship, weighed anchor and steamed around the bay in circles before tying up again at a different berth. Commissioned into the Royal Navy in 1917, *Ramillies* was placed on the reserve list in 1944, and subsequently used as a training ship in Portsmouth until sold for scrap in 1948. She displaced 33,500 tons when fully loaded, sported eight 15in guns, and had a Second World War complement of 1,146 men.

Ten miles out to sea three Japanese submarines had surfaced, and the crews feverishly worked in the heat to make ready to launch the midget submarine special attack force. The *I-18* was unable to launch her midget because the launching machinery failed to work properly, and she was forced to return to the supporting auxiliary cruisers *Aikoku Maru* and *Hokoku Maru* for repairs. Aboard the *I-16* and *I-20* the two-man midget crews prepared for the hair-raising mission to come. The *I-16*'s midget was under the command of Ensign

Katsusuke Iwase, with Petty Officer Takazo Takata as navigator. Iwase and Takata clambered into the confines of the Type A's cockpit, both armed with pistols. Iwase also symbolically carried a short *tachi* sword, denoting his officer rank and status, and highlighting the Japanese military's adherence to the *Bushido* code, 'which upheld the virtues of man-to-man combat in a machine age, and demanded that the Japanese soldier die rather than surrender'.[3] The *I-20's* midget submarine crew were both married family men: Lieutenant Saburo Akieda and Petty Officer Masami Takemoto. The two midgets slowly edged away from their mother ships and began motoring towards Diego Suarez on the surface. The crewmen planned to dive their submarines as they approached the shallow harbour, in the hope of avoiding Allied watchers, thus penetrating the port undetected. By the time they reached their target, darkness had already fallen, but the light of a full moon bathed the busy anchorage and array of ships.

Crewmen on the decks of the huge British battleship, and aboard the tanker *British Loyalty*, reported that they saw two conning towers negotiating the harbour entrance, though strangely no immediate action was taken. At 8.25 pm Akieda began his torpedo attack. Lining up on the considerable presence of HMS *Ramillies*, Akieda launched a single torpedo at the battleship. A few seconds later there was an enormous explosion that lit up the harbour, a massive plume of smoke and flame, debris and black smoke climbing into the humid night air as the *Ramillies* reeled from the torpedo strike. A 30-foot hole had been blown in the port side of the ship and water was flooding into the steaming gash in her side. Men were thrown down by the force of the explosion, or battered mercilessly against metal surfaces inside the ship, breaking limbs and cracking their skulls.

Although the damage control parties managed to save the ship from settling onto the muddy harbour bottom, intermittent power and communication failures throughout the rest of the night hampered their efforts. Fortunately for the British, Akieda must have assumed that he had crippled the battleship with a single strike, because he did not immediately launch his remaining torpedo at her. Close by, the captain of the *British Loyalty* ordered the crew to swing out the boats and raise the anchor. He rang the engine-room telegraph to 'standby'. It was to take the tanker almost an hour to begin to move away from her anchorage. In the meantime Royal Navy corvettes, fast anti-submarine vessels, raced around the port, depth charging any suspicious targets in the hope of preventing further attacks.

A signalman aboard the damaged *Ramillies* was searching the water for signs of the invisible attacker when he saw the unmistakable wake of a torpedo running fast in the bright moonlight, heading not for the warship, but travelling to intercept the *British Loyalty*. The tanker was reversing noisily in the manoeuvres from its berth, directly into the path of the oncoming Japanese torpedo that was obviously intended to finish off the stricken *Ramillies*. Another booming explosion rolled out over the harbour; ships, men and buildings lit for a second by the baleful light of hundreds of pounds of high explosives slamming into the tanker's engine-room. The *British Loyalty* began to sink rapidly by the stern and Captain Wastell ordered the 'Abandon Ship!'. Officers worked frantically to fill the boats with the mainly Indian crewmen, launch them down the straining davits, and get them to safety aboard other ships in the harbour. Second Officer Main had been standing on the gun platform when the torpedo struck the engine-room. Main had been blown flat and the gun had disintegrated. Picking himself up from the next deck where he had unceremoniously landed, Main abandoned ship along with the rest of the crew. Shortly after, he returned to the foundering ship to check whether anyone remained aboard, only to discover the chief engineer lying unconscious outside the engine-room. Drawing immense physical strength from the desperate predicament they were in, Main managed to heave the heavy engineer topside, and carry him to a waiting boat. Five engine-room crewmen had been killed by the torpedo impact and explosion. The tanker slowly sank deeper into the muddy water, coming to rest on the bottom with only the top of her funnel visible above the surface of the water.

Akieda, having successfully expended his two torpedoes, now attempted to leave the harbour and get back to the *I-20*. The Japanese knew that smaller surface craft had begun to search the immediate vicinity for the midget submarine, but in his haste to depart the scene of devastation he had created in the past hour and a half, Akieda discovered that the midget's steering appeared to be defective. At that moment Akieda's boat ran aground on a reef near the harbour entrance, and stuck firm. One opportunity still existed for the two Japanese sailors to make it back to their mother ship. Akieda was supposed to rendezvous with the *I-20* at sea, close to the shore at Cape Amber, and he had been told that the *I-20* would wait at this position for two days. If Akieda and Takemoto could get ashore, they could conceivably trek overland to Cape Amber, and the submarine could send a dinghy ashore to rescue them. The two Japanese abandoned the midget and swam to the shoreline. They emerged from the sea and started out across the barren landscape of northern Madagascar, determined to avoid capture at all costs. They would be on the loose for fifty-nine hours. On 2 June, sightings of two Japanese prompted the British to dispatch army patrols to hunt them down. A patrol of fifteen British soldiers came upon them at Amponkarana Bay and attempted to force Akieda and Takemoto to surrender. Surrender was inconceivable to the Japanese military, and now that they realized that all hope was lost of a rendezvous with the *I-20*, the Japanese determined to fight it out with the British and sell their lives as dearly as possible. With two pistols and a short sword between them, they managed to kill one British soldier and wound four others before they themselves were killed in the mêlée. Documents taken from their bodies contained details of the midget submarine attacks.

The fate of Ensign Iwase and his midget from the *I-16* remains unsolved to this day. The reported sightings of two submarine conning towers in the harbour prior to the attack on HMS *Ramillies* provides some circumstantial evidence that Iwase and Takata did successfully penetrate the port, but nothing further was ever heard from the vessel except that the day after the attack, another party of British soldiers discovered the body of a Japanese sailor on a beach outside the harbour. Presumably, if Iwase's midget had penetrated the harbour, technical malfunction must have prevented him launching an attack and resulted in both crewmen abandoning the submarine and perishing in the process. Another possible reason for the evidently calamitous end of Iwase's mission was the depth charging conducted by corvettes inside the harbour following the torpedoing of HMS *Ramillies*.

Between 5 June and 8 July the submarines sank a total of twenty-one Allied merchant vessels, with a further ship destroyed by the auxiliary cruisers, all within the Mozambique Channel. RAF and South African Air Force (SAAF) anti-submarine patrols failed to make any contact with Japanese forces. The Japanese force was bold enough to fly reconnaissance missions over the coast of Natal and even the city of Durban on 20 May, 5 June and 4 July, without being challenged by Allied air defences. The Japanese submarine offensive off Africa during 1942 was very successful, but it could have been devastating had Ishizaki launched a coordinated night attack upon the crowded anchorage of Durban. The Japanese submarine force remained interested primarily in sinking Allied warships, hence the attack on HMS *Ramillies* at Diego Suarez, rather than interdicting merchantmen. The attack at Madagascar did keep the *Ramillies* out of service for a year, adding to the inability of the Royal Navy to maintain capital ships in the Indian Ocean or Far East following the losses of the battleship HMS *Prince of Wales* and the battle-cruiser HMS *Repulse* off Malaya in December 1941, prior to the fall of Singapore in February 1942.[4] However, the overall Japanese operation in the Mozambique Channel in June and July 1942 was in reality an isolated operation, demonstrating to Germany Japan's good faith concerning serious naval cooperation within the shared operational area of the Indian Ocean.

On 18 June, under Commander Shinobu Endo, the *I-30* replenished from the Japanese auxiliary cruiser *Aikoku Maru*, and then proceeded to European waters. The *I-30*'s mission was code-named 'Sakura' ('Cherry Blossom 1') by the Japanese. Three hundred miles south of Durban, South Africa, the *I-30* was spotted and attacked by an SAAF patrol aircraft, but escaped undamaged, and on 2 August arrived in the Bay of Biscay. Initially, eight *Luftwaffe* Junkers Ju-88 bombers, which had been ordered to provide the Japanese submarine with air cover as she continued on the surface to France, met the *I-30*. Three days later, surface units of the *Kriegsmarine*, consisting of eight M-class minesweepers and a mine barrage breaker, whose job was to escort the Japanese submarine into the French port of Lorient, met the *I-30*. The Japanese submarine was secured to a floating buoy, and Commander Endo and his crew transferred to a French tender, which took them over to the deck of the U-boat *U-67*, also moored in the harbour. Drifting across the harbour was the sound of suitably martial music from the base band, the dockside lined with interested spectators and servicemen.

The arrival of the *I-30* was an occasion marked with pomp and ceremony by the *Kriegsmarine*, with none other than the commander of the German Navy, *Grössadmiral* Erich Raeder, welcoming Endo and his boat into the U-boat base. Also present was the commander of the U-boat Arm, *Admiral* Karl Dönitz, and the Japanese Naval Attaché to Germany, Captain Yokoi Tadao, who had travelled with his staff from Berlin for the occasion. Endo was decorated with a

German medal (probably the Iron Cross 2nd Class), and in a further U-boat tradition, a woman presented Endo with a large bouquet of flowers. Ashore, the quayside was lined with U-boat crews, soldiers, military nurses, women from army signals detachments, and French civilians. Berlin had previously requested 1,500kg of mica and 660kg of shellac, and Endo delivered both of these in the first underwater *Yanagi* trade. Mica was used in electrical capacitor devices and shellac was required for military munitions. The *I-30* also carried blueprints for the new Japanese Type 91 aerial torpedo. On 6 August a banquet was hosted by the *Kriegsmarine* for the Japanese in the Grand Hall, part of the old French naval arsenal in Lorient. The officers of the *I-30* dined with the Japanese naval staff from Berlin, U-boat and other German Navy officers, some German Army officers from the local garrison, and a few civilians. At that time, the base at Lorient was home to the 2nd U-boat Flotilla '*Saltzwedel*', under the command of *Kapitän zür See* Viktor Schütze (a holder of the Knights Cross of the Iron Cross with Oakleaves). Following naval tradition, German and Japanese enlisted men exchanged cap bands, and the Japanese crew was permitted access to a U-boat to take photographs. However, no German enlisted men were allowed on board the *I-30*. The successful journey of the *I-30* to France was well received in Japan, Vice Admiral Matome Ugaki, Chief of Staff of the Combined Fleet under the command of Admiral Isoroku Yamamoto, noting in his diary that: 'A big welcome given to her was made public in radio photos and announcements by Imperial headquarters.'[5]

To protect the *I-30*, and allow the Germans to refit her before her long return journey to the Far East, she was to remain inside a Keroman bunker, one of Lorient's sixteen supposedly 'bomb-proof' U-boat pens. There, the *I-30* was repainted in U-boat grey, more suitable for operations in North Atlantic and European waters, her engines were overhauled after the long journey, and a quad 20mm *Flakvierling* 38 was fitted, replacing the Japanese anti-aircraft armament which consisted of a Type 96 25mm gun. The Germans also fitted a *Metox*, or 'Biscay Cross', radar detector to the boat,[6] to assist the boat in successfully renegotiating the dangerous Bay of Biscay. A new type of radar, the *Funkmesserbeobachter 1* (FuMB1), also called '*Metox*', was introduced in July 1942. The equipment was used in conjunction with a crude wooden cross-shaped antenna strung with wire, nicknamed the 'Biscay Cross' by U-boat crews. The antenna was rotated by hand from the submarine's conning tower.

Metox emissions were detectable by Allied radar detection equipment, which unfortunately meant that anti-submarine vessels could follow *Metox* signals straight to the U-boat. *Metox* was combined in November 1943 with the FuMB7 '*Naxos*', and when the two apparatus were used in conjunction it gave the U-boat excellent all-round radar coverage. These systems were later combined into a single system in April 1944, either the FuMB24 '*Fliege*' or the FuMB25 '*Müche*' systems.

The *I-30*'s Yokosuka E14Y1 reconnaissance floatplane was repaired and was actually taken on several test flights over Lorient. Dressed in fur-lined, one-piece beige flying suits, helmets and goggles, the Japanese pilot and his crewman waved happily to their German hosts as they, most probably for subsequent propaganda purposes, filmed the flights. The later discovery of film by the Allies depicting an aircraft in Japanese *hinomaru* or rising sun disc markings airborne over France certainly contributed to rumours that the Imperial Japanese Naval Air Service had operated a unit in France. Of course, this was never the case. The Germans, however, did operate Arado Ar-196 reconnaissance floatplanes in the Far East, flying them in Japanese markings (more on this later).

While their submarine was being refitted in Lorient, Commander Endo and the crew of the *I-30* travelled to Berlin where Endo was decorated again, this time by Hitler himself, at the Reich Chancellery. During the return journey to Lorient, the crew of the *I-30* stopped in Paris for a sightseeing trip, climbing to the top of the Eiffel Tower and shopping on the Champs Élysées.

In return for the mica and shellac, the Germans loaded the *I-30* with a mass of naval equipment: a U-boat torpedo fire-control system (a kind of early computer) and five G7a (air) torpedoes, a simple torpedo, propelled by steam produced by the burning of alcohol in air, supplied from a small on board reservoir. It was driven by a single propeller, and had a top speed of 44 knots up to a range of 4.5 miles. Because the torpedo left a wake of very visible bubbles in the water, this type of torpedo was restricted to use in night attacks. Three G7e (electric) torpedoes were also loaded aboard. The G7e was an electrically powered torpedo, which was driven by a small 100bhp electric motor. It was fitted with two contra-rotating propellers and it left no visible wake in the water. Its maximum speed was 30 knots, with a range of 3.5 miles. Other items included *Bolde* sonar deflector equipment, a new search radar, a *Metox*, a hydrophone array, fifty

Enigma code machines, rocket and glider bombs, anti-tank guns, a Zeiss anti-aircraft fire-control system, 200 20mm anti-aircraft guns; a *Würzburg* air defence ground radar with blueprints and an assortment of other cargo, including one million yen in uncut diamonds. Also aboard was a Japanese engineer who was travelling home as a passenger. There had been considerable British interest in the new *Würzburg* radar developed by the Germans. On the night of 27/28 February 1942, C Company, 2nd Battalion, 1 Parachute Brigade raided a radar site at Bruneval, France, capturing vital components of a *Würzburg* radar installation, before successfully exfiltrating back to England after scattered fighting at the radar site. Also present that night were two Royal Army Dental Corps soldiers (a staff sergeant and a private), who had decided to invade France together. They had stolen a boat and crossed the Channel undetected, and were engaged in some low-grade sabotage when the Paras launched their raid on Bruneval radar station.

The *I-30* set sail from Lorient on 22 August and arrived in Penang on 8 October. The Chief of the Japanese Ministry of the Navy's Logistics Section, Admiral Hoshina Zenshiro, demanded ten of the naval Enigma machines. They were duly installed in his headquarters in Singapore, which was reached early on 13 October. After a remarkably rapid turnaround in port lasting only six-and-a-half hours, the *I-30* sailed again for Japan. However, tragedy befell the boat, the submarine striking a Japanese defensive mine near Singapore. Fourteen of the crew perished when the *I-30* sank. Admiral Ugaki summed up the feelings of Imperial Headquarters over the loss of the vessel and cargo, commenting:

> All those aboard were rescued except about a dozen petty officers and men, but the new arms and parts which our navy needed most were lost. Their transportation to our homeland was the main object of her being sent to Europe. After covering more than eighty percent of the whole trip, she met this disaster in our occupied port. Nothing could be more regrettable. I also felt my responsibility to the high command and especially to the German authorities for the loss. At least the arms on board her should be salvaged by all means.[7]

Later, some of the German naval equipment stored on board the submarine was indeed salvaged by Japanese Navy divers, including most of the 20mm flak guns. Between August 1959 and February 1960, the hulk of the *I-30* was raised and scrapped by a Japanese firm.

Although the *I-30* was lost before completing her mission, ironically a casualty of 'friendly-fire', the submarine had successfully transported a valuable cargo from the Far East to France, loaded up with an equally important exchange cargo, and made it back to friendly waters intact. The success of the *I-30*'s mission to German-occupied France demonstrated to both Germany and Japan the possibilities presented by underwater trade voyages. Although submarines were unable to transport the huge cargoes originally delivered by surface merchant ships, the high quality military merchandise transported to Japan from the Nazis was of inestimable value to the Japanese war effort, primarily in the development of their own versions of German weapons.

Following the successful run by the *I-30* to Lorient, the Imperial Japanese Navy dispatched the slightly larger submarine *I-8*, at 2,600 tons displacement. Constructed by Kawasaki prior to the Second World War, the *I-8* had been commissioned into service on 15 December 1938 at Kobe. The *I-8* was the second Japanese submarine to be ordered to conduct a *Yanagi* underwater mission to German-occupied France.

On 1 June 1943 the fully laden *I-8* left Kure, Japan, carrying a cargo consisting of wolfram and other scarce metals. In addition to this she also carried two Type 95 torpedoes, Type 95 submarine torpedo tubes, and a brand new Japanese reconnaissance aircraft. The new Type 95 torpedo had been withheld from the Germans when the *I-30* had sailed. Older steam-driven torpedoes had been substituted before the submarine sailed. The Japanese now made the new electric torpedo available for study by the Germans. Under Commander Shinji Uchino the *I-8* sailed towards Singapore. The submarine also carried an additional forty-eight Japanese submariners and their commanding officer, Lieutenant Commander Sadatoshi Norita. Norita was to assume command of *U-1224*, a German Type IXC40 U-boat, which was to be presented as a gift to the Imperial Japanese Navy from Hitler (the boat was subsequently commissioned the *RO-501* by the Japanese).[8] Other passengers travelling to France included a lieutenant commander medical officer, and a technical commander who was an expert in torpedo boat engines. His job was to study German efforts in the development of fast torpedo boats, or S-boats, enabling the Japanese to develop their own versions for use against the Americans. S-boats (*Schnellboote*) were fast motor torpedo boats erroneously known as E-boats by the Allies. The 'S' stood for '*Schnell*' or 'Fast' in German, whereas the 'E' represented 'Enemy' in the Allied term for these craft.

The *I-8* also carried an additional four naval clerks who were expert in codes and translation. The boat was crammed with 160 sailors of all ranks, and the additional crew required to train on and man the U-boat *U-1224* were housed mainly in the torpedo rooms forward. Japanese submarines did not normally suffer from the extremely cramped and dirty conditions to be found aboard German U-boats. The largest German ocean-going attack submarines, the Type IXD2 U-cruisers, were considerably smaller than the Japanese ocean-going boats of the period. Three versions of the Type IX were to be used during the coming forays into the Indian Ocean and the Far East. The Type IXC40 was the smallest, at 76.7 metres in length, displacing 1,144 tons surfaced. The larger, at 87.5 metres in length and 1,799 tons surfaced, Types IXD1 and IXD2 U-cruisers were also converted to carry freight, taking up further valuable space within the boat. The crews of these boats, conducting some of the longest war patrols of any U-boats during the Second World War, lacked much in the way of water to clean themselves. And because of the development of improved Allied anti-submarine patrols, on arrival at their destinations they were sickly pale after having to *schnorchel* under water for much of the voyage, and fully bearded as no water was available for shaving. The U-boat was designed to operate primarily on the surface, only submerging when threatened with attack or when conducting a rare daylight attack. Once forced beneath the surface the conventional U-boats, such as the Type VII and Type IX, employed by the *Kriegsmarine* prior to and alongside the belated entry of more technologically advanced Electro-boats (Types XXI and XXIII) in 1945, could only remain submerged for a limited amount of time before they had to surface to recharge the batteries that drove the underwater electric motors, and replenish the boat's fresh air supply.

When the Germans overran The Netherlands in 1940 they discovered a Dutch invention, which the Germans expropriated and named the *schnorchel*. This was a pipe system that enabled a submarine to run its diesel engines while submerged – potentially giving a U-boat a massive underwater range and greater protection from aerial detection and attack. It was to be 1944 before the Germans began using *schnorchel* technology on their U-boats, as increased Allied anti-submarine measures meant U-boats could no longer risk prolonged periods spent on the surface without inviting destruction. The *schnorchel* masts were vulnerable to damage and faults, the first caused by the hostile conditions found at sea, and the second because of poor quality control checks at factories and deliberate sabotage by foreign workers. If a U-boat exceeded 6 knots while submerged and employing the *schnorchel* the air mast would break off. Staying submerged meant that rubbish rapidly accumulated inside the boat, making the fetid air even more noxious. Previously, the boat would have surfaced and the rubbish been disposed of over the side. Crewmen had to resort to packing torpedo tubes with rubbish, and firing it into the sea while submerged. A third problem was that early models of the *schnorchel* tended to close their valves when hit by waves, which resulted in the diesel engines suddenly being starved of oxygen. The engines would then suck all the air from the U-boat, causing the crew to suffer ear pains, sometimes resulting in damaged eardrums.

Japanese submarine crews, in contrast to crews aboard German U-boats, arrived in France clean-shaven and well turned out, owing to the increased space and supplies aboard their boats. Aboard the *I-8*, because of the extra crewmen, only six torpedoes were carried as cargo. Two of these were the Type 95s, destined for German scientists and designers. The remaining four were carried in the boat's own torpedo tubes, ready for any targets that presented themselves.

When the *I-8* arrived at Penang on 11 June, additional cargo for the Germans was taken on board the submarine, consisting of raw rubber in bales, tin and quinine. The Yokosuka E14Y1 reconnaissance floatplane, along with the two pilots normally present in the boat's complement, and the four crewmen required to keep the plane airworthy and operational at sea, were disembarked, the aircraft's watertight hangar being used as valuable additional storage space on the submarine. After refuelling from the submarine *I-10* at sea, the *I-8* departed for France on 8 July. The epic journey was very hard on the *I-8* and she sustained storm damage as she battled to round the Cape of Good Hope into the Atlantic Ocean. For ten days the *I-8* had forced her way through fierce South Atlantic storms, conditions not often encountered by most of the crew aboard, with the submarine heading into an alien world of cold mountainous seas, the officers glimpsing the rocky tip of Africa through dense driving rain and howling winds, the big diesels fighting to push the huge submarine into calmer waters. In July the *I-8* encountered a U-boat inbound to France after a patrol off Freetown, West Africa, and the Indian Ocean. Lookouts on the bridge of the U-boat constantly scanned the heavy grey seas and overcast sky for any signs of Allied patrols, aircraft or a merchant ship. For a few minutes the officers and lookouts aboard the German U-boat and the *I-8* would have surveyed each other's crafts through binoculars, casting their eyes over the alien vessels. Certainly, *Korvettenkapitän* Peter-Erich Cremer[9] of *U-333*, a Type VIIC, had never seen so large a submarine in that part of the world, and he reported to U-boat Control of sighting a 'strange' submarine through his binoculars running on the surface. The *I-8* was maintaining radio silence on her run to France, so no communication occurred between U-boats and the Japanese boat at sea. The only communication was between U-boat Control and the Japanese submarine, which was monitoring her progress towards France. U-boat Control sent a message to the *I-8* on 29 July, changing her destination from La Rochelle to the U-boat base at Brest. The Germans had code-named the *I-8* '*Flieder*' ('Lilac').

Because of the great danger posed to submarines in the Bay of Biscay at this stage of the war by Allied surface and aerial submarine-hunting groups, the *Kriegsmarine* wisely chose to meet the Japanese submarine while she was still out in the Atlantic in order to fit a radar detector to the *I-8*, and pass over a German pilot to lead the *I-8* safely into port. U-boat Control would communicate with one of their submarines, and order her to locate the *I-8*. Accordingly, on 20 August, the *I-8* rendezvoused with *U-161*, a Type IXC commanded by *Korvettenkapitän* Albrecht Achilles.[10] The following day Achilles dispatched *Oberleutnant zür See* Jahn to act as pilot, and two petty officers to operate the *Metox*, or 'Biscay Cross', radar detector, which was installed on the Japanese submarine's bridge. This officer and two men were fortunate. They stayed with the *I-8* on the journey to Brest, while *U-161* parted company with the Japanese submarine and set a course for Brazil, only to be lost with all hands south-west of the Azores less than a month after the rendezvous. *U-161* was sunk on 27 September 1943 in the South Atlantic by a Mariner of Squadron VP-74, US Navy. All fifty-three crew aboard were killed.

Throughout the period 29–31 August the *I-8* negotiated the Bay of Biscay, and the *Luftwaffe* provided Junkers Ju-88 aircraft to protect the vessel on its journey into Brest. The *Kriegsmarine* dispatched the destroyers *T-22*, *T-24* and *T-25* as further protection, along with S-boats, and the *I-8* successfully arrived in the German-occupied port on 31 August 1943. As the Japanese submarine swept gracefully into the U-boat base, her crew, bedecked in their navy blue square rig, lined the casing standing smartly at attention. The conning tower was crowded with officers, one standing high up on the periscope from where a large rising sun flag hardly moved in the still air. As the little French tug eased the submarine towards one of the 'bomb-proof' bunkers housing the submarine pens, crowds lined the quayside, many frantically waving little swastika and rising sun flags at the immaculate Japanese crewmen. The officers' impassive faces, clean-shaven unlike German U-boat crews returning from patrol, gave nothing away regarding their relief at having completed the epic journey safely. Hundreds of stick figures lining the roofs of the Keroman bunkers must have awed the Japanese seamen as they disappeared into the huge gaping concrete mouth of the pens. The Germans had spared little expense in providing their sea wolves complete protection from Allied air power, but they soon realized that their U-boats were immediately vulnerable at their new French bases from Allied air attack.

Befehlshaber der U-boots (BdU), or U-boat Control, was formed in September 1939, and divided into two sections: *BdU – Operationsabteilung* (Operational Department) which controlled all U-boat operations in the Atlantic Ocean, the North Sea and the Indian Ocean, and *BdU – Organizationsabteilung* (Organizational Department), which was responsible for all U-boat personnel and training. U-boats in the Mediterranean Sea and Arctic Sea came under the control of their own *Führer der U-boots* (Leader of U-boats), and the Black and Baltic Seas were controlled by special area commands. The entire BdU organization remained under the command of Karl Dönitz for the duration of the war.

The RAF had first attacked Lorient on 27 September 1940, following the Battle of Britain. RAF raids had resulted in over 4,500 tons of bombs being dropped on Lorient, with the aim of destroying both U-boats and the facilities that serviced them, but without much success. The Germans realized that in order to maintain the effective and efficient running of the U-boat base despite the ever-present threat of aerial disruption, gigantic shelters would be required in which to move the U-boats while they were in port, and where all maintenance could be safely conducted. The first shelter, Keroman I, was begun in February 1941, followed by Keroman II in May and Keroman III, the largest at 24,000 square metres, in October 1941. It was not to be operational until May 1943. Keroman I, with a ceiling 3.5 metres thick, housed five pens, enabling five U-boats to tie up. Keroman II contained berths for eight U-boats, and the enormous Keroman III, with a concrete roof of between 6.4 and 7.4 metres thickness, contained a further eight pens. All the torpedoes required for operations by the U-boats were stored separately in six bunkers constructed to the north-west of the Keromans.

After disembarking from the *I-8*, *Admiral* Theodor Kranke, Commander of German Naval Forces West, greeted Commander Uchino, and some German medals and decorations were awarded to Japanese crewmen on the quayside while a Germany Navy band played. The entire arrival and ceremony was filmed by the Germans for propaganda purposes. In the meantime the *I-8* was towed into the 'bomb-proof' U-boat pens to protect the vessel from aerial attack.

German Naval Forces West (or Navy Group West) under the command of *Admiral* Kranke, commanded the destroyers, torpedo boats, and smaller naval vessels and shore establishments based in the ports of occupied France and the Low Countries. This military area was under the command of *Generalfeldmarschall* Gerd von Rundstedt. Kranke reported directly to *Oberkommando der Kriegsmarine* (OKM), part of central German military headquarters, meaning that von Rundstedt could not issue direct orders to Kranke, rather only request his cooperation. Navy Group West also controlled most of the coastal artillery critical to the defence of the Atlantic Wall. Once the enemy effected a landing, however, command of naval gun batteries was to be switched to local army commanders under the overall leadership of von Rundstedt.

The U-boat base at Brest at this time was home to the 1st U-boat Flotilla *Weddigen*, under the command of *Kapitän zür See* Werner Winter (a holder of the Knights Cross). The Japanese officers and men were housed by their German comrades in some luxury ashore and entertained by the officers of the 1st U-boat Flotilla. Commander Uchino was taken to meet the commander of the *Kriegsmarine*, *Grössadmiral* Karl Dönitz, with the crew of the *I-8* undertaking sightseeing and shopping in Paris in similar fashion to the crew of the

I-30. Dönitz had now taken over from Raeder as head of the German Navy. *Grössadmiral* Erich Raeder was *Chef der Marine Leitung* (Navy Chief) between 1928 and 1935, when the *Kriegsmarine* was formed from the old Weimar *Reichsmarine*. Raeder was then titled *Oberbefehlshaber der Kriegsmarine* (Commander in Chief of the German Navy) until 30 January 1943 when he was sacked by Hitler and replaced by the newly promoted *Grössadmiral* Karl Dönitz, formerly *Führer der Unterseeboote* (Senior Officer Submarines). Dönitz relinquished command of the navy to *Generaladmiral* Hans-Georg von Friedeburg on 1 May 1945, and twenty-two days later, following the suicide of von Friedeburg as a result of his feelings over signing the German surrender documents at Luneburg Heath, the last man to command the by now surrendered Nazi navy was *Generaladmiral* Walter Warzecha until 22 July 1945, when the *Kriegsmarine* was disbanded until the formation of the post-war *Bundesmarine* in 1955.

By October the *I-8* was ready to attempt the return voyage to Japan, loaded with a German *Yanagi* cargo including six of the latest German machine-guns with ammunition; aircraft bombsights and naval navigational equipment; the latest German radar and radar detection equipment (including the *Rotterdam Gerat*); several 20mm *Flakvierling* 38 anti-aircraft guns; the latest German electric torpedoes; and much needed penicillin. Additionally, and in common with all the journeys undertaken by Japanese submarines to and from Europe, she carried passengers – the former Japanese Naval Attaché to Germany, Rear Admiral Tadao Yokoi; the former Japanese Naval Attaché to France, Captain Sukeyoshi Hosoya; three *Kriegsmarine* officers (one of whom, a *Leutnant zür See* Koch, spoke Japanese); a major from the German Army; and four German scientists expert in radar and hydrophone technologies. Two pieces of equipment which the Japanese had purchased from the Germans, but had, with the difficulties of surface blockade-running, absolutely no chance of transporting back to Japan, had to remain with the manufacturers.

The Japanese had purchased two German tanks, a PzKpfw V Ausf D Panther and a PzKpfw VI Tiger in 1943. Presumably the Japanese wanted the two heavy tanks for testing and evaluation purposes, before either obtaining a licence to build them in Japan or gaining permission to copy elements of their designs for incorporation into a new heavy Japanese tank to supercede the rather flimsy medium and light tanks then employed by the Imperial Japanese Army in the war in the Pacific. Japanese tanks, although relatively successful against the armour deployed by the Chinese, proved to be no match for the Sherman tanks fielded by the Allied armies in the Far East. Although the Japanese owned the Panther and Tiger tanks, they loaned them indefinitely to the German Army when they realized they could not transport them to Japan. What the purchase demonstrates, however, is the level of interest exhibited by the Japanese military in all aspects of German military technology during the war. It was only the tenuous nature of the supply routes between the two countries, and the small lift capacity of the submarine transports, which prevented more extensive transfers of military technology. In the case of Japan, this might have enabled them to inflict reverses or even halted the inexorable progress of the Allies in the Pacific and Burma.

The *I-8* departed from Brest on 6 October, and after an eventful journey, which included an attack by Allied anti-submarine aircraft, and the sustaining of further storm damage in the South Atlantic, she arrived in Singapore, Malaya on 5 December. On 21 December 1943 the *I-8* arrived back at Kure, Japan after successfully completing an incredible round-trip journey of 30,000 miles. For achieving this astounding feat of submarine seamanship and endurance, Commander Uchino was promoted to the rank of Captain, effective on 1 May 1944. The *I-8*'s war continued in the Pacific and Indian Oceans until the final climactic battle for the Japanese island of Okinawa in 1945, when the *I-8* was presumed lost on 10 May with all hands.

Enter the Italians: The *Aquila* Missions

Blockade-running was virtually the sole means by which German industry could be supplied from outside sources with rubber, tin, tungsten and molybdenum. By early 1943 it was clear to both the Germans and the Japanese that the level of surface ship attrition meant that an alternative method of continuing the *Yanagi* trade had to be put into operation, otherwise the entire trade would collapse under the pressure of Allied attacks.

Although surface ship blockade-running would continue until January 1944, when Hitler's direct intervention halted the catastrophic losses being inflicted upon Germany's merchant fleet, the Germans had long since pinned their hopes on submarines continuing the trade undetected by the Allies. Several factors made the submarine delivery of *Yanagi* trade cargoes particularly attractive to the Germans. Primarily, the German failure to win the Battle of the Atlantic led to a reappraisal of U-boat operations generally, and the German defeat had freed up submarines that could be converted into cargo-carriers. The Germans were also interested in moving some U-boat operations into the Indian Ocean in the hope of discovering another 'happy time', striking at what were rightly believed to be poorly protected Allied convoys supplying the armies fighting in North Africa, and also supplying the Soviet Union. The long cruises already completed by Japanese submarines to Europe demonstrated that such a plan was feasible and had been successfully tested. It was also at this point that Germany was to call upon its limping ally Italy to assist them in keeping the supply line open with the Japanese.

The Royal Italian Navy possessed several submarines that were substantial enough to carry a reasonable quantity of cargo to the Far East. Earlier in the war the Italians had attempted to support the German U-boat campaign in the Atlantic by operating ten of their own submarines from the German base in Bordeaux, without significant success. The ten boats were of the 1,036-ton *Marconi*-class. The group based at Bordeaux was the XI Submarine Group, under the command of Rear Admiral Angelo Parona. As a temporary measure, while the Germans continued efforts to design and build submarines dedicated to cargo transportation to the Far East, it was decided to approach their Italian allies and obtain permission to utilize existing Italian boats. To this end, Hitler approved the plan at the Führer Naval Conference of February 1943. Dönitz had considered the Italian submarines to be unsuitable for anti-convoy operations in the Atlantic, and had suggested to Hitler that they should be used instead in the *Yanagi* trade, though still crewed by Italians.

The Italian Admiralty was not prepared to meekly hand over ten of their valuable submarines to the German Navy, and through negotiations demanded ten brand-new Type VIIC *Atlantik* U-boats in exchange for their large boats operating out of Bordeaux. However, by the time agreement was reached, with the Germans reluctantly parting with a batch of newly constructed Type VIICs, two of the Italian submarines had been lost on operations in the Atlantic. The remaining eight were taken out of service, and conversion to cargo-carriers was begun by the Germans under the code-name 'Aquila'.

The Royal Italian Navy also possessed two *Romolo*-class transport submarines, which would not have required any conversion work, and could have been employed immediately running *Yanagi* cargo to the Japanese while the Germans converted the '*Aquila*' boats in France and further prepared their own U-boats as transport submarines. The *Romolo*-class submarines were just being completed by the Italians, built originally with the idea of delivering supplies to Italian forces in North Africa. However, by that stage of the war, Italian forces in North Africa had been severely defeated and the large cargo submarines were of no further use to them. The Italians, for reasons that remain unclear, turned down the German request for the two boats in June 1943.

After a six-week conversion in the yards, the eight Italian submarines were ready to begin operations as cargo-carriers. Each boat could carry 150 tons of cargo, 90 tons stowed in bunkers on the boat's superstructure and the remaining 60 tons secured inside the submarine. In theory at least, each boat would be able to make two round-trip voyages to the Far East each year, meaning that the Italians would transport 4,800 tons of supplies annually to the Third Reich's war machine, and deliver a further 4,800 tons annually in return to the Japanese. It can be seen immediately that the cargo tonnage was pathetically small when compared with the lift capacity of surface blockade-runners, but this tonnage was calculated to increase as U-boats were diverted as cargo submarines, and the delivery was considered safer under the water rather than upon it.

Each Italian boat's 100mm deck gun was removed to make space for the cargo bunkers, and the eight torpedo tubes and ammunition storage magazines were converted into diesel fuel storage bunkers. However, the boats would still require refuelling on the outward and return legs of the voyages, necessitating the Germans to provide U-tankers in the Atlantic and Indian Oceans for this task. This would take them away from their intended operational use of refuelling U-boats conducting war patrols enabling the Germans to extend their convoy interdiction ranges and durations.

In May 1943 the first three Italian submarines sailed, followed by two more in June. However, by August only three of these boats had reached Singapore. These were: *Aquila II* (formerly the *Guiliani*), *Aquila III* (formerly the *Cappellini*) and *Aquila VI* (formerly the *Torelli*). *Aquila VI* departed from Bordeaux for Singapore on 14 June carrying a mixed cargo consisting of mercury, steel, 800 Mauser MG

151/20 cannons, one example of a 500kg SG500 bomb, and German torpedoes. She also embarked passengers for the voyage, including Colonel Kinjo Satake, a Japanese officer who had undergone extensive training on the latest communications techniques in Germany, and Heinrich Foders of the German company Telefunken, who was travelling to Japan accompanied by two mechanics, and finally, a set of blueprints for the new *Würzburg* anti-aircraft radar system. The MG 151 aircraft cannons were destined to be fitted to a Japanese fighter design that provides an excellent example of German–Japanese technical cooperation during the war. Kawasaki had purchased a licence to build the German DB. 601 liquid-cooled aircraft engine in 1937, which the Japanese modified and lightened to produce the Ha-40. The Japanese determined to produce a fighter aircraft based on the German Messerschmitt Bf-109E, and they had received, through the *Yanagi* trade, a working example of the famous German fighter. From this design the Japanese produced the Kawasaki Ki-61 *Hien* (Flying Swallow), and the prototype was tested extensively against both the Bf-109E and a captured American P-40E Warhawk. The Ki-61 performed well in comparison, and full construction began. The MG 151 cannons were fitted to many of the earlier versions of the Ki-61, the Japanese eventually producing 2,654 examples of the Ki-61-1 and the 61-1a versions of the fighter. Employed by the Imperial Japanese Army Air Service in the campaign in New Guinea in April 1943, the Allies assigned the code-name 'Tony' to the type. The *Hien* was further updated in 1944; the Ki-61-II being built in limited numbers, and engine production became inadequate. Many airframes were completed, but they lacked engines, until in early 1945 some engineers fitted an airframe with the Ha-112 radial engine, instead of the more complex liquid-cooled Ha-40.

The result was an amazing fighter aircraft, one of the best of any nation during the Second World War, which came to be designated the Ki-100. The Japanese were unable to manufacture a sufficient number to turn the tide of the war in 1945, but the Ki-100 remains an excellent example of the German–Japanese cooperative design effort, and during one of its first engagements with US Navy aircraft during the Battle of Okinawa in 1945 a unit of Ki-100s shot down fourteen Grumman F6F Hellcat fighters without any loss to themselves. The Ki-100, along with early German and Japanese jet interceptors such as the Messerschmitt ME-262 and the Types XXI and XXIII

Electro-boats, are examples of 'too little too late'. Even with technically superior weaponry the Germans and the Japanese were doomed to lose the war in any event. The *Yanagi* trade was vital to the cross-fertilization of ideas and examples of technologically advanced weaponry between Germany and Japan, with the Japanese benefiting greatly from the exchanges.

On 12 August *Aquila VI*'s fuel situation had become critical, with every chance that the boat would run out of fuel in the Indian Ocean. However, the Italians managed to successfully rendezvous with *U-178* under *Korvettenkapitän* Wilhelm Dommes[11] (later the commander of the German U-boat base at Penang in Japanese-occupied Malaya, and then Chief of the Southern Area with responsibility for all U-boat operations in the Far East). The two boats travelled the remainder of the route together, arriving in Penang on 29 August 1943. On 31 August, *Aquila VI* arrived in Singapore and unloaded her passengers and cargo. With Mussolini deposed and the future of Italy in the Axis alliance in doubt, the Japanese prevented *Aquila II*, *Aquila III* and *Aquila VI* from departing from Singapore to begin the return journey to France, and the Germans delayed sending the remaining three *Aquila* boats that were still in Bordeaux. In common with *Aquila II* and *Aquila III*, the Italian crews were all taken prisoner by the Japanese on the orders of the commander of the 9th Base Unit at Sabang, Vice Admiral Kumeichi Hiroaki, following the Italian surrender on 8 September 1943.

The armistice was to prove a disaster for Italian military and naval forces in the Far East. Italian surface assets suffered a mixed fate, with the auxiliary cruiser *Calitea II* being scuttled by her crew in Kobe harbour, the gunboats *Carlotto* and *Lepanto* and the steamboat *Conte Verde* scuttled in Shanghai, and the colonial sloop *Eritrea* managing to flee to Colombo in Ceylon (now Sri Lanka), where she was surrendered to the British. The Italian submarine *Cagni* made a dash for South Africa where she also surrendered to the British, with the remaining Italian soldiers and sailors garrisoning concessions in Beijing and Tientsin in China, fighting Japanese forces sent to disarm and intern them. There was particularly savage resistance from one hundred soldiers and sailors defending the radio station inside the Italian concession in Beijing under Lieutenant Commander Baldasarre who held off a 1,000 strong Japanese infantry regiment for twenty-four hours before surrendering. Afterwards, all but twenty-nine of the Italian defenders declared themselves willing to

71

fight on for the Axis, the rest ending up enduring the brutality of a Japanese prisoner of war camp in Korea.[12]

The subsequent operation of former Italian submarines by the Germans was known as '*Merkatur*' or Mercury.

Notes

1. Boyd, C. & Yoshida, A., *The Submarine Force and World War II*, Naval Institute Press, Shrewsbury, 1995, pp. 24–6.
2. *Ibid.*, p. 40.
3. Mollo, A., *The Armed Forces of World War II*, MacDonald & Co. (Publishers) Ltd, London, 1981, p. 252.
4. David, S., *Military Blunders*, Robinson Publishing Ltd, London, 1997, pp. 63–5.
5. Ugaki, M., *Fading Victory: The Diary of Admiral Matome Ugaki 1941–1945*, University of Pittsburgh Press, Pittsburgh, 1991, p. 234.
6. The FuMB1 *Metox* 600A was a German radar detector installed in U-boats from August 1942 onwards. The system proved to be problematic and was eventually superceded on the introduction of the *Naxos* radar detector from November 1943 onwards.
7. Ugaki, M., *Fading Victory: The Diary of Admiral Matome Ugaki 1941–1945*, University of Pittsburgh Press, Pittsburgh, 1991, p. 234.
8. Blair, C., *Hitler's U-Boat War: The Hunted 1942–1945*, Cassell & Co., London, 1998, p. 558.
9. Wynn, K., *U-Boat Operations of the Second World War: Volume 1: Career Histories, U-1–U-510*, Chatham Publishing, Chatham, 1997, p. 222.
10. *Ibid.*, p. 124.
11. Wynn, K., *U-Boat Operations of the Second World War: Volume 1: Career Histories, U-1–U-510*, Chatham Publishing, Chatham, 1997, p. 134.
12. Felton, M., 'Commands: Italy's Far Eastern Army and Navy Forces', *World War II*, September 2004, p. 12.

Chapter 5

The U-Boats
Move East

The Polar Bear Group

The Germans collected initial reports concerning the commerce raiding possibilities around the Cape Town area during April 1942, prompting Dönitz to divert U-boats from the Battle of the Atlantic to form *Gruppe Eisbär* (Polar Bear Group). An initial Wolf Pack of four boats, long-range Type IXCs, supported by a single '*Milchküh*' U-tanker would sortie south.

The first to depart was *U-172* under the command of *Kapitänleutnant* Carl Emmermann, which left Lorient on 19 August, followed that same day by *Korvettenkapitän* Fritz Poske and *U-504*. Poske was to prove to have a long career in the German Navy, first joining in 1923. He transferred to the U-boat service in 1940 and commissioned *U-504* in July 1941, without first serving as a Watch Officer or commander under training on any other boats. After the war Poske joined the *Bundesmarine* and served West Germany between 1951 and 1963, before retiring. He died in 1984.

On 20 August a further two U-boats also departed from Lorient: *U-156* under *Korvettenkapitän* Werner Hartenstein and *U-68* under *Korvettenkapitän* Karl-Friedrich Merten. Fuel was to be provided on-station by the U-tanker *U-459* under the command of *Kapitänleutnant* Georg von Wilamowitz-Möllendorff, based at Bordeaux.

The *Laconia* Incident

One of the most famous incidents of the U-boat war was the sinking of the *Laconia*. On 12 September Hartenstein was hunting in the South Atlantic, midway between the West African nation of Liberia and Ascension Island. He located a large Allied ship travelling unescorted – an ideal target. After sinking the unidentified ship with torpedoes, Hartenstein surfaced *U-156* hoping to collect intelligence from the ship's officers. However, when Hartenstein stepped onto the U-boat's bridge he was confronted with a nightmare scene of human tragedy. The sea was filled with the upturned faces of many hundreds of people struggling for survival, appalling Hartenstein and his officers with the scale of the disaster. A great many of the survivors were being attacked by scores of sharks attracted to the scene by the loud explosions of the *Laconia*'s boilers on contact with cold sea water as the ship sank. Hartenstein immediately ordered a rescue operation. *U-156* had sunk the Cunard White Star liner *Laconia*, a 19,700-ton ship crewed by 136, and carrying eighty British civilian women and children, 268 British soldiers, 160 Free Polish troops and approximately 1,800 Italian prisoners of war. Hartenstein's two torpedoes had struck the areas used to transport the Italian prisoners of war, and the explosions had killed several hundred. The troops guarding other groups of prisoners had refused to unlock the holding cages, and eventually abandoned their charges to an unpleasant death by drowning. Several hundred other Italians had managed to break out of their holding areas and make it to the boat deck, where crew struggled vainly to properly launch lifeboats and rafts as the ship lurched over severely. British and Polish soldiers refused the Italians access to the lifeboats at gunpoint, and the Italians could do little but join hundreds of other people of all nationalities in the shark infested sea.

The task of rescuing all these people was immense and *U-156* could do little on its own. Considerations of space inside a fighting U-boat meant that only a handful of women survivors could be taken below. Within minutes the U-boat's casing was providing a lifeboat for around 200 assorted nationalities. Clearly more help was required to prevent a tragedy in loss of life approaching the *Titanic* disaster of 1912. Hartenstein sent a radio message to Dönitz, apprising him of the situation and requesting assistance. Dönitz diverted *U-506* under *Kapitänleutnant* Erich Würdemann and *U-507* under *Korvettenkapitän* Harro Schacht to race to the scene, to be joined by the Italian submarine *Cappellini* (later to figure prominently in the *Yanagi* trade). Hartenstein also took the unprecedented step of broadcasting details of the operation, and his position, in plain English to all nearby ships, requesting further assistance. He also promised in the transmission that he had ceased offensive operations. According to Clay Blair in his book *Hitler's U-Boat War: The Hunted 1942–1945*, when Dönitz reported to the Führer the details of the sinking and the rescue operation then under way, Hitler callously suggested that the Italians were expendable: 'Professing to be humiliated and outraged by the loss of Italian comrades, Hitler declared that Hartenstein should have said nothing, quietly submerged, and left the scene.'[1] Blair suggests that Hitler wanted nothing to interfere with the *Eisbär* operation, the 'surprise attack on Cape Town, which was designed to deliver a crippling blow to military supplies destined for the British in Egypt and the Soviets, via the Persian Gulf'.[2] Fortunately for the survivors, Hartenstein, though a loyal officer, chose to save lives rather than end more.

On 15 September the other three submarines arrived at the scene and began taking lifeboats crammed with survivors in tow, as Hartenstein already had four lifeboats secured to his U-boat. The submarines were quickly overwhelmed by hundreds of survivors sheltering on their decks, making it impossible for the submarines to submerge without endangering lives if they were attacked. Hartenstein ordered that Red Cross flags be draped across the gun positions, further identifying their intentions to any Allied patrols. Vichy French warships were racing from Senegal and Dahomey (now Benin) to rendezvous with the rescue flotilla, which was slowly making its way towards land.

On 16 September the submarines were spotted by a US Navy B-24 Liberator based at Ascension Island, which circled the boats menacingly. Hartenstein signalled to the pilot for assistance and the Liberator reported what they had discovered back to base, and Hartenstein's request. The pilot's immediate superior considered the options: he could allow the rescue operation to proceed, which would have meant that the submarines would escape to continue commerce raiding at a later date, or he could take this opportunity to attempt to sink at least one of them. He chose the latter, ordering the circling Liberator to commence an anti-submarine attack. The big bomber dove down and deposited bombs and depth charges over the terrified survivors and submarines, one bomb landing in the midst of a group of lifeboats, another narrowly missing *U-156*. Hartenstein ordered the tow-lines to the lifeboats to be cut, and shouting at the huddled survivors crowding the U-boat's decks, told them to get back into the sea as he had no choice but to dive. Men, women and children tumbled into a roiling sea of exploding aerial bombs and depth charges, hundreds being killed or wounded, and the rescue submarines hastily made off. Later that day Vichy French ships arrived to rescue most of the survivors, 1,041 people in all being recovered from the sea, lifeboats and rafts. A further two *Laconia* lifeboats came ashore in Africa some time later, containing another twenty people.

Blame for the tragedy can be laid at the feet of Hartenstein for initially sinking the *Laconia*, but it was his duty and his mission to intercept Allied commerce. Once he realized the scale of the tragedy unfolding before his very eyes he made extraordinary efforts to save lives, putting his boat and crew in peril of losing their lives as well. The British could be blamed for underestimating the Axis threat to commerce in the region and allowing such a ship to travel totally unescorted. Blame can certainly be laid before the US Navy for their decision to attack a humanitarian rescue mission in such a fashion.

Up until the debacle of the sinking of the *Laconia* and the rescue effort, U-boats had often provided the survivors of the ships they had torpedoed with supplies, medical assistance and directions to the nearest piece of land. This was, however, in contravention of German naval orders issued earlier by Dönitz, Standing Orders 154 and 173. These orders instructed U-boat commanders not to put their boats at risk by rescuing survivors. Dönitz was furious that the Americans had attacked U-boats participating in a rescue mission, clearly displaying Red Cross symbols, and actively asking for assistance from the enemy. Dönitz used the Americans' actions to reinforce what he already felt about the enemy – you could not trust them, and therefore he issued a stronger version of his two previous orders to all U-boat skippers. He ordered that henceforward U-boat skippers were prohibited from assisting survivors in any way, and they were to be left to survive as best they could. This order was brought up at Dönitz's war crimes trial at Nuremberg after the war, but proved to be another accusation against the Admiral which had been taken out of context. Hitler had gone so far as to suggest that survivors of U-boat attacks should be eliminated, but this was dismissed by Dönitz as ludicrous. As for Hartenstein, his leadership in organizing his partially successful rescue of the survivors of the *Laconia* was not officially acknowledged by Dönitz on his return to base. Dönitz criticized him for presuming that he could organize a truce with the enemy, though he was awarded the Knights Cross. The sinking of the *Laconia* had raised Hartenstein's kills to seventeen ships.

Dönitz reserved his praise for Hartenstein's well-executed patrol to the south.

Following the *Laconia* incident Hartenstein was ordered home, his place in *Gruppe Eisbär* being filled by *U-159* under the command of *Kapitänleutnant* Helmut Witte. As related earlier, the Japanese had already launched an attack on Madagascar, so theoretically the British should have been prepared and alert for further Axis attacks in the region of southern Africa. The *Eisbär* boats were able, however, to score many kills over the following months.

Emmermann in *U-172* sank two ships on 7 October, the American *Chickasaw* (6,196 tons) and the Panamanian *Firethorn* (4,700 tons). The next day he dispatched the Greek *Pantelis* (3,845 tons), following this success on the 10th by sinking the British ship *Orcades*. At the end of October, Emmermann found and sank the British *Aldington Court* (4,891 tons) and scored three kills in November – on the 2nd sinking the British *Llandilo* (4,966 tons), the British *Benlomond* (6,630 tons) on the 23rd, and finishing with the American *Alaskan* (5,364 tons).

Poske and *U-504* were also quite successful, highlighting the poor state of British anti-submarine forces in the region. Intercepting Convoy JJ13 on 17 October, Poske sank the 5,970-ton *Empire Chaucer*. On the 23rd he sank another British ship, the 5,669-ton *City of Johannesburg*, and three days later attacked and sank the American Liberty ship *Anne Hutchinson* for 7,176 tons. Two kills were achieved on the 31st, both British ships: *Empire Guidon* (7,041 tons) and *Reynolds* (5,113 tons). Poske's final kill was the Brazilian *Porto Alegre* (5,187 tons) on 3 November. Poske was free to launch attacks on Brazilian commerce and warships following the activities of Harro Schacht and *U-507* off the coast of Brazil in August 1942. Schacht had managed to sink six neutral Brazilian ships, and the Brazilian government had subsequently declared war on Germany and allowed the US Navy to establish a base at Recife.

Merten and *U-68* were particularly successful in the new southern Africa zone of operations. On 12 September Merten sank the British ship *Trevilley* (5,296 tons), followed three days later by the Dutch *Breedijk* (6,861 tons). Intercepting Convoy GR59 on 8 October, Merten accounted for four ships: the Greek *Koumoundouros* (3,598 tons), the Dutch *Gaassterkerk* (8,579 tons), the American *Swiftsure* (8,207 tons) and the British *Sarthe* (5,271 tons). The next day Merten attacked Convoy GR59 again, sinking the American *Examelia* (4,981 tons) and the *Belgian Fighter* (5,403 tons). Merten's final kill of the patrol was on 6 November, sinking the British *City of Cairo* (8,034 tons).

Hartenstein's replacement, Witte, and *U-159* were to prove highly successful, sinking a total of eleven ships during the patrol, seven British, three American and an Egyptian. Bad weather was to preclude a more successful run by all four boats, with *U-172* and *U-68* heading for home in mid-October, while the other two extended their patrols around Durban. At the same time Dönitz sent south four of the latest long-range U-cruisers, the Type IXD2, many of whose commanders were to figure prominently in future operations in the Indian Ocean and later the Far East. The four Type IXD2s were *U-179* under *Fregattenkapitän* Ernst Sobe, which departed on 15 August 1942; *U-178* under the command of *Kapitän zür See* Hans Ibbeken on 8 September; *U-181* under U-boat ace *Kapitänleutnant* Wolfgang Lüth (later *Kapitän zür See*) on 12 September; and *U-177* under *Kapitänleutnant* Robert Gysae on 17 September. All of the boats departed from Germany. Larger than the older Type IXCs employed by *Gruppe Eisbär*, the IXD2 did not require any refuelling during the long haul to South Africa and back.

U-179, although the first to arrive off South Africa around 8 October, was destroyed soon after. Sobe attacked Convoy GR55 on 8 September, sinking the British ship *City of Athens* (6,558 tons) close to Cape Town, but was turned on by one of the convoy escorts, the Royal Navy destroyer HMS *Active*. *Active* lived up to her name, depth charging *U-179* to the surface and promptly ramming the stricken U-boat, which was lost with all sixty-one crew.

Gruppe Seehünd

Dönitz's second foray into the Indian Ocean was named *Seehünd* (Seal), and would witness the dispatch into southern waters of five Type IX U-cruisers, accompanied part of the way by the Type XIV U-tanker *U-459*. Although the *Seehünd* boats were designated a *Gruppe* or Group, each commander was to hunt independently.

U-160 under Knights Cross holder *Korvettenkapitän* Georg Lassen was the first of the hunters to score a kill. On 7 February 1943, *U-160* was in the South Atlantic and attacked an American Liberty ship, the 7,191-ton *Roger B. Taney*, firing two torpedoes, one of which struck the merchantman. However, the US Navy gunners stationed aboard the freighter immediately returned fire at the surfaced U-boat, forcing it to dive. Lassen attacked again, also firing two torpedoes and achieving a strike with one. The Liberty ship went to the bottom along with most of her crew, apart from a few who were plucked from lifeboats barely alive nearly a month later.

Georg Lassen was born on 12 May 1915 in Berlin-Steglitz. He entered the *Kriegsmarine* in 1935, and would end the war in 1945 a *Korvettenkapitän*, having accumulated an impressive array of decorations (besides the Knights Cross with Oakleaves, Lassen was awarded both the Iron Cross 1st and 2nd Class and the U-boat War Badge with Diamonds) and an equally impressive tally of kills: Lassen sank twenty-seven ships and damaged four others. He would eventually become a tactics instructor and the chief of the Officers Company in the *1st U-Boot Lehrdivision* (U-Boat Training Division).

Following his successful kill on 7 February, *U-160* proceeded to hunt off Cape Town. On the night of 2 March, Lassen came upon Convoy DN21, which was en route from Durban to the Suez Canal in Egypt. Lassen tracked the convoy until after midnight on 3 March, when he fired a pattern of eight torpedoes and claimed a total of six enemy vessels sunk and one probable. In reality, Lassen's claim was close to the mark, and his devastating attack on the poorly protected convoy resulted in the destruction of four ships, with a further two damaged. U-boat Control was extremely pleased by Lassen's brilliant attack on Convoy DN21, and Dönitz approved the award of the Oakleaves to Lassen's Knights Cross on 7 March. Throughout the following week Lassen and *U-160* remained off Durban, and augmented his kill tally by sinking the 7,176-ton US Liberty ship *James B. Stephens* on 8 March and the 4,986-ton British freighter *Aelybryn* on 11 March. Following these attacks, and with only three torpedoes remaining, Lassen informed U-boat Control that he was coming home. Lassen's war patrol to South Africa and the Indian Ocean had been an unmitigated success with around 45,200 tons of shipping sent to the bottom. Returning north through the Atlantic his total might have been even more impressive when he fired two of his remaining torpedoes at an unescorted freighter – but he missed. *U-160* arrived back in France on 10 May. In accordance with U-boat Control's efforts to keep some of the more senior and highly decorated officers alive, Lassen was transferred to an instructors post until the end of the war. A new commander, *Oberleutnant zür See*

Gerd von Pommer-Esche led *U-160* out on a final war patrol as part of *Gruppe Monsun* at the end of June 1943 and was sunk bound for the South Atlantic, all hands being lost.

U-506 under *Kapitänleutnant* Erich Würdemann, another U-boat ace, arrived off Cape Town on 7 March. Würdemann was born on 15 January 1914 in Hamburg and had entered the navy in 1933. He was to sink a total of sixteen ships and damage three others before his own early death on 12 July 1943 in the cold wastes of the North Atlantic. Almost immediately after arrival off Cape Town, Würdemann torpedoed the 5,212-ton British freighter *Sabor*, but then his boat was involved in a collision with a submerged unidentified object which damaged the U-boat's periscope and fouled the propeller, forcing *U-506* to stop hunting and withdraw south of Cape Town to a quiet area to make repairs. Two days later, on 9 March, Würdemann came upon the Norwegian freighter *Tabor* and finished her with three torpedoes and shells from the deck gun. U-boat Control informed Würdemann by radio on 14 March that he had been awarded the Knights Cross because his previous accumulation of kills amounted to sixteen ships sunk (Würdemann had previously been awarded the Iron Cross 1st and 2nd Class, and the U-boat War Badge). Würdemann now headed east of Cape Town to interdict coastal convoys, but because the Allies had broken Enigma they were aware of *U-506*'s general position and naval staff were able to re-route convoys around the dangerous U-boat. The success of Allied decryption of German naval codes meant that Würdemann was forced to hang around an unpromising area for several days, until on 19 March he informed U-boat Control that he was returning home. He refuelled from the Type XB U-tanker *U-117* (*Korvettenkapitän* Hans-Werner Neumann) near the Azores on the way home, and arrived back in France on 8 May after a disappointing patrol.

U-509 would have little more luck than *U-506* hunting around South Africa. Commanded by *Korvettenkapitän* Werner Witte (born 5 January 1915 in the Berlin district of Friedenau and joined the navy in 1935), who was on his third patrol, he was on-station off Cape Town by the beginning of February. On 11 February Werner Witte attacked the 4,937-ton British freighter *Queen Anne* with a single torpedo, and sank her. However, a Royal Navy anti-submarine trawler HMS *St. Zeno*, which opened up with gunfire and dropped seven depth charges, in turn attacked the U-boat, but Witte evaded the warship and remained lurking off Cape Town for several more days. Frustrated by a lack of targets and by his own misfortune (Witte had fired torpedoes at several passing ships, but missed on every occasion), U-boat Control had him double back on himself to the north-west of Cape Town, to Saldanha Bay. Witte wasted two weeks patrolling this area without any targets presenting themselves, and by 28 March, short of food, he began the long journey back to France. As *U-509* motored up the south-west coast of Africa, Witte came upon a small convoy south of Walvis Bay on 2 April. Firing blind, relying only on sonar bearings, he shot four torpedoes from maximum range and struck the 7,129-ton British freighter *City of Baroda*, before disengaging and making for a refuelling rendezvous with *U-117*. A disappointed Witte arrived back in France on 11 May.

Fregattenkapitän Gerhard Wiebe managed to slightly augment the success of the *Gruppe Seehünd* effort aboard *U-516*, but also had a poor run in comparison to the success of Lassen and *U-160*. Wiebe was one of the older skippers in the U-boat service. Born on 24 January 1907 in Lautenburg, he had joined the *Reichsmarine* in 1925. The patrol began well for Wiebe, and between 11 and 27 February he sank the British freighter *Helmsprey*, the American freighter *Deer Lodge*, and most significantly of all, a Dutch submarine tender, the *Colombia*. When the tender sank, several Royal Netherlands Navy submarine crews went down with her – a serious blow to Allied personnel. However, the patrol began to deteriorate soon after. *U-516* firstly collided with floating wreckage off Cape Town, which required the boat removing herself to a quiet spot to the south to make repairs, and then on 11 March *U-516* reported to U-boat Control that she was removing herself entirely from the operation and returning home. This was because Wiebe was suffering from severe stomach pains, and had been forced to temporarily hand over command of the boat to his First Watch Officer. However, *U-516* was not out of the war, and on 20 March she sank the 3,663-ton Panamanian freighter *Nortun*. When *U-516* arrived back in France on 3 May, Wiebe was removed from command and sent off to spend the rest of the war as a staff officer, never to command a U-boat again.

Kapitänleutnant Asmus Nicholai Clausen had been awarded a Knights Cross in March 1942 after sinking a total of eighteen ships while commanding the Type VII *U-37* and Type IX *U-129*, and was given command of the brand new Type IXD2 *U-182*, which he took south from Norway with the intention of patrolling

Madagascar. Clausen, known as 'Niko', was born on 2 June 1911 in Flensburg. He joined the *Reichsmarine* as an ordinary seaman in 1929, transferring in September 1935 from the sailing school ship *Gorch Fock* to the U-boat service. Following training Clausen joined *U-26*, under the command of *Kapitänleutnant* Werner Hartmann in April 1936. Selected for officer training at the Navy School at Mürwik, Clausen was commissioned in 1937 and spent two years serving aboard the battle-cruiser *Admiral Graf Spee* and the minesweeper *M-134*. On the outbreak of war in 1939 Hartmann requested him back aboard *U-37* as the First Watch Officer. After completing three war patrols aboard *U-37* and being awarded the Iron Cross 2nd Class, Clausen commissioned into service the Type IID *U-142*, in August 1940. However, he was soon back aboard *U-37*, this time as commanding officer. Clausen completed a further three war patrols, sinking a total of twelve Allied ships, earning himself the Iron Cross 1st Class. In May 1941 *U-37* was relegated to a training flotilla and Clausen took command of *U-129*. His first three war patrols resulted in no kills, but on his fourth outing in the Caribbean Sea, Clausen accounted for seven Allied ships, which earned him the Knights Cross. He then left the boat and in July 1942 commissioned *U-182*, which he would take to the Indian Ocean.

On the journey south Clausen sank the 7,173-ton British Liberty ship *Ocean Courage* west of Freetown, and on 17 February 1943 he rounded the Cape of Good Hope and sank another British freighter, the 4,836-ton *Llanashe*. He then cruised through the Mozambique Channel, patrolling off Durban in South Africa, Lourenço Marques in Portuguese Mozambique and the west coast of Madagascar. However, during the month expended on this section of the patrol, Clausen only destroyed one ship, another Liberty, the American 7,177-ton *Richard D. Spaight*. Beginning the return trip to Norway he augmented his total tonnage by sinking the 5,047-ton British merchantman *Aloe* and a Greek freighter, the 5,838-ton *Adelfortis*, before happening across part of Convoy UGS8, which was en route across the Atlantic from the United States to Gibraltar carrying tanks. A pair of brand new American destroyers, USS *MacKenzie* and USS *Lamb*, were escorting fourteen Landing Ship Tank (LST) vessels. As Clausen approached the convoy in the surfaced *U-182* on the night of 16/17 May, *MacKenzie*'s radar picked up the U-boat. Both destroyers charged down the bearing as *U-182* dived. The destroyers now locked onto the U-boat with their sonar and plastered the area with depth charges before losing contact with the submarine. Strangely it was only around an hour later that two large underwater explosions were picked up by sonar, and Clausen (with twenty-three confirmed kills aboard the three U-boats he had commanded) and his sixty-man crew were never heard from again.

The *Seehünd* operation had been only a modest success. The five U-boats employed in the group had managed to sink twenty Allied ships for approximately 123,000 gross registered tons. In their reports to Dönitz, the surviving four commanders reported that they had been frustrated by Allied anti-submarine operations, as well as the instigation of convoys in southern waters, and many in U-boat Control remained worried that the naval Enigma code had been broken, allowing the Allies to re-route convoys away from the *Seehünd* boats. Although the Germans had not lost any U-boats in the Indian Ocean, the loss of Clausen and the brand-new *U-182* was keenly felt for such a small tonnage sunk. The Japanese had also operated in the Indian Ocean during March, deploying three submarines of the Eighth Submarine Group (Submarine Squadron 8) out of Penang. The *I-27* commanded by Lieutenant Commander Toshiaki Fukumura had sunk the 7,100-ton British freighter *Fort Mumford* off India, along with four other merchantmen totalling 25,000 gross registered tons. The *I-37* sank a further two freighters and the *I-29* sortied to a prearranged rendezvous with *U-180* in the Indian Ocean – the 'High Seas Exchange'.

High Seas Exchange

Thus far the Japanese had successfully sailed two large cargo-carrying submarines to German-occupied France, the *I-30* and *I-8*. Strangely, the first German mission to the Japanese was not based primarily upon trade, but upon an exchange of personnel.

A U-cruiser, *U-180*, a brand new Type IXD1 boat commanded by thirty-eight-year-old Berliner *Fregattenkapitän* (later *Kapitän zür See*) Werner Müsenberg, was chosen to carry out the mission. Although the U-boat was the fastest in the fleet, with a top speed of 20.8 knots surfaced, she was in fact a design failure. Propulsion was provided by six Mercedes-Benz 1,500 horsepower water-cooled diesel engines, which were adapted from those propelling German S-boats. Although fast, *U-180*'s engines smoked heavily and created intense heat throughout the boat, which made her unsuitable for operating in the tropics. Armed with four bow and two stern torpedo tubes, she carried twenty-seven torpedoes (which included twelve stored in canisters mounted on the superstructure), and was fitted with a 105mm gun on the deck in front of the conning tower. The submarine's complement numbered sixty-three. *U-180*'s mission was to sail into the Indian Ocean and meet the Japanese submarine *I-29*. The two submarines were then to 'cross-deck' cargo and personnel in mid-ocean, and then the submarines would part company and return to their respective home bases.

The night before departing from Kiel, Germany, *U-180* gained two passengers – the Indian Nationalist leader Subhas Chandra Bose and his aide Dr Habib Hasan. In contrast to Mahatma (born Mohandas) Gandhi, Bose preached an aggressive confrontation with the British Imperial authorities in India and viewed the war in Europe as weakening the British grip on India. The British had placed Bose under house arrest in Calcutta, but in January 1941 he had slipped away into Afghanistan, and from there had entered the Soviet Union. After failing to find support from the Soviets for an insurrection in India, they suggested he go to Nazi Germany. Bose duly arrived in Berlin in April 1941. German forces in Libya had recently captured the 3rd (Indian) Motorized Brigade, largely intact, and after six months of intensive recruiting, Bose, with German assistance, announced the formation of the *Jai Hind* or Indian National Army. By mid-1943, now designated the 'Free India Legion', the unit numbered around 2,000 men. Shortly afterwards the unit was renamed Infantry Regiment 950 of the German Army. From May to August 1943 it was used by the Germans on garrison duties along the North Sea coast of The Netherlands, after which the unit was transferred to France where it was involved in anti-partisan duties until August 1944 when, following D-Day and the advance of the Anglo-American armies, Infantry Regiment 950 retreated towards Germany (an officer and two NCOs were killed by the French resistance during this evacuation). Based temporarily in Alsace, the American advance caused the unit's redeployment at Heuberg, Germany. At this time the regiment came under the administrative control of the *Waffen*-SS. In April 1945 Infantry Regiment 950 surrendered to the Americans in the region of Lake Constance.

Bose intended to travel to Japan in order to organize the so-called 'Provisional Government of Free India'. He also wished to attempt

1. The Japanese submarine *I-8* entering the protective bunkers at the German U-boat base at Brest, 31 August 1943. *(Author's collection)*

2. *Korvettenkapitän* Heinrich Timm, skipper of *U-862*, pictured in the tropics. Timm was the only U-boat commander to patrol in the Atlantic, Indian and Pacific Oceans during the Second World War.

(Courtesy of Ted Agar)

3. *U-862*, a Type IXD2 U-cruiser, resupplying in 1944. This photograph shows the anti-aircraft armament and *Wintergarten* area behind the conning tower bridge. *(Author's collection)*

4. *Grössadmiral* Karl Dönitz, Commander in Chief of the German Navy, 1943–45 and father of the Second World War U-boat service. After 1942 Dönitz realized the potential in extending U-boat operations into the Indian Ocean, and establishing bases within the Japanese sphere of control. *(Author's collection)*

5. *Fregattenkapitän* Wilhelm Dommes, the skipper of *U-178*, who assumed command of the first German U-boat base in the Far East at Penang in Malaya in August 1943. Later Dommes was stationed in Singapore as Chief of the Southern Area, responsible for U-boat bases and facilities at Batavia, Surabaya, Penang, Singapore and Kobe.
(Author's collection)

6. Japanese submarines which visited Europe were equipped with a Yokosuka E14Y1 reconnaissance floatplane, seen here being launched by catapult. The Germans later test flew an example over France. *(Author's collection)*

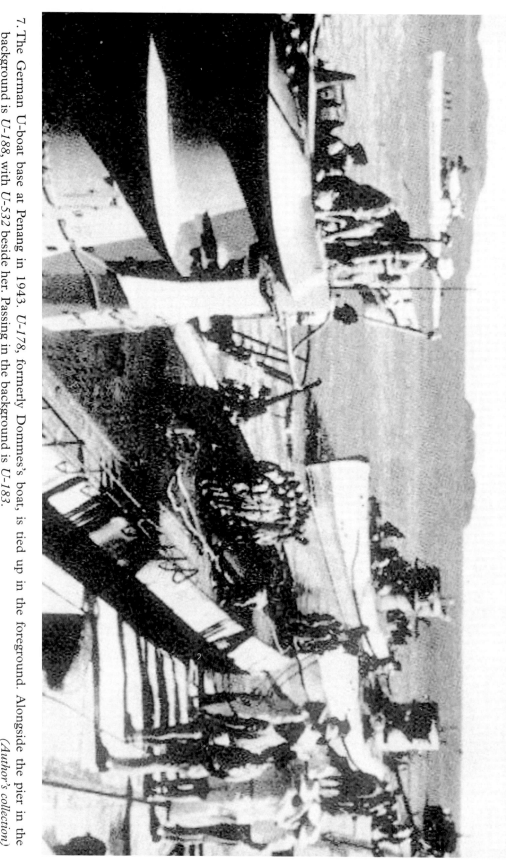

7. The German U-boat base at Penang in 1943. *U-178*, formerly Dommes's boat, is tied up in the foreground. Alongside the pier in the background is *U-188*, with *U-532* beside her. Passing in the background is *U-183*. (*Author's collection*)

8. *Fregattenkapitän* Heinrich Schäfer, commander of *U-183* and later of the former Italian submarine *UIT-23*, shooting the sun with a sextant in the tropics. He eventually died in Singapore in 1944. *(Author's collection)*

9. German and Japanese officers pictured with officials at the Henschel tank factory in Germany. The Japanese purchased a Panther and a Tiger tank for shipment to Japan. This proved to be logistically impossible, so both tanks were loaned to the German Army for the remainder of the war. *(Author's collection)*

10. A Japanese Navy launch alongside *U-511* at the U-boat base at Penang in 1943. *U-511*, code-named '*Marco Polo I*' was Hitler's gift to the Japanese, and would serve the Imperial Japanese Navy as *RO-500*.
(*Author's collection*)

11. The German version of a reconnaissance aircraft for use by submarines – the *Bachstelze* 330 rotary-winged kite, pictured aboard *U-523*. Powered only by the forward motion of the U-boat, the pilot would ascend to around 500 feet, remaining tethered to the U-boat and in contact by telephone with the bridge. Safe only for use in southern waters where Allied anti-submarine patrols were less active.
(*Author's collection*)

12. Mess facilities aboard a Japanese submarine – considerably superior to those found on a German U-boat. Note also the clean shaven appearance of Japanese crewmen; evidence of more access to washing facilities aboard larger Japanese submarines. *(Author's collection)*

13. The Japanese submarine *I-52*, sunk in the Atlantic by American aircraft on her way to France with a valuable *Yanagi* cargo in June 1944. *(Author's collection)*

14. 'Hedgehog' – a devastating new Allied anti-submarine weapon that successfully destroyed several U-boats employed on the run to the Far East. Unlike a depth charge, each Hedgehog bomb only exploded on impact with a submerged submarine. *(Author's collection)*

15. *Kapitän zür See* Wolfgang Lüth, one of Germany's greatest U-boat aces, who took *U-198* into the South Atlantic and Indian Ocean against Allied commerce. *(Author's collection)*

to raise another 'army' from Indian prisoners of war held by the Imperial Japanese Army in Asia, mainly collected following the fall of Singapore in 1942 and the Japanese advance through Burma. The authorities in Tokyo were sceptical about Bose, but some believed that his agitation might be useful to the Japanese military in causing internal trouble for the British authorities in India, and thereby tying up large Imperial forces on internal security duties throughout the subcontinent. Arrangements were made to transfer Bose and his aide from Germany to either Singapore or Japan.

The Allies had, by this stage of the war, successfully decrypted the Japanese diplomatic codes used in communications between Berlin and Tokyo, and were able to monitor the departure of Bose by U-boat from Kiel on 9 February 1943. Importantly, because the Allies had cracked German and Japanese diplomatic codes, they were able to track *U-180*'s mission under Müsenberg. *Fregattenkapitän* Müsenberg was required to replenish his fuel stocks from a U-tanker positioned for this purpose in mid-Atlantic in March, before rounding the Cape of Good Hope into the Indian Ocean.

The *I-29*, under Commander Juichi Izu, was a submarine from the same class of vessels as the *I-30*. The *I-29* had successfully sunk six Allied ships during its career. The boat did not require extensive refuelling stops on its journey to the Indian Ocean, unlike the *U-180*, whose unusual engine configuration consumed a large quantity of the diesel fuel on board. On 5 April 1943 the *I-29* departed from Penang on its top-secret mission. Although under the command of Izu, the boat also carried Captain Teroaka, the commanding officer of Submarine Division 14.

On 3 March *U-180* duly rendezvoused with the Type XIV U-tanker, *U-462* (*Kapitänleutnant der Reserve* Bruno Vowe). Allied code breakers noticed that on 20 March, *U-180* was scheduled to meet an Italian submarine in mid-ocean, close to the equator – apparently to provide the Italian vessel with medical assistance. However, this rendezvous was cancelled, the German commander being unable to locate the Italian submarine.

Although *U-180* was undertaking a groundbreaking mission for the *Kriegsmarine*, traditional U-boat hunting as if the boat were on a normal war patrol was not prohibited. Indeed, Müsenberg scored a notable kill on 18 April, soon after negotiating the Cape of Good Hope, sinking the 8,132-ton British tanker *Corbis*. He tried his luck again on 20 April on another merchant vessel travelling unescorted, but the U-boat partly surfaced, or breeched, during the submerged attack and the merchantman escaped.

On 23 April, 450 miles to the south-east of Madagascar, *U-180* successfully rendezvoused with the *I-29* in heavy seas. The sea conditions prohibited the safe 'cross-decking' of Bose and his aide, or the valuable cargo, and so the two submarines travelled together until the ocean calmed. Commander Izu suggested to *Fregattenkapitän* Müsenberg that the two submarines should make for Sabang in Indonesia, but the German refused. Some food and drink items were exchanged between the two boats as they travelled together. The transfers took place on 27 April.

After Bose and Hasan had been successfully transferred to the *I-29*, the U-boatmen began delivering their cargo to the Japanese. A torpedo tube containing a gun barrel of an unspecified type, together with accompanying ammunition was one of the items sent across. Others included a case of documents, and blueprints of the latest German military designs for weapons, aircraft and submarines (of particular note were blueprints for the Type IXC40 U-boat). Three cases containing 432 *Bolde* noisemakers or sonar decoys also accompanied the case of design materials. Finally, an example of a German hollow charge was sent over to the Japanese.

Once *U-180* had deposited her passengers and cargo she began taking on cargo from the Japanese submarine. Two Japanese naval officers, Commander Tetsushiro Emi, a submarine commander, and Lieutenant Commander Hideo Tomonaga, a submarine designer and engineer who would be involved specifically in the German Navy's midget submarine development programme, clambered aboard the German U-boat. Emi and Tomonaga were charged with observing the construction of German U-boats. Following them came three 21in Model No. 2 aerial torpedoes, some 1.3 tons of the latest Japanese weapons and blueprints (including blueprints of the aircraft carrier *Akagi*, which the Germans wished to use during the construction of their own aircraft carrier the *Graf Zeppelin*, a Type-A midget submarine of the type recently used in the attacks on Pearl Harbor and Madagascar), half a ton of documents, mail and drawings from the German Embassy in Tokyo, and several cases containing valuable quinine. The Japanese delivered three *Kaiten* Type 1 suicide torpedoes to the Germans. The craft displaced 8.3 tons each, were fuelled by a mixture of kerosene and pure oxygen, and had an operational range of about 4 miles at 30 knots. Each *Kaiten* was designed to be launched from specially modified Japanese submarines and was carried on the deck of the mother boat. However, the submarines required for these suicide operations against Allied shipping did not actually become operational themselves until early 1945. Finally, 146 large cases were securely stowed aboard *U-180*; cases containing 2 tons of gold ingots which were destined for the Japanese Embassy in Berlin, where they were used to finance the Japanese diplomatic mission throughout Europe. The two submarines then departed, *U-180* for France, and *I-29* for Japan. The crew of *U-180* were to be plagued by cockroaches and beetles from the Far East that had secreted themselves among the boxes and machinery exchanged with the Japanese. They also picked up some lice during the exchange, which was to make the return journey somewhat uncomfortable.

As *U-180* approached the coast of South Africa, close to New London, the smoke created by the boat's diesels while running on the surface attracted the attention of two Allied aircraft. Investigating the smoke, an unarmed Avro Anson training aircraft of No. 44 Air School SAAF came close on 12 May, but *U-180*'s 20mm flak barrage saw it off.[3] The second aircraft, a Handley Page Hampden bomber, was armed and attempted to attack the surfaced German submarine. However, the U-boat flak crew shot it down.

Müsenberg's luck continued into the Atlantic where on 3 June he sank the 5,166-ton Greek merchant ship *Boris*. However, the unusual engine design continued to hamper effective operation of the U-boat because the engines, though powerful and creating the fastest surfaced U-boat in the fleet, were using up a considerable amount of fuel. Once again *U-180* was forced to rendezvous at sea to refuel, requiring both U-boats to be surfaced and therefore becoming vulnerable to attack for some time. The Type IXC40 *U-530* (*Kapitänleutnant* Kurt Lange), serving in a provisional role as a tanker, met *U-180* on 19 June, west of the Canary Islands, with *U-180* finally arriving in Bordeaux on 3 July.

The *I-29* made her way back to Singapore, but Bose and his aide had disembarked at Sabang. The *I-29* arrived in Singapore on 14 May. Bose was to find little support for his scheme to 'liberate' India from the British and proved to be an increasing irritation to the Japanese. In August 1945 Bose boarded a Japanese military aircraft to travel from Singapore to Japan. Somewhere over the Chinese island of Formosa (now Taiwan) his plane crashed and Bose was presumed to have been killed in the accident. Since then, numerous theories have been proposed concerning Bose's disappearance – that he went into hiding in exile, that he was captured by the Red Army, and that he survived the plane crash but died of his injuries later and was cremated in Japan.

U-180, once safely ensconced in the concrete U-boat pens at Bordeaux, was decommissioned and declared unfit for combat. She had only completed a single war patrol, but the propulsion experiment had failed. U-boat Control decided to refit the boat with two conventional *Germania* supercharged F-46 1,400 horsepower diesel engines, which did not emit any exhaust smoke, and turn *U-180* into a cargo submarine capable of carrying 252 tons. The traditional engine configuration reduced the U-boat's surface speed to 16.5 knots, but they were more reliable.

The 146 cases containing Japanese gold were all safely delivered to the embassy in Berlin. Several such gold deliveries were made throughout the Second World War because Japan needed to pay its expenses in Germany and throughout Europe.

Fast Cargo Submarines: *U-180* and *U-195*

The German Navy had seriously considered that to possess an effective replacement for surface blockade-runners, they would have to design and build an entirely new kind of U-boat, a submarine designed primarily to carry cargo to the Far East and return equally heavily laden to Europe, with a particular emphasis placed upon fuel capacity needed to get to the Far East unaided and deliver their cargo. The Italian submarines taken into service under the code-name *Aquila*, and later operated under the cover name *Merkator*, were not capable of delivering a decent quantity of cargo and would require an intricate refuelling network. In 1942 design work had started on a transport U-boat, designated the Type XIX. The design was based upon the already operational Type XB minelayer U-boat. However, this design was abandoned in favour of a U-boat theoretically capable of carrying 800 tons of cargo and which at a displacement of 3,425 tons, was considerably larger than the big Japanese submarines such as the *I-29* and *I-30*, both of which had already visited France. On 15 March Hitler approved the construction of thirty big cargo submarines of an improved design. The design was designated the Type XX, being based upon the Type XB design, but with a greater beam and draught and a larger keel. However, following repeated delays this type was also cancelled in May 1944 alongside the projected Type XIX. Although rejected as a cargo-carrying design, work on the construction of three Type XX U-boats was restarted in August 1944, with *U-1701*, *U-1702* and *U-1703* under construction as hydrogen peroxide carriers. Work ceased early in 1945 before completion of the boats.

The revolutionary new Electro-boat, the Type XXI, offered submarine designers a possible new cargo submarine, and a variant of the Type XXI was proposed, designated the Type XXIE, designed to be capable of carrying 665 tons of cargo. This large cargo tonnage proved an overestimation and technically impossible, so a final variant of the type was proposed. Carrying only 275 tons of cargo, the Type XXIT was also cancelled before production began. Instead, the German Navy designers settled upon two existing U-boat types to meet their idea of a dedicated cargo-carrying U-boat. The first was the Type VIIF, four of which were specifically constructed as specialized torpedo transports. The second type involved the conversion of a pair of Type IXs, *U-180* and *U-195*, into the new Type IXD1. This was achieved by reducing the number of diesel engines in each boat from six to two, removing all six torpedo tubes and creating more deck storage space by the disposal of the 105mm deck gun. A *schnorchel* was also fitted to both boats to allow them to run their diesel engines while submerged. Although now effectively clawless, the two Type IXD1s thus built could each carry 252 tons of cargo, close to the design estimate for the cargo capacity of the cancelled Type XXIT. Both *U-180* and *U-195* were converted between October 1943 and April 1944 at Bordeaux, both boats leaving for the Far East in August 1944.

The German Far East U-Boat Bases

In December 1942 the Imperial Japanese Navy had contacted the German Navy High Command (*Oberkommando der Kriegsmarine – OKM*) with the suggestion that the Germans should establish a U-boat base in the Far East, in territory recently captured by Japanese forces. The Japanese suggested two possible locations for the base, Sabang or Penang. With U-boat operations active in the Indian Ocean, and off the Cape of Good Hope and Madagascar Strait, the advantage of having a base on the eastern side of this area, with concomitant fuel, port and repair facilities on hand, could only have been advantageous to the German Navy. No longer would U-boats have to sail the length of the Atlantic and negotiate the Cape of Good Hope, requiring them to be refuelled at sea, before beginning a patrol because the boats could be semi-permanently based within the Japanese sphere of operations and support. This would allow their more effective employment in the Indian Ocean against Allied merchant shipping.

Allied anti-submarine defences in place around southern Africa were rudimentary at best, when compared with the improved Allied defences off South America and the West African coast (the Freetown area), which had eroded the Germans' ability to successfully interdict shipping in these areas without a greater risk to their U-boats. Another factor contributing to *Kriegsmarine* interest in the Indian Ocean was the deteriorating military situation on land, specifically *Generalleutnant* Erwin Rommel's failure to capture the Suez Canal in Egypt. During the latter half of 1942 Rommel and his Afrika Korps were in full retreat, and it was imperative that U-boats attacked Allied ships on the Persian Gulf and Red Sea supply routes, delivering supplies to both British and Empire forces in Egypt, and the Soviet Union. By spring 1943 the Battle of the Atlantic had clearly been lost by Germany necessitating a withdrawal of the surviving U-boats from the North Atlantic. They were redeployed to areas such as the Indian Ocean, where targets were abundant, and Allied countermeasures were considerably less well developed.

Dönitz had not been particularly enthused by the idea of basing some of his U-boats in the Far East when first approached by the Japanese in 1942. The Atlantic was the main theatre of U-boat operations, with the Indian Ocean and Far East being seen essentially as distractions and sideshows. Tactical considerations on land made a concerted German–Japanese submarine offensive in the Indian Ocean unlikely. The defeat of German and Italian forces in North Africa during 1943 following Operation Torch, coupled with Rommel's earlier failure to capture the Suez Canal and push on into the Caucasus, meant there would be no possibility of a linkup between German and Japanese forces in India. This was made even more remote by the Imperial Japanese Army's failure to invade India from newly-conquered Burma in 1942–43. The Japanese deduced that expending great effort and massive quantities of supplies assisting the Germans in attacks on Allied shipping in the Indian Ocean was more beneficial to Germany than Japan, and therefore probably not the best use of Japanese military resources. Such an attitude certainly appears to be in line with the inability of both allies to coordinate their military efforts. The Imperial Japanese Navy throughout the Second World War preferred to use its submarines to support fleet activities and attack Allied warships. Japan did not enact a concerted effort to sink Allied commerce. This meant that cooperation with the *Kriegsmarine* was difficult because of the two very different tactical deployments of their respective submarine forces.

There was also present, aside from the official treaties and cooperation agreements signed between the Nazis and the Japanese government, a general distrust exhibited by the Japanese in cooperating with the Germans. However, the Germans managed to persuade Japan to grant them a base for Far East operations, but only after considerable prevarication on the part of Japan. This was in marked contrast to their earlier encouragement in 1942. In September 1944, through negotiations with Japan, an officer was chosen by Germany to over-see control of all Far East activities, *Kapitän zür See* Vermehren. With the later creation of a Southern Area command, actual command of the base that would be established at Penang was placed under *Korvettenkapitän* Wilhelm Dommes, who brought *U-178* to the Far East and who controlled all operations of U-boats in the Far East until the end of the war. Dommes was born in Büchberg in West Prussia on 16 April 1907, and began his career in the *Reichsmarine* in January 1933 after serving in the Merchant Navy. The first years of his career as a junior officer were spent on the light cruiser *Nürnberg* and the battle-cruiser *Scharnhorst* until he transferred to the U-boat service in April 1940. Dommes commanded *U-431* in the Mediterranean before taking command of *U-178* at Bordeaux, preparatory to leaving for Penang in March 1943. Appointed base commander at Penang in August 1943, he remained in this position until January 1945 when he was promoted to *Fregattenkapitän* and created commander of the Southern Area, based at Singapore. This placed him in direct command of all U-boat activity in the Far East. During his U-boat career Dommes sank twelve ships and damaged a further two, earning a series of decorations (Knights Cross, Iron Cross 1st and 2nd Class, U-boat War Badge, and U-boat Front Clasp). Dommes died in Hannover in 1990.

The first suggested location for a base, Sabang, was a small port on an equally small island located at the north-western tip of Sumatra (in present-day Indonesia). The second location proposed by the Japanese, Penang, was an island off the west coast of the Malay Peninsula. The Germans eventually decided upon Penang for the practical reasons that it possessed more substantial and better equipped port facilities than Sabang, and was closer to the main Japanese supply lines, bearing in mind that all U-boat operations this far to the east would be principally reliant upon the Japanese for most of their material needs. Other supplies, such as torpedoes and spare parts for the boats, would have to be delivered along the precarious underwater supply route from Europe. However, one advantage possessed by Sabang was that it was located 300 miles closer to the U-boat hunting grounds in the Indian Ocean, which would have meant the Germans being able to conduct longer duration patrols before returning to refuel, but the better port facilities at Penang quickly won the Germans over and it became the obvious choice. Dönitz, therefore, ordered that *U-511* (*Kapitänleutnant* Fritz Schneewind), operating at that time in the South Atlantic, be diverted from its patrol. It was directed to proceed to Penang at once where it was to be handed over to the Japanese as a gift from Hitler. Concurrently in France a group of nine Type IXCs were being worked up, preparatory to sailing to the Indian Ocean to conduct war patrols. On completion they were ordered to base themselves at the new U-boat facility at Penang. Because of the great distances to be travelled, the nine Type IXCs were due to arrive in the Indian Ocean in September 1943, at the end of the rainy season, known as the monsoon. Accordingly, this flotilla was given the name *Gruppe Monsun* by U-boat Control.

At the beginning of the war, many ships of the German merchant marine and naval auxiliaries had been effectively trapped in Far Eastern ports soon overrun by the Japanese. The Allied blockade of European ports and the intensive sea and aerial patrolling of the routes to and from the Far East meant that these ships, unless ordered to join the German blockade-running programme, would stay in the Far East for the time being. From these vessels, Dönitz would draw the personnel initially required to construct and staff a German naval base in the Far East. These men were, along with the subsequent arrival of German auxiliary cruisers, to become known as the Special Naval Service.

Penang was to be the operational base for the *Gruppe Monsun* boats from where offensive combat patrols could be mounted. The former Royal Navy base at Singapore, now being used by the Imperial Japanese Navy, would provide a facility for major repairs and dry-docking.

In July 1943, *U-511* under the command of *Kapitänleutnant* Fritz Schneewind was the first U-boat to arrive at Penang. Schneewind took over as temporary commander of the base until the arrival of Dommes aboard *U-118* in August. Schneewind had actually been born at Padang in Sumatra on 10 April 1917, and had been commissioned into the *Kriegsmarine* in 1936.

The Japanese cooperated in the provision of base facilities for the U-boats, but in little else. Essential services and supplies were of a poor quality, and after his arrival and assumption of command Dommes was forced to enter into protracted negotiations with local Japanese bases in order to obtain supplies. For example, the U-boat crews and the crews of the blockade-runners in port, had to load, unload and carry out repairs on their own vessels. The Japanese refused to allow the Germans to recruit local labour and would not divert their own personnel to provide assistance to their allies. The Germans were also forced to store their torpedoes alongside Japanese munitions. The Japanese had great difficulty in providing the U-boats with the correct quality diesel fuel and lubricating oil, without which operations would have ceased. Germany had requested a base within the Japanese sphere of operations, close to their supply routes. This was specifically to alleviate the problem of providing a lengthy and complex refuelling net for U-boats based in France but operating in the Indian Ocean. The extremely poor quality of the fuel provided by the Japanese threatened to scupper the effective operation of U-boats from the convenience of Penang. The fuel damaged the U-boats' diesel engines, leading to the engineering departments aboard the boats attempting to solve the problem *in situ*. The engineers conducted purification experiments and ingeniously managed to solve the problem and halt the wear and tear on the engines.

Friction also existed between the Germans and the Japanese regarding personnel matters. Penang was, in addition to being a new U-boat base, home to the Japanese 8th Submarine Group under the command of Rear Admiral Hisashi Ichioka. The senior *Kriegsmarine* officer at Penang was Dommes, holding the relatively junior rank of *Korvettenkapitän* or Lieutenant Commander. Berlin had appointed a full captain, Vermehren, as the officer with overall responsibility for

U-boat operations in the Far East, but he was based thousands of miles away in Tokyo and was forced to go through Japanese channels when communicating with Dommes, effectively preventing him from directly intervening alongside Dommes regarding the fuel and supply problems being experienced with the Japanese. The German Naval Attaché in Tokyo, *Admiral* Paul Wennecker, was of flag officer rank, but the nature of his duties constrained him also. Wennecker eventually informed Berlin that Dommes required more authority in dealing with the Japanese, and he was duly promoted to *Fregattenkapitän* or Commander towards the end of the war in 1945. He still remained too junior an officer to make much of an impression upon Ichioka, or on the supply problems manifesting themselves in all areas of his command. According to U-boat historian and authority Mallmann Showell,[4] during March 1944 Dommes was ordered by U-boat Control to take command of all U-boat operations in the Far East under the title 'Chief of the Southern Area'. However, Dommes soon realized that considerable refuelling and repair facilities were additionally required, necessitating an expansion of German bases to an eventual two in Malaya, two in Java and one in Japan. Each base had its own officer commanding and headquarters responsible to Dommes (see Appendix II).

Because of the problems encountered in working with the Japanese, reference was made to the existing Special Naval Service to provide support for the boats that were making the long journey from France, and later Norway. To this end, *Admiral* Paul Wennecker, German Naval Attaché in Tokyo, directed the Special Naval Service to provide Dommes and his command with all necessary supplies purchased from the Japanese and locals.

Penang itself was not a particularly great success as a base for U-boats. Although the position of the base enabled U-boats to theoretically harass Allied commerce throughout the Indian Ocean, in reality the endless supply problems, exacerbated by a lack of Japanese cooperation, resulted in operational U-boats being pressed into service as cargo-carrying submarines. In addition, the unwanted diversion of dispatching *Yanagi* cargo to Germany had, as has been noted, resulted in the utilization of Italian submarines as well, with mixed results. This process defeated the object of basing U-boats in the Far East and limited their potential to attack Allied shipping, which was the reason Dönitz had dispatched the U-boats in the first place. As will be seen, the Italian submarines utilized by the

Kriegsmarine were unable to fulfil their allotted task as cargo-carriers satisfactorily, forcing the Germans to rely more on their own U-boats and to re-role the Italian boats to local operations within the Southern Area.

By October 1944 Penang was no longer a suitable base. Allied submarines constantly patrolled the Malacca Strait, and because of the ineptitude and neglect of Japanese anti-submarine defences, Allied submarines were routinely able to lay off the entrance to Penang harbour waiting for targets of opportunity – be they German, Italian or Japanese – to present themselves. Admiral Ichioka had also realized that Penang was no longer a viable asset and planned to withdraw his force elsewhere.

On 25 October 1944 Batavia (now Jakarta, Indonesia) was named as the new U-boat base in the Far East. Penang was relegated to the status of an emergency repair facility and run down. On 15 November it was decided to transfer major repair facilities out of Singapore to Surabaya in Java. By 1 December the last U-boat, *U-843* under *Kapitänleutnant* Oskar Herwartz, had left and Dommes took command at Singapore on 1 January 1945.

The Germans had already been using Batavia for much of the war. Surface blockade-runners had often docked at both Batavia and Surabaya, so a level of German organization was already in place before the work-up for the transfer. The Germans had also maintained seaplane bases in both ports for some time, operating Arado Ar-196 floatplanes in Japanese markings.

Notes

1. Blair, C., *Hitler's U-Boat War: The Hunted 1942–1945*, Cassell & Co., London, 1998, p. 59.
2. *Ibid.*, pp. 59–60.
3. Franks, N. & Zimmerman, E., *U-Boat versus Aircraft*, Grubb Street, London, 1998, p. 203.
4. Mallmann Showell, J., *German Navy Handbook 1939–1945*, Sutton Publishing, Stroud, 1999, pp. 150–1.

Chapter 6

U-Boats Hunt in the Indian Ocean and the Japanese Return to France

With the collapse of the German U-boat offensive in the North Atlantic in May 1943, Dönitz had been forced to search elsewhere for new hunting grounds for his Wolf Packs. Cooperation with Japanese forces in the Indian Ocean appeared to provide the Germans with a chance to regain some of the initiative against Allied mercantile shipping – and perhaps even the chance of a return to another 'happy time' for the U-boats. German operations in the Indian Ocean occurred in several distinct phases, allied to the establishment of U-boat bases in the Far East and the growing importance of the underwater *Yanagi* trade with Japan.

The Emperor's New Boat: *U-511*

At the Führer Naval Conference of March 1943, Hitler revealed to Dönitz that the Imperial Japanese Navy had requested that the Germans should present them with two U-boats. Admiral Kichisaburo Nomura, the Japanese Naval Attaché in Berlin, had said that the Japanese wished to copy the German design, then mass-produce the boats and deploy them against the US Navy in the Pacific. Dönitz was against any such 'gift' being made to the Japanese. He argued that the Japanese were incapable of mass-producing U-boats, and anyway, they could not produce enough to change the course of the war. However, the *Yanagi* trade had proved to be extremely useful to the German war effort and Japan had sent a vast quantity of material to the Germans. In the interests of protecting Germany's valuable *Yanagi* trade, Hitler informed Dönitz that he must give the Japanese at least one U-boat as a gesture of goodwill and friendship between the two uncommon allies. Such a gift would also have compensated the Japanese in some way for the large quantities of valuable raw

96

materials and medicines they had generously provided to German blockade-running merchant vessels which had subsequently been lost when the merchantmen had been sunk attempting to run the Allied anti-blockade gauntlet.

Two U-boats were selected and prepared for delivery to the Japanese. The first was *U-511*, a Type IXC, which had already completed three war patrols since being commissioned in December 1941. She was in reasonable condition despite these patrols, and on 10 May 1943 she sailed from France under the command of *Kapitänleutnant* Fritz Schneewind. Code-named '*Marco Polo I*', *U-511* carried the usual *Yanagi* cargo, and six passengers, including Vice Admiral Nomura who was returning to Japan from his diplomatic post in Berlin, and Dr Ernest Woermann who was the new German Ambassador to Japan. *U-511* refuelled in late May west of Freetown from the *Milchkuh U-460* (*Kapitänleutnant der Reserve* Ebe Schnoor), and successfully rounded the Cape of Good Hope on 27 June, south-east of Madagascar. Although the boat was being delivered as a gift to the Japanese, Schneewind took the opportunities presented by the hunting in the Indian Ocean, and torpedoed and sank the *Sebastiano Cermeno* for 7,194 tons. He followed this success with the sinking of the *Samuel Heintzelmann* (7,176 tons) on 9 July east-south-east of Chagos Archipelago (which now forms the modern British Indian Ocean Territory).

U-511 reached the German U-boat base at Penang on 20 July and unloaded spare torpedoes, which were placed into storage ready to rearm the *Gruppe Monsun* boats when they eventually arrived. At this stage Admiral Nomura disembarked and flew on to Japan. *U-511* embarked a Japanese naval officer who was to act as pilot and translator/communicator for the final journey to Japan.

The U-boat reached Kure, Japan, on 7 August and was commissioned into the Imperial Japanese Navy as submarine *RO-500* on 16 September. Schneewind and the German crew of the former *U-511* boarded a Japanese ship and sailed back to the U-boat base at Penang, which was just being established. The redundant crew was to act as a pool of trained replacements at the U-boat base as tropical sicknesses, injuries and accidents necessitated a steady flow of quality manpower – something which the crews of German naval auxiliaries were unable to provide at Penang due to the particular training requirements and standards of submariners. *RO-500* continued to serve the Imperial Japanese Navy for the rest of the war, finally being surrendered to the US Navy at Maizuru, Japan in August 1945. The Americans scuttled the boat in the Gulf of Maizuru on 30 April 1946.[1]

Independent U-Boat Operations in the Indian Ocean, May–August 1943

Dönitz decided, following the limited success of *Seehünd*, to dispatch seven U-cruisers into the Indian Ocean to operate independently, and all commanded by highly experienced skippers. In fact, of the seven U-boats sent south, six were commanded by officers who held the Knights Cross and several of them were relieved of commanding desks at U-boat Control following great success earlier in the war. Dönitz was keen for the seven boats to operate for an extended period in the Indian Ocean, taking supplies and fuel from captured merchant ships if need be, and preying on lone ships as well as the less well-protected convoys to be found there. However, Dönitz and U-boat Control still had not realized that scientists at Bletchley Park in Britain had cracked the German Naval Enigma code, giving the Allies a massive advantage over the U-boats. Allied commanders were apprised immediately of the movements of all seven boats as they motored to their respective patrol areas.

Forty-year-old *Kapitän zür See* Werner Hartmann, who had been awarded his Knights Cross early in the war in May 1940, was taken from a desk job and given command of the Type IXD2 *U-198*. Hartmann was born in Silstedt in the Harz Mountains on 11 December 1902 and entered the *Reichsmarine* in 1923. His early career saw him command the torpedo boats *Seeadler* and *Albatros* before he transferred to the U-boat service in 1935. During the Spanish Civil War Hartmann patrolled in *U-26* off the Spanish coast, his First Watch Officer being Günther Prien, later famous when as commander of *U-47* he sank HMS *Royal Oak* in Scapa Flow in 1939. During the early part of the war Hartmann commanded *U-37* and 2nd U-boat Flotilla. Following staff appointments he took command of 27th U-boat Flotilla at Gotenhafen in 1941, before commanding *U-198* in the Indian Ocean. After the war Hartmann served for several years in the *Bundesmarine*, the modern Federal German Navy, before his death in 1963. During his service in the *Kriegsmarine* Hartmann was awarded the Knights Cross with Oakleaves, Spanish Cross in Silver, Iron Cross 1st and 2nd Class, and the U-boat War Badge, sinking a total of twenty-six ships and making him an undisputed U-boat ace.

Hartmann struck first in the same area as *Gruppe Seehünd* had two months previously, attacking Convoy LMD17 on 17 May 1943 in the lower Mozambique Channel. He quickly sank the 4,392-ton British ship *Northmoor*, but was pounced upon by an escorting Royal Navy anti-submarine trawler which plastered *U-198* with fifty depth charges, and an aircraft that dropped a further five. The U-boat escaped serious damage, but in the meantime the convoy escaped.

On 18 May, off Durban, Hartmann discovered two freighters steaming in company and manoeuvred to attack, only to have his attack ruined by an Allied aircraft, which attacked him immediately. The subsequent pounding from Allied aircraft and small surface vessels was unrelenting for the rest of the day, and most of the night, although Hartmann's flak crew successfully drove off a depth-charge equipped Catalina from No. 262 Squadron RAF. But once again Hartmann was himself driven off the convoy and was forced to hunt elsewhere. On 26 May he attempted to interdict another convoy in the same area, but was again repelled by escorts. At this point he motored 400 miles east into the Indian Ocean, hoping for more luck and a less well organized Allied response to his attacks. On 29 May he sank the 5,231-ton British merchantman *Hopetarn*, and two days later attempted another convoy attack, this time against a small convoy that did not appear to be especially well escorted. A corvette tracked *U-198* on sonar, forcing Hartmann to dive deep, and following several depth charge attacks the U-boat discovered that one of the topside torpedo canisters had been crushed by the force of the underwater explosions.

Hartmann's colleague, thirty-six-year-old *Korvettenkapitän* Eitel-Friedrich Kentrat who was aboard the Type IXD2 *U-196*, had not been to sea in a year. Born on 11 September 1906 in Stahlheim, Metz, Kentrat had joined the *Reichsmarine* as an ordinary seaman in October 1925 and was selected for officer training in 1928. Commissioned in 1932, he served on the warships *Hessen*, *Deutschland*, and *Schlesien* before transferring to U-boats in October 1939. In May 1940, after a war patrol aboard *U-25*, he took command of *U-8*, but an injury sustained on board kept him away from the sea for several months. After recovering, Kentrat commanded *U-74* on seven war patrols, sinking five ships including the Canadian corvette HMCS *Levis*.

He also managed to damage the British auxiliary cruiser HMS *Worcestershire*, and successfully infiltrated his boat through the heavily defended Straits of Gibraltar into the Mediterranean. A staff appointment followed before he commissioned *U-196* in September 1942. Kentrat was destined to serve in several staff positions in Japan, only returning to Germany from Allied captivity in the Far East in October 1947. Kentrat was awarded the Knights Cross in 1941. He died in 1974.

Kentrat patrolled near Durban, and on 11 May sank another British freighter, the 4,962-ton *Nailsea Meadow*, but was then forced to wait for two weeks for another target to present itself. Eventually Kentrat found a convoy and fired two new T-5 electric torpedoes. One of the torpedoes, which were all fitted with magnetic triggers, malfunctioned in the tube and refused to budge. The torpedo propeller was in motion inside the tube and the crew expected the magnetic trigger to fire at any moment, which would have sunk the U-boat immediately, killing most of the crew. Kentrat reacted quickly to save his boat, ordering the bow to be angled steeply downwards and the malfunctioning torpedo slid out of the tube harmlessly. *U-196* hung around the area for another week without any success, until on 1 June she turned east to rendezvous with the *Charlotte Schliemann*.

U-195 was under the command of thirty-four-year-old *Korvettenkapitän* Heinz Büchholz. Born in East Prussia in the town of Goldap on 3 August 1909, he had attended the commissioning course at Mürwik in 1929. First serving as Second Watch Officer aboard *U-8* in 1935–36, Büchholz had been promoted to the post of First Watch Officer on *U-34* and then *U-22*, until in 1937 he was given command of his own boat, the Type IIB *U-24*. Two months later, in October 1937, Büchholz was transferred to command another Type IIB, *U-15*, which would take him into the Second World War. He was, however, destined to miss out on the 'happy time' at the beginning of the war, being employed as a staff officer until Dönitz gave him command of *U-195* in September 1942. *U-195* was the second of the fast experimentally engined U-boats (the other being *U-180* until the problems she experienced following her rendezvous with the Japanese submarine *I-29*). On 12 April 1943 Büchholz was west of the Canary Islands in the Atlantic where he found and sank the 7,200-ton American Liberty ship *James W. Denver*. After crossing the equator on 7 May *U-195* struck again, sinking another US Liberty ship, the *Samuel Jordan Kirkwood*. Her run of luck continued and on 12 May she attacked and damaged the American 6,797-ton freighter *Cape Neddick*, but surprisingly the merchant captain engaged the U-boat with her guns and attempted to ram *U-195*. Büchholz dived and fired another torpedo, which missed. However, the same engine problems that had afflicted Müsenberg on *U-180* manifested themselves and Büchholz reported severe engine faults on 30 May. He aborted his patrol and arrived back in Bordeaux on 23 July. *U-195* followed *U-180* to the workshops to undergo a refit into a two-engined, stripped down, cargo-carrying submarine.

U-197, under the command of *Korvettenkapitän* Robert Bartels, had virtually no success, and it was only on the boat's forty-eighth day out from France that thirty-two-year-old Bartels attacked and sank the 4,763-ton Dutch tanker *Benekat* in mid-Atlantic. Born in the Pries district of Kiel in 1911, Bartels had entered the Naval Academy in 1934 and served as First Watch Officer aboard *U-37* between 1937 and 1940, before commanding *U-139* in 1940, and *U-561* until September 1942. He had been awarded the German Cross in Gold in August 1942 following his successful command of that boat. As *U-197* proceeded to the rendezvous with the *Charlotte Schliemann*, aircraft attacked the U-boat. During the attack one of the crewmen was killed. Bartels reached the replenishment rendezvous on 22 June.

Kapitän zür See Wolfgang Lüth, commander of the Type IXD2 *U-181*, was one of Germany's leading U-boat aces by the time he took the boat to the Indian Ocean,[2] and this highly experienced U-boatman had become a national hero in Germany. Born in Riga, Latvia, on 15 October 1913, Lüth had begun his naval career in April 1933, after abandoning his law studies. He spent the summer of 1933 undergoing basic training aboard the sailing school ship *Gorch Fock*, then joined the light cruiser *Karlsruhe*, in which he spent nine months touring the world, calling at ports in India, Indonesia, Australia, and North and South America. Lüth spent another year aboard the light cruiser *Königsberg* before transferring to the U-boat service in February 1937. During the Spanish Civil War he served aboard *U-27* as Second Watch Officer, before transferring as First Watch Officer on *U-38* in which he found himself out on patrol when war commenced. After further training in the Baltic, Lüth was given command of the coastal Type IIB *U-9*, which he took out on six war patrols, his most notable success being the sinking of the French submarine *Doris* in May 1940, which earned him the Iron Cross 1st

Class (he had already been awarded the Iron Cross 2nd Class in January 1940).

Lüth proved to be a commander who cared deeply for the well being of his crew and behaved in a paternalistic manner towards them. Throughout his several commands, Lüth attempted to control the behaviour and activities of his crews to a remarkable degree, for example: books brought on board had to be approved by him; pornography and pin-ups were forbidden; smoking and drinking were strictly regulated; and proper dress was expected while on patrol. However, Lüth was very popular with his men and he tried hard to create diversions for them, organizing a newsletter for the boat produced by the crew themselves and holding a multitude of contests designed to keep the crew fit and alert. These and many other inventive man-management techniques were pioneered by Lüth and his officers to stave off boredom and low morale. His ideas were laughed at by many other U-boat commanders, mainly for the fact that Lüth sank most of his ships in the less well-defended seas off Africa and the Indian Ocean. This afforded him fewer worries concerning immediate Allied attack, whereas commanders who were battling in the North Atlantic had their hands full just keeping themselves and their crews alive for the duration of a war patrol, quite apart from having the time or the energy to regulate what the crewmen were reading. Lüth was also quite vocal in his adherence to Nazism, but this does not seem to have detracted from the high standing he was held in by successive crews, and U-boat Control evidently had complete faith in his methods and command style.

Following his successes in command of *U-9* Lüth commissioned the Type IID *U-138*, distinguishing himself by sinking four ships on the night of 20/21 September 1940. The following month, as he was returning from his second war patrol aboard *U-138*, he sank another ship and damaged one more. Dönitz awarded him the Knights Cross and gave him command of *U-43*, a much larger Type IXA U-boat. Over five war patrols Lüth sank another twelve ships. In April 1942 he departed from *U-43* to command one of the latest versions of the Type IX, the IXD2 *U-181*. Following his first war patrol to the waters around South Africa and into the Indian Ocean between September 1942 and January 1943, Lüth sank a total of twelve ships, leading to the award of the Oakleaves to his Knights Cross.

On 11 April 1943, 400 miles south of Freetown, Lüth attacked the 5,983-ton British freighter *Empire Whimbrel*, but failed to sink her with torpedoes. Instead he ordered the 37mm flak crew to finish the job, but a shell jammed in the breech and exploded, severely wounding three of the crew – one mortally. The submarine's deck gun was used instead, firing twenty rounds before the *Empire Whimbrel* eventually sank. As Lüth proceeded south he met the returning *Gruppe Seehünd* boat *U-516* and on 12 April was able to transfer the wounded men to *Fregattenkapitän* Wiebe's boat. On learning of the sinking of the *Empire Whimbrel*, Dönitz awarded Lüth with the Swords to his Knights Cross with Oakleaves, because Lüth had by that stage of his career sunk a confirmed thirty-eight ships grossing around 189,633 registered tons. More bad luck was to follow, however, because when Lüth started to patrol off Lourenço Marques he fouled his propeller on a steel fishing net. One brave seaman, kitted out in cumbersome diving equipment, went over the side with a cutting torch and removed the offending net, but not before other crewmen had killed a large shark that threatened the diver as he worked.

For a month, from 11 May to 11 June, Lüth patrolled the lower Mozambique Channel, sinking three ships: the 5,232-ton British freighter *Tinhow*, the 1,633-ton Swedish merchantman *Sicilia* (which was, incidentally, a neutral), and finally the less than impressive 193-ton South African coaster *Harrier*. Lüth also arrived at the refuelling point on 22 June, undoubtedly annoyed that after ninety-two days at sea he had only sunk four small ships for approximately 14,000 gross registered tons.

Another Knights Cross holder, *Korvettenkapitän* Robert Gysae, arrived at the Cape of Good Hope aboard the Type IXD2 *U-177* on 28 May, and found Convoy CD20, which was proceeding from Cape Town to Durban in South Africa. Gysae sank the American freighter *Agwinonte* for 6,679 tons and the 7,886-ton Norwegian tanker *Storaas*. This raised his confirmed kills to twenty ships for around 116,000 gross registered tons, and Dönitz had Gysae awarded the Oakleaves to his Knights Cross by radio on 1 June. Born on 14 January 1911 in the fashionable neighbourhood of Charlottenburg in Berlin, Gysae's naval career began in April 1931 and was to last until March 1970. He transferred to U-boats from torpedo boats in April 1940 and was able to completely skip the normal path to command followed by officers, through positions

103

such as Second and First Watch Officer, commissioning *U-98* in October. Gysae would complete six war patrols in command of *U-98* before being given command of *U-177*.

U-177 was fortunate to survive her next encounter with the enemy. During foggy conditions Gysae stumbled into the middle of a convoy and was fired upon from the surrounding ships, as well as having three depth charges dropped on him from a Catalina. Following this, one of his crewmen fell ill, so *U-177* rendezvoused with Büchholz's aborting *U-195* and transferred the man to him to take back to France. By the time Gysae arrived at the refuelling point on 23 June, *U-177* had been at sea for eighty-three days and only sunk two ships for 14,565 gross registered tons.

U-178, a Type IXD2 under the command of *Kapitänleutnant* Wilhelm Dommes who was on his way to Penang to assume command of the base, attacked a small convoy off Cape Town on 24 May. In turn *U-178* was attacked by a Royal Netherlands Air Force Catalina anti-submarine aircraft armed with depth charges. The U-boat flak crew fought back, but when another Catalina appeared at the scene, Dommes sensibly dived and lost the convoy.

At the end of May, Dommes picked up information transmitted by Gysae in *U-177* reporting a convoy en route to Cape Town. Dommes intercepted it, discovering the group of ships some 60 miles south of Durban. On 1 June *U-178* attacked, sinking the 6,586-ton Dutch merchantman *Salabangka*. This was to be Dommes' only kill on the outward-bound leg of the journey to the Indian Ocean, and he arrived at the refuelling point on 22 June. Between them, seven of Germany's leading U-boat commanders had only managed to sink fifteen ships, totalling around 77,400 gross registered tons.

Following the successful refuelling of all the U-boats by the *Charlotte Schliemann*, each U-boat commander was assigned a new patrol sector by U-boat Control. All boats were to remain in the Indian Ocean and continue to target small escorted convoys and freighters travelling unescorted. The less than outstanding total tonnage figure of approximately 77,400 tons was not the result U-boat Control had hoped for when it originally dispatched the seven experienced skippers south, but keeping the boats on station much longer than the previous efforts of Groups *Eisbär* and *Seehünd* could yet yield good results for the venture. If the six remaining independent boats could launch simultaneous attacks on shipping throughout a variety of patrol areas, some real damage could be inflicted upon the Allies' supply chain. To this end *U-181* was to patrol around the island of Mauritius, *U-198* would lurk off the neutral Portuguese port of Lourenço Marques, *U-196* was ordered to sweep north to south down the Mozambique Channel, while *U-178* swept in the opposite direction, *U-177* would conduct a patrol to the south of the large island of Madagascar, and finally, *U-197* would patrol close to the African coast between Lourenço Marques in Mozambique and Durban in South Africa.

Gysae immediately took *U-177* well to the south of Madagascar, where he could operate a new German addition to submarine warfare – a primitive helicopter. The Germans had equipped *U-177* with the Focke-Achgelis Fa-330 *Bachstelze* helicopter. Perhaps 'helicopter' is a slightly disingenuous description, for the aircraft was little more than a manned, rotary-winged observation kite. The aircraft was carried aboard the U-boat in a metal cylinder and could be quickly and easily assembled by the crew. To get the rotor started, the crew could either flick the rotor tips by hand or use a pull-rope wound around a drum on the rotor hub. The aircraft did not have an engine, but relied upon the updraft created by the passage of the U-boat motoring on the surface to stay aloft. Once airborne, the pilot would rise to an altitude of between 300 and 500 feet, and from this position on a clear day he could see a distance of 25 miles. The *Bachstelze* increased the lookout's range considerably, allowing searches to be conducted over a much wider area than could be achieved by the normal lookouts positioned on the submarine's conning tower. If the pilot spotted a potential target, he would communicate with the U-boat's bridge by telephone, a line running down the tow-cable. Recovery of the aircraft was simple. The crew would activate an electric winch to bring the aircraft gently down to the U-boat's deck, where it could be hastily disassembled and stowed. In an emergency situation, such as an imminent Allied warship or aircraft attack, successfully winching the aircraft and pilot back to the submarine would have been impossible because of the time factor. In this instance, the U-boatman (usually a specially-trained petty officer) who took to the skies in the Fa-330 would become more akin to his colleagues in the *Luftwaffe*. The pilot would reach up and pull a lever above his head that released the rotor assembly. This automatically released a parachute attached to the pilot and the remains of the glider. The tow-cable was also automatically released at this point. Once the rotors were clear, the rest of the aircraft would be automatically released when the pilot disengaged his safety harness, leaving the pilot to descend into the sea by parachute. Once in the water, and having inflated his life-jacket, the pilot would await rescue from the U-boat, which would ideally have picked him up before diving. In reality, the U-boat would most likely have crash dived immediately and abandoned the pilot to his fate, the reasoning being that it was better to sacrifice one man than risk losing the U-boat and over sixty crewmen while attempting a recovery as Allied anti-submarine assets bore down upon them.

Weser Aircraft at Hoykenkamp, near Bremen, manufactured approximately 200 Fa-330s, and the Germans traded two examples with the Japanese in exchange for a pair of Yokosuka E14Y1 floatplanes (not a very good deal when the specifications of the two aircraft are compared). The Japanese reconnaissance aircraft were used by the Germans alongside Arado Ar-196As that had been removed from German auxiliary cruisers at their U-boat bases in Penang and Surabaya. All aircraft operating in Japanese *Hinomaru* (blood-red roundels) were flown by German pilots. As the war was drawing to a close, Weser Aircraft began work on a powered version of the Fa-330, but the project was curtailed by the German surrender in May 1945.

The *Bachstelze* immediately provided results for Gysae and *U-177*, as witnessed by the sinking of two ships over a five-day period at the beginning of July. Although Gysae attacked a third ship with two torpedoes, he missed and the freighter escaped. The second target, the 7,129-ton Canadian merchantman *Jasper Park*, was not so lucky and Gysae sent her to the bottom with a spread of three torpedoes. He followed this on 10 July with the destruction of another American Liberty ship, the 7,176-ton *Alice F. Palmer*, with two torpedoes and an extraordinary ninety-nine rounds from the U-boat's deck gun. Returning to the south of Madagascar, Gysae sank the 4,952-ton British ship *Cornish City*, before wasting time and fuel chasing an American Liberty ship almost to the shores of Madagascar before giving up the hunt. However, on 5 August the *Bachstelze* again proved its worth when the pilot spotted the 4,195-ton Greek ship *Afthalia Mari*, which was subsequently sunk. Following a fire in the engine-room Gysae turned *U-177* for France, and after a 184-day patrol the U-boat arrived safely in Bordeaux. During the patrol Gysae had sunk six ships for around 38,000 gross registered tons and thereafter was sent to the Baltic to command

25th Training Flotilla. Command of *U-177* was given to Heinz Büchholz after Gysae's departure in 1943, whose own boat, the experimentally engined *U-195*, was undergoing conversion into a fast cargo-carrying submarine.

In April 1945 Gysae was to command *Marinepanzerjagd-Regiment 1* (1st Navy Tank-Hunter Regiment) during the final desperate battles in the final month of the war in Europe, where U-boatmen armed with hand-held *Panzerfaust* rocket-propelled grenades took on Soviet tanks in the ruins of the Reich. After a few weeks in Allied captivity, Gysae then served for a couple of years in the *Deutscher Minenraumdienst* (German Minesweeping Service), which was tasked with clearing up and disposing of the detritus of the recent conflict. He then joined the *Bundesmarine*, serving firstly as German Naval Attaché to the United States, and then as *Flottillenadmiral* in command of *Marinedivision Nordsee* (Naval Division North Sea). *Flottillenadmiral* Gysae retired in March 1970 and died in 1989.

Wilhelm Dommes, commanding *U-178*, was having a harder time of it in the Indian Ocean, and although he was still sinking ships (netting the 2,669-ton Norwegian freighter *Breiviken* and the 4,774-ton Greek merchantman *Michael Livanos* at the start of July), he reported to U-boat Control that he was ill, though would carry on in command of the boat. *U-178* hung around to the north of Lourenço Marques with some success. Between 11 and 16 July Dommes dispatched the 4,771-ton Greek ship *Mary Livanos* and the 7,119-ton US Liberty ship *Robert Bacon* to watery graves. However, by this stage he had expended all his torpedoes, and U-boat Control directed him to rendezvous with the eastbound Italian cargo submarine *Torelli* to give her some fuel before she attempted to reach the far side of the Indian Ocean. After completing this task, U-boat Control wanted to know whether Dommes was well enough, and his U-boat in a good enough condition, to motor to the Japanese base at Penang, Malaya, where *U-178* could be refuelled and refitted. U-boat Control's idea was that once *U-178* had been overhauled and rearmed, Dommes could then undertake a full combat patrol back through the Indian Ocean and thence to France. Dommes replied that both he and the boat were able to go to Penang, and in company with the *Torelli* they arrived in the Far East port on 29 August 1943. *U-178* had been on patrol for 155 days, and sunk six ships for about 32,800 gross registered tons. As previously related, it was just before Dommes arrived in Penang at the end of August that Dönitz and the Naval High Command (OKM) decided upon their audacious plan to found a U-boat base at Penang, enabling U-boats to be permanently relocated to the Indian Ocean theatre. Dommes was still unwell when he docked his U-boat in the Japanese-controlled port, and by agreement with U-boat Control, the First Watch Officer of *U-177*, *Kapitänleutnant* Wilhelm Spähr, would assume command later. Dommes was reassigned to command the new German U-boat base at Penang and in due course made a full recovery from his tropical illness.

Spähr eventually sailed *U-178* back to France, leaving on 27 November 1943 and arriving 180 days later on 25 May 1944. *U-178* was simply worn out by such long patrols and the boat never sailed again. Indeed, she sat at Bordeaux in urgent need of repairs to her batteries, but the local dockyard could not carry out the work. Due to the deteriorating situation around the German U-boat bases in France following the Allied invasion of Europe in June 1944, and Hitler's decision to evacuate the bases soon after, *U-178* was deliberately wrecked by her crew and then scuttled on 20 August 1944, to avoid the boat being captured intact by the Allies. Wilhelm Spähr was evacuated from the port and sent to a staff post. He survived the war and died in 1978.

Hartmann, aboard *U-198*, scored some good kills in early July 1943 to the south of Lourenço Marques. On 4 July he almost violated international law by lining up to fire on a freighter, only to realize at the last moment that she was a Portuguese neutral. Two days later, however, he sank the 4,476-ton Greek merchantman *Hydraios* and the following day the 4,742-ton British freighter *Leana*. Indeed, the *Leana* proved hard to sink, requiring Hartmann to expend an incredible 147 rounds at her from his deck gun, before finishing her off with a single torpedo. Air activity and attacks disrupted patrolling for the next three weeks, although on 1 August he sank the 8,457-ton Dutch ship *Mangkalibat* before heading home. *U-198* arrived back in France on 25 September 1943 after an incredible 201-day patrol. Hartmann had sunk seven ships for around 36,778 tons, and Dönitz promoted him to command all U-boats in the Mediterranean, a post he assumed on New Year's Day 1944.

After obtaining a volunteer seaman from the *Charlotte Schliemann* to help fill the crew shortage following the three men wounded and removed from the boat after the accident with the 37mm flak gun, Lüth, aboard *U-181*, proceeded to the waters around the British colony of Mauritius, and his designated patrol sector. He quickly found the British ship *Hoihow* and sank her, managed to escape air attack, then pursued a Royal Navy cruiser towards Madagascar, where he sank two more British ships. He torpedoed the 2,852-ton *Empire Lake* on the 15 July, and the next day destroyed the 7,135-ton *Fort Franklin*. U-boat Control was not happy about this unauthorized excursion to Madagascar and ordered Lüth to return to Mauritius. The hunting was good around the colony, Lüth bagging three more British ships, the 4,558-ton *Dalfram* on 4 August, the 4,419-ton *Umvuma* on the 7th, and a refrigerator ship, the 10,528-ton *Clan MacArthur*, on the 11th. On 9 August Hitler awarded Lüth the Diamonds to his Knights Cross with Oakleaves and Swords, Germany's highest award, while he was still at sea. Lüth's award of the Diamonds to the Knights Cross was only the seventh given to a member of the German Armed Forces in the Second World War, and the first occasion it had been awarded to a member of the *Kriegsmarine*. The Knights Cross with Oakleaves, Swords and Diamonds was only superceded in precedence by the Grand Cross of the Knights Cross of the Iron Cross, and this had only been awarded once, to *Reichsmarschall* Hermann Göring, head of the *Luftwaffe*.[3] Lüth's tally of ships sunk now stood at forty-seven since the beginning of hostilities in 1939. Thereafter Lüth was ordered to rendezvous with Bartels aboard *U-197* several hundred miles south of Madagascar, to collect new Enigma keys that would be needed on the voyage back to France.

Following the refuelling stop, morale aboard *U-197* deteriorated severely. For over two weeks Bartels had failed to sink any Allied shipping, except one neutral Swedish tanker, the 9,583-ton *Pegasus*, and the crew had grown despondent. On 30 July another opportunity presented itself in the shape of an American Liberty ship, the 7,181-ton *William Ellery*, but although Bartels hit the merchantman, she failed to sink, and after being driven off by air attack the Liberty ship was towed to Durban and survived.

In order to arrange a rendezvous with Lüth, and Lüth in turn with Kentrat on *U-196*, the boats had to talk to each other, and this placed them in a dangerous and unfamiliar situation. The Allies intercepted enough of the radio traffic to enable them to get a rough fix on where the rendezvous site was located, and they scrambled Catalina anti-submarine flying boats to search the area in the hope of getting lucky. After meeting Bartels, Lüth sailed off to meet Kentrat, leaving

Bartels motoring along on the surface. On 20 August RAF Catalinas out of Durban began searching the recent rendezvous site. Bartels' boat was discovered and attacked. Although the flak gunners shot back, the No. 259 Squadron aircraft raked the U-boat with machine-gun fire and dropped its full load of six shallow-set depth charges as *U-197* performed a crash-dive. The Catalina now marked the spot where Bartels had disappeared with smoke and after calling up reinforcements, commenced circling the area. Bartels' boat had been damaged during the initial depth charge attack and could not remain submerged, shooting back to the surface while emitting distress calls to other nearby boats. Although the flak crew opened fire immediately, another Catalina of No. 265 Squadron arrived (both this pilot and the No. 259 Squadron pilot being highly experienced sub-hunters, with both having been previously awarded the Distinguished Flying Cross), and after a preliminary strafing run it too deposited all six depth charges it was carrying over the crippled *U-197*, with devastating effects. The U-boat blew up in a tumultuous, roiling cloud of water, oil and debris, killing Bartels and all sixty-six crew instantly.

Lüth and Kentrat were exchanging Enigma keys and chatting at their rendezvous point when reports came in to their respective radio operators of Bartels' distress calls, and through Enigma, U-boat Control directed both boats to go to the aid of the stricken *U-197*. Indeed, so confident was U-boat Control of the ability of the Type IX U-boat to fend off air attack, and bearing in mind that they had issued a standing order to all U-boat commanders not to dive when attacked by aircraft, that they came up with a plan for Lüth and Kentrat to rescue Bartels from his predicament. The three U-boats would sail in company using their combined firepower of three 37mm and three 20mm flak guns. However, when Lüth arrived at the site where Bartels was supposed to be he found nothing. Lüth was fortunate that poor weather had halted further Allied anti-submarine patrols over the area as it is fair to suggest that *U-181* might have found itself in a similar predicament to the late Bartels and *U-197*. For five days Lüth searched in vain for Bartels. Finally he admitted defeat and turned for home in the company of Kentrat.

U-181 arrived back in Bordeaux the day before Lüth's 30th birthday, after a patrol that had lasted 206 days and bagged ten ships for around 45,331 tons. Lüth met Hitler again on the 25 October in Berlin, when he was formally presented with the Diamonds to his Knights Cross with Oakleaves and Swords, which had been awarded to him while he was still at sea. His Chief Engineer, Carl-August Landfehrmann, was also awarded the Knights Cross for his efforts on the highly successful patrol of *U-181*. Thereafter, the most highly decorated officer in the *Kriegsmarine* was transferred to a safer command in October 1943, the 22nd U-boat Flotilla at Gotenhafen and Wilhelmshaven, commanding 2nd U-boat Training Division between January and July 1944.

Kentrat's miserable bag of two ships sunk during an operational patrol lasting 225 days seemed to pass by Dönitz without remark, but as Kentrat already held the Knights Cross it was probably put down to bad luck. He retained his command of *U-196*.

Overall, although the operation had not netted a large tonnage of Allied merchant ships sunk, it had perhaps highlighted an area that was ripe for further exploitation by U-boat Control, namely where Allied defences were not well-developed and where they did not necessarily expect large-scale U-boat activity. Undoubtedly the thirty-six ships that had been sunk made the Allies realize that they would have to divert convoy escorts and anti-submarine forces from elsewhere to counter the threat, perhaps relieving some of the strain upon U-boats operating in the Atlantic, Arctic and Mediterranean. Another outcome of the operation was the establishment of a U-boat base within the Japanese sphere of operations, which meant that, theoretically, Germany could attempt the continuous interdiction of Allied shipping throughout the Indian Ocean without the need for a network of refuelling vessels on station permanently in southern waters.

Gruppe Monsun Heads South – The First Wave

On 9 June 1943 Dönitz ordered eleven U-boats to sail into the Indian Ocean, to be supported by two U-tankers. This group of boats, the first of the so-called *Gruppe Monsun*, was due to arrive in the Indian Ocean at the beginning of September, the start of the tropical monsoon season or *monsun* in German. Both U-tankers were lost en route to the Indian Ocean necessitating the diversion of some *Monsun* boats to refuel one another. Even U-boats returning from patrols in the Atlantic were used for refuelling. Eventually *Gruppe Monsun* was reduced to five U-boats by the time the flotilla reached the South Atlantic. One Type IXD2 boat, *U-200*, which had departed from Norway on 11 June, was sunk in the Iceland–Faroes Gap by a Catalina flying boat from US Navy Squadron VP-84. Its supposed mission before entering the Indian Ocean had been to land a special unit of German troops, called *Brandenburg* Commandos, in South Africa, presumably to ferment trouble between the Afrikaans-speaking Boers and the British South African authorities. As the Catalina dived in to attack the U-boat, accurate defensive flak damaged the aircraft's port wing and fuselage, causing hydraulic problems and a leak in the fuel tank within the wing itself. The Catalina managed to dump only two depth charges over the U-boat, but the subsequent explosions caused *U-200* to sink rapidly. Of the estimated fifteen crewmen who went into the water, none was picked up. *U-200*'s commander, *Kapitänleutnant* Heinrich Schönder, who had been awarded the Knights Cross in August 1942, perished along with sixty-one U-boatmen and an unspecified number of *Brandenburgers*.

Three of the Type IXs sent as part of *Gruppe Monsun* were also lost while making for the Indian Ocean. The first was the Type IXC *U-514*, which had departed from Lorient on 3 July. *Kapitänleutnant* Hans-Jürgen Auffermann was taking *U-514* on her fourth war patrol since the boat's commissioning in January 1942. His first war patrol in late summer 1942 had seen the boat operating off the mouth of the Amazon River, and Auffermann had successfully sunk six ships over all four patrols. On 8 July 1943, *U-514* was attacked by an RAF Liberator bomber of No. 224 Squadron north-east of Cape Finisterre, an experimental aircraft fitted with rockets and *Fido* homing torpedoes. The pilot flew into the heavy flak screen being thrown up by the U-boat and fired eight rockets, hitting the German with six, and *U-514* sank immediately. The pilot decided to make sure, and released a *Fido* homing torpedo. This top-secret weapon ran out of control, forcing the pilot to destroy it with two depth charges to prevent its recovery by Franco's Spanish government, and the technology inevitably being made known to the Germans. The experimental rocket attack resulted in the loss of all fifty-four men on board. At the time of her sinking, *U-514* was in the midst of a flotilla of neutral Spanish fishing boats, but this did not deter the determined British attack that followed. Hans-Jürgen Auffermann was posthumously awarded the German Cross in Gold on 7 January 1944.

U-506, also a Type IXC, which departed from France on 6 June 1943, did not survive very much longer. Under the command of

Kapitänleutnant Erich Würdemann (who had been awarded the Knights Cross in March 1943), *U-506* had already sunk sixteen ships over four previous war patrols and damaged a further two, including taking part in the relatively unsuccessful *Gruppe Seehünd* operation. This run of luck came to an abrupt end on 12 July while west of the town of Vigo in northern Spain. *U-506* was attacked by another Liberator, this time from 1 Anti-Submarine Squadron, United States Army Air Force (USAAF), which released seven Mk IX depth charges that straddled the U-boat. The pilot then came about, preparatory to a second depth charge run, but *U-506* was observed to be breaking in two and approximately fifteen U-boatmen went into the water. The rapid destruction of *U-506* resulted in the deaths of forty-nine members of the crew, including Würdemann, and only six of the fifteen in the water survived to be taken prisoner by a Royal Navy destroyer on 15 July.

The final fatality suffered by the outward-bound *Gruppe Monsun* occurred on the same day, 15 July, when the Type IXC *U-509* was sunk near Madeira. *Kapitänleutnant* Werner Witte was the second officer to have command of *U-509*, taking over from *Korvettenkapitän* Karl-Heinz Wolff, who joined U-boat Headquarters as a staff officer in September 1942. The two previous war patrols completed under Witte's command had resulted in the sinking of four Allied merchant ships, with three more damaged. On this occasion he departed from France on 3 June as part of *Gruppe Monsun*. On 15 July 1943, while south-west of the Azores, an Avenger–Wildcat team from US Navy Squadron VC-29, based on the escort carrier USS *Santee*, sent the U-boat to the bottom of the Atlantic. The Wildcat strafed the U-boat and, as the submarine crash-dived, the Avenger released an Mk-24 *Fido* homing torpedo. A large underwater explosion resulted and *U-509* and her crew of fifty-four were never heard from again. Witte was also posthumously awarded the German Cross in Gold on 7 January 1944.[4]

U-847, the other *Gruppe Monsun* U-cruiser lost en route to the Indian Ocean, had departed from Kiel on 6 July under *Korvettenkapitän* Herbert Kuppisch. Born on 10 December 1909 by the sea in Hamburg, Kuppisch had joined the *Reichsmarine* as an officer cadet in 1933. Unlike most of his U-boat skipper contemporaries, Kuppisch only ever served in the U-boat service. His first command was *U-58* in February 1939, and he followed eight successful war patrols aboard this boat with command of *U-94* in August 1940. A further five war patrols was followed by a year on the staff of U-boat Control Operations (BdU Op), Kuppisch having been awarded the Knights Cross in April 1941. A further staff appointment in December 1942 at *Oberkommando der Kriegsmarine* (Navy High Command) came to an end in July 1943 when Kuppisch took command of *U-847*. After colliding with an iceberg in the Denmark Strait she was appointed to be an auxiliary tanker following the loss of all U-tankers supporting the group. On 27 August 1943 signals traffic referring to a refuelling rendezvous was intercepted by the Allies, which allowed the aircraft carrier USS *Card* to launch an attack. An Avenger–Wildcat team from US Navy Squadron VC-1 attacked the Type IXD2 nearly 800 miles south-west of the Azores, sinking *U-847*. This resulted in the deaths of all sixty-two crew. The eerie underwater explosions and death throes of *U-847* resulting from the *Fido* torpedo attack were heard by *U-508* which was several miles away at the time. Kuppisch sank a total of sixteen ships before his death.

Both U-tankers assigned to *Gruppe Monsun* were also lost. On 13 July 1943 a combined Avenger–Wildcat team from the American aircraft carrier USS *Core*, attacked the Type XIV *U-487*, commanded by *Oberleutnant der Reserve* Helmut Metz. Incredibly, when the US Navy aircraft intercepted *U-487*, they found that Metz had allowed the majority of the crew out onto the casing of the submarine where they were busy working on their suntans. Metz seemed to have assumed that his position south of the Azores was out of reach of Allied aircraft. The Avenger–Wildcat team followed a standard attack procedure, the Wildcat strafing the U-boat and the Avenger following to deposit four depth charges across the boat, two of which exploded, catching the sunbathers in a mad dash to man their battle stations. In fact, although the crew were fairly disorganized and caught unexpectedly by the carrier aircraft attack, the flak crews managed to put up a ferocious barrage, shooting down the Wildcat and killing the pilot. But in the meantime two more Avengers had arrived and the U-boat was blasted four times close to, by exploding depth charges. *U-487* sank rapidly by the head, while many of the crew threw themselves clear of the submarine into the water. The stern soon became visible, standing up in the water for a few moments, and then slid under. The destroyer USS *Barker* plucked thirty-three men from the sea, with a further thirty-one men, including Metz, being lost in this action. It was probable that the U-boat's crew

114

casualties would have been considerably higher, certainly around 80 to 95 per cent, had Metz not inadvisably allowed his men the privilege of sunbathing in a war zone.

U-462, also a Type XIV, under the command of *Kapitänleutnant der Reserve* Bruno Vowe, was caught on the surface along with *U-504*, and attacked by an RAF Halifax of No. 502 Squadron in the Bay of Biscay on 30 July 1943. The U-boat was lost, but all of the crew, except one man who was killed, were later rescued by the Royal Navy and taken prisoner.

The destruction of the two Type XIV U-tankers stretched the German Navy's ability to actually get *Gruppe Monsun* into the Indian Ocean to the limit of its logistical support. Even before *U-487* had been sunk, U-boat Control had redirected *U-160*, a Type IXC, to give assistance to the *U-487*. *U-160* had left Bordeaux on 28 July, and was on her way to rendezvous with *U-487*, unaware that the latter vessel had already been sunk. Commanded by *Oberleutnant zür See* Gerd von Pommer-Esche, *U-160* had been on operations since October 1941, having already completed four successful war patrols to the United States, the Caribbean Sea and South Africa under the command of *Korvettenkapitän* Georg Lassen. The crew had already suffered fatalities in December 1941, though not through enemy action. While 'working-up' in Danzig, seven crewmen were killed and one injured when a fire broke out on board.

Pommer-Esche assumed command of the boat from Lassen in June 1943. On 14 July a pair of American aircraft spotted *U-160* as she made her way to rendezvous with *U-487*, while patrolling from the escort carrier USS *Santee* of US Navy Squadron VC-29. The Avenger–Wildcat team immediately attacked the boat, which was some 300 miles south of the Portuguese Azores. The Wildcat strafed the U-boat as it began to crash-dive (a manoeuvre that was contrary to German Navy standing orders), and the Avenger followed by dropping depth charges and a *Fido* homing torpedo over the roiling water where *U-160* had just submerged. The pilot registered the shock of an underwater explosion, which was followed by foam and oil rising to the surface, indicating that *U-160*, Pommer-Esche and his fifty-three subordinates were no more.

The loss of *U-160* further complicated the refuelling situation for the Germans. This is aptly demonstrated by the revised refuelling plan issued by U-boat Control shortly after the sinking of *U-160*. At the rendezvous site a herd of eight thirsty U-boats had gathered expecting to meet *U-487* and *U-160*. After some of the boats had notified U-boat Control that the U-tankers appeared to be missing, U-boat Control attempted to contact the destroyed *U-487*. Obtaining no response, the Germans correctly determined that the Type XIV had been lost, though they did not assume the loss of *U-160*. Prioritizing the U-boats of *Gruppe Monsun*, U-boat Control directed that the destroyed *U-160* was to refuel four of the *Monsun* U-boats (*U-516*, *U-532*, *U-533* and the destroyed *U-509*), with another Type IXC, *U-155* which was outbound towards a patrol area off the Americas, diverted to refuel the remaining three *Gruppe Monsun* boats (*U-168*, *U-183* and *U-188*). After completing this mission *U-155* was directed to abort her mission and return home. However, *U-155* would herself require refuelling in order to get home after giving most of her fuel away to the *Monsun* boats. U-boat Control redirected the Type VII *U-648*, which was returning from a patrol off the Americas, to refuel the Type IXC40 *U-527*, which was also returning home from the Americas, and then travel the remaining way in company with *U-155*. When the thirsty *Monsun* U-boats reported that *U-160* was missing around 19–20 July, U-boat Control thought fast and the solution presented itself in the form of one of the *Monsun* boats themselves. *U-516* had reported mechanical difficulties which required port facilities to make good, and Control directed that she should refuel *U-532*, *U-533* and *U-509* on 26 July, and then sail south independently to meet the Americas-bound *U-662* to receive ammunition and a *Metox*, and then return home. (At this stage Control was unaware of the loss of *U-509*.)

U-155, the Type IXC that had been redirected by Control from her Americas' war patrol, successfully refuelled *U-168*, *U-183* and *U-188* on 23 July. On 24 July *U-155* refuelled *U-306*, which was heading home from a patrol off the coast of West Africa, and both boats successfully returned to Lorient in August. The five surviving U-boats sailed into the Indian Ocean via the Straits of Madagascar, and discovered that the hunting was considerably easier than in the Atlantic, where anti-submarine hunter-killer groups were taking a heavy toll of U-boats. Indeed, merchant ship sinkings in the Indian Ocean throughout late 1943 and 1944 amounted to half of all those sunk in all theatres taken together by the German Navy.

At the beginning of September 1943, *Gruppe Monsun* refuelled south of the island of Madagascar from the German tanker *Brake*. *U-177*, which was still in the area, also rendezvoused with the

16. Wilhelm Dommes
    pictured in tropical
    kit in Singapore.
    (Courtesy of Ted Agar)

17. The port side of the wreck of *U-534*, one of only two examples of the Type IX
    U-boat left in the world. *U-534* is preserved at Birkenhead near Liverpool, England.
    The other example, *U-505*, is on display in Chicago.   *(Courtesy of Ben Felton)*

18. The conning tower bridge and *Wintergarten* with 37mm anti-aircraft gun. *U-534*, Birkenhead, England.
(*Courtesy of Ben Felton*)

19. The American escort carrier USS *Bogue*, whose air group was to prove a deadly menace to U-boat and *Yanagi* operations in the South Atlantic. (*Author's collection*)

20. The wreck of *U-852* off the coast of British Somaliland (now Somalia) in May 1944 after being scuttled by her skipper, *Kapitänleutnant* Heinz Eck. Eck was to be the only U-boat commander found guilty of war crimes and executed after he ordered the machine gunning of survivors from the Greek ship *Peleus*. *(Author's collection)*

21. The deck of *U-156*, under the command of *Kapitänleutnant* Werner Hartenstein, crowded with survivors from his sinking of the liner *Laconia* in September 1942. Hartenstein organized a rescue operation with three other U-boats and an Italian submarine, only to be attacked by American aircraft during the attempt. *(Author's collection)*

22. *Korvettenkapitän* Robert Gysae returning from a successful patrol of southern Africa aboard *U-177*.
(*Author's collection*)

23. *U-183* coming alongside the German tanker *Brake* in the Southern Ocean, September 1943.
(*Author's collection*)

24. *U-182* commissioning ceremony at the Deschimag wharf in Bremen, 30 June 1942. Her skipper, *Kapitänleutnant* Nicholai Clausen is pictured left.   *(Author's collection)*

25. The Japanese submarine *I-29* in Lorient harbour, France 1943.   *(Author's collection)*

26. Rear Admiral Sadamichi Kajioka, commander of the Japanese submarine force. *(Author's collection)*

27. The former Italian submarine *Commandante Cappellini* in service with the German Navy as *UIT-24*. *(Author's collection)*

28. *U-459*, a Type XIV 'Milkcow' tanker supporting U-boats in the Indian Ocean.

(Author's collection)

29. Lieutenant General
Hiroshi Oshima, Japanese
Ambassador to Berlin
between 1938 and 1945.
(Author's collection)

30. *Korvettenkapitän* Jürgen Oesten, commanding *U-861*. *(Author's collection)*

31. *Korvettenkapitän* Werner Winter, commanding *U-103*. *(Author's collection)*

tanker at the same time. However, as soon as refuelling had been accomplished, the U-boats went their separate ways and maintained a strict radio silence – which defeated British attempts to track the group by decoding their radio transmissions to U-boat Control, and each other.

The ultimate fate of Büchholz and *U-177* was sealed four months later. Assigned to 12th U-boat Flotilla, *U-177* departed from La Pallice on 2 January 1944 bound for the Indian Ocean. On 6 February Büchholz was in the vicinity of Ascension Island in the South Atlantic when his surfaced boat was spotted by a Liberator bomber of US Navy Squadron VB-107, a unit that had proved to be one of the greatest menaces to U-boats travelling to and from operations in the Far East. The Liberator dumped depth charges all over *U-177*, wrecking the submarine. Fifty of the crew, including the hapless Büchholz, followed their stricken boat to a watery grave, and another ten were eventually plucked from the sea by Allied forces and made prisoners of war.

Because both German and Japanese submarines were now operating in the Indian Ocean, the two allies attempted to fix a demarcation line to create two zones of operations, German to the west and Japanese to the east, along the imaginary line 70E. However, such a demarcation was not rigid, as shown by the location of the German U-boat base at Penang, well within the Japanese zone of operations.

Gruppe Monsun – Second Wave Reinforcements

Operations in the Indian Ocean were continuing to provide the Germans with rewards in tonnage sunk, and *Admiral* Dönitz decided to reinforce the group in November 1943. He ordered five U-cruisers, to be known as the Second *Gruppe Monsun*, to proceed to the Indian Ocean.

Operations by *Gruppe Monsun* were suspended for a brief period, November 1943 to January 1944, as all the boats headed for Penang and the new U-boat base, to effect repairs, rearm, refuel, and rest their crews over Christmas. In the meantime, although the new German base at Penang contained four U-boats (*U-183*, *U-168*, *U-532* and *U-188*), U-boat Control had decided to supplement hunting potential in the Indian Ocean by the dispatch of further boats from Europe. The first to depart was a brand-new Type IXD2, *U-848*, under the command of Knights Cross holder

Fregattenkapitän Wilhelm Rollmann. Born on 5 August 1907 in the naval town of Wilhelmshaven, Rollmann's naval career began in the *Reichsmarine* in 1926. After service on several warships, Rollmann transferred to U-boats in May 1937, taking command of *U-34* in October 1938. During command of *U-34* he sank, among others, the Royal Navy destroyer HMS *Whirlwind* and the submarine HMS *Spearfish*. He was awarded the Knights Cross in July 1940. On completing his seventh war patrol in command of *U-34*, he subsequently became an instructor in *Unterseeboots-Lehr-Division 2* (2nd U-boat Training Division). On the 20 February 1943 Rollmann re-entered active sea duty when he commissioned *U-848*.

On his way south as part of the *Gruppe Monsun* second wave reinforcement group Rollmann attacked and sank the 4,573-ton British freighter *Baron Semple* near Ascension Island on 2 November, which had the unfortunate effect of alerting Allied anti-submarine aircraft based at the British colony. Rollmann continued with his mission to the Far East, but a B-24 US Navy Liberator bomber of Squadron VB-107, based on Ascension, discovered *U-848* cruising on the surface 300 miles south of the island on 5 November. Rollmann observed *Kriegsmarine* standing orders regarding aerial attack and did not dive, and his flak crews put up a fearsome anti-aircraft barrage into which the Liberator twice dived to deliver its attacks. After twelve depth charges had exploded close to the U-boat, *U-848* was severely damaged and leaking large amounts of fuel oil into the ocean. The B-24, having expended its payload of depth charges, now called in reinforcements in an effort to finish Rollmann off. A second aircraft appeared, also braving the flak barrage, to deposit another twelve depth charges. Missing the target it was forced to return to Ascension to rearm and return later. A third B-24 was summoned, but the German flak crew managed to shoot out one of the aircraft's engines, leaving the pilot with no choice but to immediately abort his sortie and return to base.

Thus far, although gravely damaged, *U-848* had successfully beaten off the second and third aerial attacks and was still afloat, though unable to dive. However, it was relatively straightforward for the first Liberator to stay on station and circle the stricken U-boat, just out of range of the boat's anti-aircraft guns, marking Rollmann's location for the expected Allied reinforcements. Four hours passed until a flight of three USAAF B-25 Mitchell medium bombers, armed with conventional aerial bombs, appeared and rather optimistically attempted to sink *U-848* by bombing her from an altitude of 1,500 feet. The attempt failed. Not to be put off, the second B-24, which had missed *U-848* during both its previous attacks with depth charges, now reappeared and lost no time in launching an attack run. The resulting twelve depth charge explosions destroyed the U-boat, breaking it in two and leaving around twenty-five to thirty crewmen floundering in the water a long way from rescue. The American aircraft dropped three life-rafts and then turned for home, leaving the Germans to their fate. One month later, a single German survivor from *U-848* was plucked from the Atlantic, but he was in such a poor condition that he died soon afterwards and is buried in Recife, Brazil.

U-849, also a brand new Type IXD2 U-cruiser, under the command of yet another experienced skipper, *Kapitänleutnant* Heinz-Otto Schültze, sortied from Kiel on 2 October bound for Penang. Schültze followed a family tradition by becoming a U-boat skipper. His father, Otto, had commanded *U-63* during the First World War and had sunk an astounding fifty-two ships. Kaiser Wilhelm II had decorated Otto Schültze with Imperial Germany's highest award before the advent of the Knights Cross – the *Pour le Merite* (which was sometimes known as the 'Blue Max'). Heinz-Otto Schültze was born in 1915 in Kiel, and began his naval career in 1934, joining U-boats in 1937. After a couple of school boat commands, Schültze eventually commissioned *U-432* in April 1941 and completed seven war patrols in the North Atlantic and off the east coast of the United States. He was awarded the Knights Cross in July 1942. Schültze would sink a total of nineteen ships and damage two others before his early death.

The same US Navy Liberator bombers on Ascension Island that had sunk *U-848* also discovered *U-849*. On 25 November Schültze was attacked on the surface by a single Liberator, which flew so low during its attacking run that one of the six depth charges released actually bounced off the U-boat and struck the aircraft's tail plane, causing some damage. The damage done to *U-849* was, however, terminal, and in an eerie replay of the death of *U-848*, the U-boat sank quickly leaving around thirty German sailors struggling in the roiling water. Following standard procedure, the B-24 dropped three life-rafts to the U-boatmen and then departed quickly for home. None of the thirty Germans was ever recovered from the sea off the Congo Estuary, and one can only imagine the miserable deaths that these U-boatmen suffered during the weeks they were adrift. It was a common enough fate that awaited those U-boatmen who were lucky enough to survive the sinking of their boat by aerial attack, and on many occasions Allied aircraft reported that practically half of a destroyed U-boat's crew made it into the water. Sadly though, few were subsequently recovered. Those U-boatmen whose boats were sunk on the surface by Allied naval vessels generally had a better chance of being picked up, whereas boats destroyed while submerged generally never yielded survivors.

Departing France for Penang on 22 November 1943 was the youngest officer in command of a U-boat, twenty-two-year-old *Oberleutnant zür See* Hermann Hoffmann in the Type IXC *U-172*, the boat having previously patrolled in the Indian Ocean under the command of *Korvettenkapitän* Carl Emmermann in 1942. Unfortunately, on this occasion *U-172* would not reach southern waters. She was attacked in the Bay of Biscay on the night of 3 December by an RAF Coastal Command bomber, but managed to escape without serious damage. Because of the penetration of U-boat Enigma the Allies knew when and where *U-172* would meet and refuel from *U-219* and they had the aircraft carrier USS *Bogue* move into the area. American aircraft, however, failed to find the rendezvous and it was only two days later, on 12 December, that a lone Avenger discovered *U-172* motoring on the surface and immediately attacked. Hoffmann was extremely lucky because the *Fido* homing torpedo dropped by the Avenger failed to locate the U-boat, and Hoffmann was able to go to maximum depth in an attempt to outsmart his pursuers. The *Bogue*, and the four destroyers forming her escort, now began a painfully thorough search for the U-boat. The search lasted for twenty-seven hours and employed further *Fido* torpedoes and bomb drops from the carrier's air group, and Hedgehog and depth charge attacks from the destroyers. By 13 December Hoffmann was forced to surface, but he did not surrender, preferring instead to fight back. The U-boat skipper personally manned a machine-gun and fired at the USS *Osmond Ingram*, killing a sailor and wounding six others, before the combined firepower of the four destroyers killed thirteen of the U-boat's crew, with the rest abandoning ship. The US Navy recovered Hoffmann and forty-five survivors from the water and took them as prisoners of war to Norfolk, Virginia.

U-850, a brand-new Type IXD2, departed from Kiel for Penang on 18 November commanded by one of the most experienced officers in the U-boat service, *Kapitän zür See* Klaus Ewerth, aged thirty-six. Ewerth's career had been long, having first commanded the Type IIA *U-1* between 1935 and 1936, then the Type VIIA *U-36* from 1936 to 1938. His next command had been the Type IA *U-26* between 1939 and 1940, followed by a long period on the staff between 1940 and 1943, then command of *U-850*. On 20 December 1943 U-boat Control had just informed Ewerth of the good news that his wife had safely delivered their fifth child, when an Avenger torpedo bomber from the USS *Bogue* discovered *U-850* on the surface. The U-boat was taken completely unawares by the subsequent attack and failed to mount any flak defence. The Avenger completely missed with the six depth charges it was carrying, but in the meantime frantically radioed for reinforcements. These materialized in the form of two Wildcat fighters and a further two Avengers. Ewerth was crash-diving the boat when two *Fido* homing torpedoes struck. One of the aerial torpedoes slammed into the starboard side, while the other impacted close to the conning tower. *U-850* sank quickly by the stern. All sixty-six crew perished in the resulting demise of the boat even though two US Navy destroyers were at the scene of the sinking relatively quickly. They found only tattered clothing, some wood and lifebelts, and pieces of bodies floating on the oily pool where Ewerth and his men had been killed.

Of the original boats that had hunted independently in the Indian Ocean and had been based at Penang, *U-178*, now under the command of *Kapitänleutnant* Wilhelm Spähr (formerly the boat's First Watch Officer under Dommes), managed to sink the 7,244-ton American Liberty ship *Jose Navarro* close to the Maldives before the meeting with the *Gruppe Monsun* second wave reinforcement boat *U-510*, commanded by *Kapitänleutnant* Alfred Eick, who had departed from France on 3 November 1943. The tanker *Charlotte Schliemann* finally arrived in the Indian Ocean at the end of January 1944, and met with *U-178* and *U-510* on 27 January. Allied intelligence was aware of the tanker and her mission. Both boats were refuelled, with *U-178* obtaining the latest cipher materials from the homeward-bound *U-510*. *U-178* also took on board ninety days provisions, and in addition to the 30 tons of rubber that had been loaded in Penang, she took on a further 19 tons, as it was expected that the U-boat would depart for Germany. This brought *U-178*'s total *Yanagi* cargo to 172 tons of rubber, tin and tungsten. In addition, *U-178* had taken aboard 400 tons of diesel fuel from the *Charlotte Schliemann*. This meant that the boat could be utilized as an auxiliary tanker in the Indian Ocean as she sailed for the Cape of Good Hope. It was as well, because the British had discovered the meeting between the *Charlotte Schliemann* and the two U-boats, and an aerial search by British aircraft based in Mauritius soon located the merchant tanker allowing naval forces to intercept the ship. HMS *Relentless*, a destroyer, had closed in on the *Charlotte Schliemann* on 12 February, and to avoid capture the tanker had scuttled herself. Some of the crew were rescued by *U-532*, who in turn was forced to refuel from *U-178* on 27 February. Allied intelligence subsequently reported that the *Charlotte Schliemann*'s orders,

> were to R/V (*rendezvous*) with three Italian and two German U-Boats in position considerably further South of position in which she was sunk about 17th February. Possibly these vessels bound for Europe.[5]

After refuelling from the *Charlotte Schliemann* on 28 January, *U-510*, the Type IXC under the command of *Kapitänleutnant* Alfred Eick, formerly of *U-176*, patrolled up into the Arabian Sea on a line between Oman and India. On 22 February Eick intercepted and attacked Convoy PA69, which was en route between the Persian Gulf and the British fortified harbour at Aden. During this one attack Eick managed to sink the 7,385-ton British vessel *San Alvaro* and an American freighter, the 9,181-ton *E.G. Seubert*, and also damaged the 9,970-ton Norwegian tanker *Erling Brovig*. Eick's successes continued into March, attacking Convoy MQ67 on 7 March and sinking the 7,229-ton Norwegian freighter *Tarifa*. He struck again on 19 March, this time attacking Convoy MR63, sinking the 7,176-ton American ship *John A. Poor* and finally (before reaching Penang) claiming the tiny 249-ton Norwegian vessel *Maaloy* on 27 March. On 5 April *U-510* arrived safely in Penang. Two days later Eick was notified that he had been awarded the Knights Cross for sinking ten ships totalling 57,221 tons and damaging several others during all of his war patrols.

U-532, *U-168*, *U-188* and *U-183*, all original *Gruppe Monsun* first wave boats, received orders on 4 January 1944 while in Penang to sail for Europe as soon as they had achieved war readiness. Allied intelligence noted that these boats, although retaining their fighting abilities, were primarily being loaded up by the Germans with a large *Yanagi* cargo. Since mid-November 1943, when *U-168* had arrived in Penang, preparations had been going on for loading this cargo.

> On 16/11/43 they were told that an order to carry with them as keel cargoes ores important for the war effort (wolfram concentrate) they were to have tin boxes fabricated.[6]

Allied intelligence noted that,

> Some difficulty was expected and apparently experienced in the construction of tin boxes. On 18/12, following a report ... from the Senior CO Monsun Boats he was ordered to 'continue with the manufacture of zinc boxes for the keel loading of U-boats, for boats that are later going to Japan'.[7]

The Germans were determined to load these boats with the maximum cargo they could transport, and such a move would necessitate stripping the U-boats of much of their normal equipment and fittings, for example:

> On 19/11 further orders came; the 10.5cm gun [105mm deck gun] and all ammunition was to be landed, keel ballast removed. Wolfram ore or molybdenum were to be put in the magazine and in tin boxes in the keel, and the keel ballast replaced by tin bars.[8]

By 15 December U-boat Control issued more precise instructions: '*U183* and *U532* were to load tin in the keel, wolfram concentrate in sacks in the magazine',[9] *U-168* and *U-188* were to follow suit and:

> on 25/12 all four U/Bs (U-boats) were told to remove keel ballast iron from pressure frame compartments 37–48 on both starboard and port sides and to have these compartments empty; to remove iron ballast in other keel ballast compartments and replace this with an equivalent weight of zinc ingots; to stow the 2cm and small arms ammunition in No. 2 magazine and the remainder in the fore compartment and to 'stow

wolfram ore in sacks (about 290 tons) in No. (Roman) 1 magazine'. In addition to these ores the boats are to use any remaining space to dump as much opium, quinine and vitamin concentrates as possible.[10]

The remaining German surface tanker in the Indian Ocean, the *Brake*, sailed from Penang on 26 February, and three U-boats, *U-532*, *U-188* and *U-168* were ordered to refuel from her. The commander of *U-168*, Helmuth Pich, was born on 26 June 1914 in Babziens, Rastenburg. He began his officer training in 1934, and rose to the rank of *Kapitänleutnant* in February 1942. In September 1942 Pich assumed command of *U-168*, attached to the 4th Training Flotilla. *U-168* became operational as a 'front-boat' with 2nd Flotilla in March 1943, based at Lorient. After arriving in the Far East, Pich and *U-168* were assigned to 33rd Flotilla under *Korvettenkapitän* Georg Schrewe, with flotilla headquarters nominally located at Flensburg in Germany. Schrewe and many of the flotilla's boats were actually based at Penang and Djarkarta. Pich and *U-168* had been in Penang since he was reported to have been suffering from nervous exhaustion on 24 October 1943.[11] Once again, the penetration of German signals' codes by the Allies allowed the valuable *Brake* to be located. The British knew from the decrypts the date and location of the refuelling rendezvous, and accordingly diverted naval forces to destroy the ship and the U-boats. On 12 March, aircraft from the carrier HMS *Battler*, noted by Pich on *U-168* to be 'Albacore type A/C'[12] found the *Brake* while she was in company with several U-boats, including *U-188*, *U-532* and *U-168*. Fleet Air Arm aircraft had directed British warships towards the rendezvous and the U-boats had wisely dispersed before they arrived on the scene. The unfortunate *Brake* was faced with the same fate as the *Charlotte Schliemann*, being forced to scuttle herself. After the Royal Navy had departed from the scene, carrier aircraft remained on station waiting to see if any of the U-boats would return to rescue the survivors from the *Brake*. The British were rewarded by the appearance of *U-168*, which began to rescue survivors from the water. Aircraft pounced at the opportunity to destroy the U-boat, and *U-168* narrowly avoided destruction as she was bombed during her subsequent crash-dive. Fortunately for *U-168* the single bomb that hit the U-boat failed to explode.

Junker on *U-532* reported to Control at 1809 hours that '*Brake* sunk. Entire crew aboard'.[13] He also reported that he had partially fuelled from the tanker before its destruction. Pich reported that it was his intention to cooperate with Junker in taking care of the *Brake*'s crew, but U-boat Control considered carefully the problems of so many new mouths to feed and bodies to stow in the cramped confines of his boat: 'Pich and Junker to divide up BRAKE's crew at an agreed R/V proposed by Pich tonight. If Pich can carry out return of crew unaided, Junker return home.'[14] This strategy was successful and *U-168* was able to return safely to Penang with only minor damage. Assisted by *U-188*, the two boats managed to bring 196 crewmen from the *Brake* to Penang. On 25 March the U-boat base at Penang reported to Control that 'German S/M U 168 arrived at 2100 on the 24th with 135 of the crew of the "BRAKE"'.[15] These men were integrated into the U-boat base's pool of trained manpower. *U-188* had enough diesel to attempt the long journey back to France without any further need for refuelling, but the journey proved to be so hard on the boat that on her arrival in Bordeaux she was decommissioned, never to sail again. When Allied forces surrounded Bordeaux following the Normandy Landings, *U-188* was scuttled on 20 August 1944.

The loss of the tankers *Charlotte Schliemann* and the *Brake* removed the means by which *Gruppe Monsun* could be refuelled at sea. U-boats trading fuel and provisions from one another while on patrol was the only available solution. The sinking of the *Charlotte Schliemann* and the *Brake* within such a short space of time, coupled with the fact that Allied aircraft always seemed to arrive when U-boats met at a rendezvous for refuelling finally convinced both the U-boat commanders themselves and U-boat Control in Kiel that the Allies had penetrated the U-boat Enigma code. Therefore, in order to immediately prevent the Allies using German naval communications to decimate U-boat operations, the Enigma settings and keys were changed. The code was changed to the 'Shark' key, placing the Allies once more in the dark. The entire process of altering the method by which messages were encrypted aboard U-boats and at U-boat Control caused confusion and anger at the British code breaking station at Bletchley Park, and at the US Navy decryption centre in Washington DC. The code breakers themselves, and members of both governments, were furious that Allied commanders had given the game away concerning the penetration of U-boat Enigma by so obviously attacking U-boat refuelling at pre-arranged rendezvous points.

Penang was now the only place available for U-boats to refuel within the Indian Ocean area of operations, necessitating boats to shorten their patrols in order to sail back to Penang. This was combined with improved Allied defences throughout the region, the introduction of escorted convoys and increased aerial activity. These factors caused *Gruppe Monsun*'s successes to fall appreciably. Penang was also not the best place from which to attempt to operate a U-boat offensive. The climate and tropical diseases wore down the U-boatmen, there was a great shortage of skilled labour in Penang (as compared with occupied France), and the Japanese were not given to actively supporting U-boat operations, now that the U-boat base was fully operational. Indeed, batteries and other technical components needed by the U-boats had to be imported from Japan. The problem of quality components, especially batteries, was so bad that it led the Germans to establish a small base at Kobe, Japan, which included a battery repair and construction facility. By March 1944 the small base was placed under the command of *Korvettenkapitän* Eitel-Friedrich Kentrat.

The former crew of *U-511*, who had successfully delivered the U-boat to the Japanese, became a much-needed resource for the German base at Penang. They provided a highly trained core of men who could be drafted aboard other U-boats as crew replacements, and they could provide the skilled engineering team needed to maintain the fighting boats so far from home. *Korvettenkapitän* Wilhelm Dommes, the former commanding officer of *U-178* who had been appointed commander of the U-boat base at Penang by Dönitz, also quickly realized that his men required rest and relaxation following patrols, and established a U-boat rest home for the crews in the mountains close to Penang.

Radio messages intercepted and decoded at Bletchley Park indicate the poor maintenance facilities and spares situation at Penang. On 10 July it became necessary to divert Schrewe's boat, which was ordered by U-boat Control 'to proceed via Djakarta (Batavia) on return passage to hand over a propeller to Pich (*U-168*)'.[16] The continual and well-documented problem with the quality of U-boat batteries in the Far East prompted Pich to inform U-boat Control in August: 'Exchange of battery must be carried out. Cannot be responsible for return passage with battery capacity reported.'[17] It was to be a problem for the Germans until the end of the war, and one which the battery repair and overhauling facility at Kobe would stop from becoming completely critical.

False Start – The *I-34*

The Japanese submarine *I-34* was completed at the Sasebo dockyard and commissioned into the Imperial Navy on 31 August 1942 under the command of Commander Kinzo Tonozuka, who had previously skippered the *I-3*. Under Tonozuka the submarine was engaged throughout late 1942 and into early 1943 in Japanese operations in the Aleutian Islands, the only sections of mainland United States occupied by Japanese forces during the Second World War. On 20 March 1943 Commander Tatsushi Irie was appointed as the new skipper while the boat was undergoing a refit at Yokosuka. Thereafter the *I-34* was employed to run supplies to the garrison in the Aleutians, and later helped evacuate Japanese troops following the American effort to retake the islands.

On 15 September the *I-34* was reassigned to Penang and prepared in Japan for a *Yanagi* mission to France. She departed from Kure on 13 October under the Japanese code-name '*Momi*' (Fir), having also been assigned the German code-name '*U-Tanne*' for the duration of her mission. Her mission, cargo, passengers and route were all intercepted by the Allies through deciphering the diplomatic correspondence circulated between Tokyo and Berlin. On 22 October the *I-34* arrived in Singapore to embark five passengers for the journey to Europe, the most prominent of these being the new Japanese Naval Attaché to Berlin, Rear Admiral Hideo Kojima, as well as a pair of engineers from Mitsubishi. However, the departure of the submarine from Singapore was delayed as the loading of the considerable quantity of *Yanagi* cargo was taking far longer than expected. Kojima and the other passengers decided to leave the submarine and travel by train up to Penang, and there rejoin the *I-34* when she called in. It was a decision which was to save their lives.

Finally, on 11 November, the *I-34*, fully loaded with rubber, tungsten, tin, quinine, opium and examples of Japanese weapons, pulled out of Singapore harbour and headed for the Japanese base at Penang. When approximately 30 miles south of Penang, on the morning of 13 November, she was located by the British submarine HMS *Taurus*, patrolling the waters around the busy port. *Taurus*'s skipper, Lieutenant Commander M.R.G. Wingfield, had been alerted by a special Ultra intelligence report of the likely location of the *I-34*, and he now closed his submarine in on the Japanese submarine, which was running on the surface escorted by a small submarine chaser. At 0730 Wingfield fired six torpedoes at the *I-34*, one of which struck the starboard side just below the conning tower. The heavily laden submarine began to sink rapidly. Twenty crew members managed to open a deck hatch in the after section of the *I-34* and get out, thirteen of whom survived to be rescued by a junk from Penang later in the day. The other eighty-four members of the crew all perished in the sinking.

The Japanese sub-chaser immediately attacked HMS *Taurus*, Wingfield diving his boat deep to escape the depth charge attack that followed, unfortunately jamming the submarine's bows into the soft mud at the bottom of the Malacca Strait. The explosions of the depth charges, causing no damage to the boat, did manage to dislodge the bows from the mud and Wingfield ordered *Taurus* brought up to periscope depth. Deciding that the Japanese sub-chaser was too small fry to expend a torpedo on, Wingfield surfaced the boat and began to engage the enemy with his deck gun. After scoring several hits on the Japanese, severely damaging the small craft, a Japanese aircraft appeared overhead. HMS *Taurus* dived deep and made good her escape.

Rear Admiral Kojima and the other passengers eventually left for France aboard the *I-29* on 16 December 1943. The final act in the story of the ill-fated *I-34* occurred during December 1962, when a salvage company from Singapore raised the wreck of the submarine for scrap.

The Japanese Return to France

The Japanese submarine *I-29* had already successfully rendezvoused with a German U-boat, Müsenberg's *U-180*, at sea in April 1943 and returned to the Far East unscathed. She had subsequently had a lucky escape off the coast of East Africa while on patrol and still under the command of Izu. Just after noon on 14 July 1943 the *I-29* was spotted running on the surface by an RAF Hudson VI bomber of 8 Squadron.[18] The keen-eyed crewmen had discerned the great Japanese submarine from 6 miles away and immediately prepared to launch an attack. The Hudson swooped down low out of the sun, simultaneously releasing three out of four depth charges carried aboard (the fourth refused to release or 'hung up'), the bombs straddling the *I-29* as Izu ordered an immediate crash-dive. When the depth charges detonated beneath the waves the submarine appeared to the circling RAF crew to have been forced back to the surface, only to slink once more beneath the water. The Hudson continued to circle the disturbed patch of sea where the submarine had dived, the crew noting a black oil slick bubbling to the surface and leading off along the *I-29*'s presumed submerged course. The depth charges had evidently caused the *I-29* serious damage, as the oil slick was to grow by the hour until eventually it formed a trail 1.5 miles in length and 300 yards wide. The Japanese were lucky and escaped this time to return to service as a *Yanagi* delivery boat. On 17 December 1943, the *I-29*, defined as a U-cruiser by the Germans and accordingly given the code-name '*U-Kiefer*', sailed from Japan with orders to travel considerably further this time than the Indian Ocean.

Before departing for Europe, the *I-29*'s anti-aircraft armament was improved, with the total firepower increased to three duel-mount 25mm guns. Commander Takakasu Kinashi assumed command on 10 October 1943, and on the submarine's arrival in Singapore on 14 November Kinashi had an opportunity to talk to Commander Uchino of the *I-8*, recently returned from Brest. They discussed weather conditions in the Atlantic and the strength of Allied naval forces. Kinashi also obtained permission to remove the *I-8*'s German FuMB1 *Metox* radar detector, which was duly fitted to the *I-29*.

The *I-29* set out for France on 16 December 1943, loaded with 80 tons of rubber, 80 tons of tungsten, 50 tons of tin, 2 tons of zinc and mixed 3 tons of quinine, opium and coffee. Also aboard were sixteen passengers, including Rear Admiral Hideo Kojima (the new Japanese Naval Attaché to Germany), Commander Senmei Muchaku (the new Japanese Naval Attaché to fascist Spain) and Commander Kazuto Ogi (the new Japanese Assistant Naval Attaché to Germany). Commander Yoshio Nahamori, an expert in aircraft ordnance, was also aboard along with two Mitsubishi engineers. Before rounding the Cape of Good Hope into the Atlantic the *I-29* refuelled from a small German supply vessel, the *Bogota*. The 120 tons of diesel fuel that the submarine took on board was sufficient to see the *I-29* into the Atlantic. On 12 February 1944 the *I-29* made a rendezvous at sea, but not for the purpose of fuelling. South-west of the Azores the *I-29* was scheduled to meet *U-518*, under the command of *Oberleutnant zür See* Hans-Werner Offermann. According to the

'*Offizier Cypher*' Offermann was sent by U-boat Control. He would recognize the Japanese submarine '*Kiefer*' by her size and distinctive hull features:

> Size 2,600 tons, forward of conning tower 14cm [reference to the 140mm deck gun]. Double turret, abaft of conning tower retractable a/c [aircraft] hangar and a catapult.[19]

The importance of *I-29*'s mission was reinforced in the mind of Offermann when he was ordered by Control: 'Do not hinder under any circumstances.'[20] At the rendezvous three German technicians from *U-518* clambered aboard the Japanese submarine, and fitted the new FuMB7 *Naxos* radar detector on to the bridge. *U-518* then departed, continuing on her mission to patrol in the Caribbean Sea. *U-518* and the entire fifty-seven man crew were lost on 22 April 1945 north-west of the Azores, following depth charging by American destroyer escorts during 'Operation Teardrop'.

On 13 February the *I-29* rendezvoused again, this time with the U-tanker *U-488* commanded by *Oberleutnant der Reserve* Bruno Stüdt.[21] While refuelling, the two submarines were spotted on the surface by an RAF patrol aircraft, but both boats successfully escaped. The *I-29* arrived too early in the Bay of Biscay, and spent the night of 9–10 March sitting on the seabed. However, on the morning of 10 March, five Junkers Ju-88C-6s arrived to provide the Japanese submarine with air cover for the journey to Lorient. In the afternoon, German destroyers *Z-23* and *ZH-1*, and the S-boats *T-27* and *T-29* joined them. Because the Allies had successfully penetrated both German and Japanese military codes, they were aware of the *I-29*'s position and attempted to attack the German–Japanese flotilla on 10 March. Four RAF Mosquitos of No. 248 Squadron provided an escort for two further specially modified Mosquitos, each armed with 57mm cannon. They found the warships close to Cape Penas, with German air cover circling above the ships. The escorting Mosquitos managed to shoot down one of the Junkers Ju-88s protecting the *I-29* and her German escort ships, before heading back to their base in England. Later that day a further effort was mounted by the RAF to destroy the *I-29*, this time by B-24 Liberator heavy bombers, escorted by Bristol Beaufighters, whose task was to deal with the ship's flak batteries, but the *I-29* was undamaged by either attack. Accordingly, on 11 March 1944 the *I-29* arrived at the U-boat base at Lorient. After the submarine was secured next to *U-190*, the German U-boat crew cheered the arrival of their Japanese ally. Later, to protect the boat from Allied air attack, the *I-29* was moved into one of the Keroman bunkers.

The officers of the *I-29* were entertained by the officers of the 2nd and 10th U-boat Flotillas at a dockside bar in Lorient. The entire crew of the *I-29* was housed in a luxury chateau overlooking the town of Chateauneuf-du-Faou, where the Japanese engaged in sports events and partied with their German counterparts. They also travelled to Paris for sightseeing and shopping. Commander Kinashi was presented to Hitler in Berlin and decorated with the Iron Cross 2nd Class for his earlier sinking of the American aircraft carrier USS *Wasp*. Once again, as they had done with the *I-30*, the Germans overhauled the Japanese submarine and improved her anti-aircraft defences. The four Japanese Type-96 25mm flak guns were removed and replaced with a Krupp 37mm gun, and a quad-barrel 20mm *Flakvierling* 38.

On 16 April the *I-29* set sail for Japan, having taken aboard a cargo consisting of the very latest in German radar technology, including radar apparatus, radar detectors and jamming equipment. More *Bolde* were loaded aboard, along with ten Enigma code machines and the usual medicines such as stocks of opium and quinine. Also taken aboard was a V-1 Flying Bomb fuselage, TMC acoustic mines, bauxite and a mercury-radium amalgam. Among the passengers (which included four Germans), was Commander Eiichi Iwaya who carried blueprints of the latest German jet aircraft, the Messerschmitt ME-163 *Komet* and ME-262 jet interceptor. Also carried aboard was an HWK 509A-1 rocket motor from an ME-163 *Komet* and a Jumo 004B rocket engine from an ME-162, as well as photographs of the BMW-003 axial-flow turbojet, which became the basis for the Japanese NE-20 engine.

On 11 June the *I-29* passed the *I-52*, another Japanese submarine heading for France loaded up with *Yanagi* cargo. They did not communicate, but Commander Kinashi picked up German signals traffic bound for the *I-52*. The *I-29* reached Singapore on 14 July after a quiet run home, and some of the passengers disembarked, taking with them most of the secret German blueprints and documents. These were flown directly to Tokyo.

American intelligence intercepted the coded signals traffic from the *I-29*, giving her position, cargo and route to Japan. On 22 July the *I-29* departed Singapore bound for the Japanese port of Kure, having taken aboard ten Japanese naval cadets. Once en route to Japan the submarine met with disaster. On 26 July, near the island of Luzon in the Philippines, the American submarine USS *Sawfish* sank the *I-29*. Only one crewman survived the sinking, Kinashi and his 104 crew and passengers were all lost. Kinashi was held in such high regard in Japan that following his death he was posthumously promoted to the rank of Rear Admiral.

The German aircraft that were stowed aboard the *I-29* were lost, helping to slow the development of effective jet aircraft by the Japanese. However, the blueprints and documents, which had been flown directly to Japan from Singapore, proved their value. The Japanese copied the two designs, resulting in the creation of the Nakajima *Kikka*, closely based on the ME-262, and the Mitsubishi J8M1 *Shusui*, a copy of the ME-163.

The *I-52* was completed at the Kure naval yard in 1943. She could carry 300 tons of freight and sail 21,000 nautical miles without refuelling, with a ship's complement consisting of eleven officers and eighty-four enlisted men. Along as passengers on the voyage to Europe were a mixed group of fourteen men – six Imperial Japanese Navy officers, one civilian translator and seven civilian engineers.

In mid-March 1944 the *I-52*, under Commander Kameo Uno, slipped out of Kure harbour and sailed to Singapore. Once in port she took on board an important *Yanagi* cargo bound for Nazi Germany consisting of 2.88 tons of opium, 3 tons of quinine and 54 tons of baled rubber. The departure of the *I-52* was noted by US Navy intelligence, which had successfully broken the Japanese 'purple code' used in diplomatic exchanges between Japan and Germany.

A slow month dragged by for the passengers and crew as the *I-52* made its way through the Indian Ocean. As a precaution against aerial attack, the *I-52* travelled on the surface at speed only during the hours of darkness – during daylight hours she remained submerged. This meant that only absolutely necessary movement was permitted aboard the submarine during the daytime, because oxygen supplies had to be maintained until the boat could be aired at night. Negotiating the Cape of Good Hope on 15 May, the *I-52* entered the Atlantic. Because of the unknown nature of the Atlantic to Japanese submariners, it had been decided that the submarine would effect a rendezvous with a German U-boat in mid-ocean, the Germans passing a pilot over to the *I-52* to assist with getting the submarine successfully into the U-boat base at Lorient. Along with the pilot, new radar detection apparatus to increase the submarine's ability to detect incoming Allied anti-submarine warfare attacks, and two German enlisted men to operate it, would also be transferred to the *I-52* at the exchange.

U-530, under *Kapitänleutnant* Kurt Lange, was waiting to meet the *I-52* at a pre-arranged rendezvous site, the meeting scheduled to occur at dusk on 23 June. After meeting, both submarines remained on the surface, allowing the pilot, *Leutnant zür See* Schäfer, and the two U-boat radiomen with the radar detector equipment, Petty Officers Schulze and Behrendt, to row themselves over to the *I-52* in a rubber dinghy. The sea was rough and the box containing the radar set tumbled overboard from the dinghy, but a resourceful Japanese sailor dived in and retrieved it before it sank. After remaining on the surface for two and a quarter hours, *U-530* set sail to the west while the *I-52* remained surfaced.

The Americans had not been idle regarding the *I-52*, and intended to attack and destroy the submarine before she could get to Lorient and deliver her cargo. Using Ultra intelligence decrypts to establish the likely position of the Japanese submarine, the carrier USS *Bogue* launched a Grumman Avenger torpedo aircraft. Then, using a sonobuoy, which was a kind of primitive marine sound detector, the aircraft managed to locate underwater propeller sounds. Suddenly, the Avenger encountered the surfaced *I-52*, which was battling through the waves at a speed of between 10 and 12 knots. As the Japanese submarine attempted to crash-dive, the Avenger released two depth charges. The aircraft circled back and launched a Mark-24 acoustic torpedo, the deadly *Fido*, at the *I-52*. The sonobuoy recorded the death throes of the Japanese submarine beneath the waves. Forty-five minutes after the Avenger attack the *Bogue* deployed a second sortie; this aircraft dropped another *Fido* after locating further propeller sounds at the site where the *I-52* had sunk. Seventeen minutes after the second torpedo attack, a sustained explosion was recorded by the sonobuoy. The *I-52* and the 112 men aboard her, were not heard from again.

Japanese diplomats in Berlin grew increasingly worried about the fate of the *I-52* when she failed to turn up in Lorient. Awaiting her on the dock was a valuable return cargo consisting of radar units, aircraft bombsights, vacuum tubes, optical glass, ball bearings, mercury, machine-gun ammunition, specialist alloy steel for the manufacture of aircraft engines; various chemicals; platinum, and two of the recently developed T-5 acoustic torpedoes.

Japanese diplomats and naval officers, led by the Japanese Assistant Naval Attaché to Germany, Yoshikazu Fujimura, were already in Lorient to greet the overdue *I-52* – this was following a coded message, subsequently believed to have been sent by the British as part of a misinformation campaign, but purportedly from the *I-52* stating that she was thirty-six hours from port. To this end a German Navy warship left Lorient and stood by at sea for four days to meet the Japanese submarine. At this stage of the war, Lorient was surrounded by Allied forces and under siege. The Japanese naval officers and officials decided to escape from Lorient, and using a bus they managed to get through the Allied lines and drive to Paris, arriving intact on 8 August. Before Lorient was evacuated, German troops destroyed most of the cargo sitting on the docks awaiting the lost *I-52*. The one item that was not destroyed, however, was 500kg of uranium oxide. The Japanese took this back into their possession, and the material only surfaced again when *U-234* was captured following Germany's surrender while en route to Japan.

Lorient was extremely important to the *Kriegsmarine*, so it was heavily defended. Considerable flak batteries protected the U-boat base and facilities from Allied bombing raids, and the town was named *Festung* (Fortress) Lorient. Following the D-Day landings in Normandy on 6 June 1944, elements of the US 4th Armored Division entered the suburbs of Lorient on 7 August, only to be halted by determined German resistance. Remaining U-boats were evacuated to Norway or scuttled. *General* Wilhelm Fährmbacher, commanding 15,000 army and navy troops managed to defend the town until 8 May 1945 and the general German capitulation that ended the war in Europe.

Notes

1. Wynn, K., *U-Boat Operations of the Second World War – Volume 2, U511–UIT25*, Chatham Publishing, Chatham, 1998, pp. 3–4.
2. Vause, J., *Wolf: U-Boat Commanders in World War II*, Naval Institute Press, Annapolis, 1997, pp. 162–80.
3. For full details of U-boat Service Knights Cross holders see: Sharpe, P., *U-Boat Fact File: Detailed Service Histories of the Submarines Operated by the Kriegsmarine 1935–1945*, Midland Publishing Limited, Earl Shilton, 1998, Appendix 2.

4. Sharpe, P., *U-Boat Fact File*, Midland Publishing Limited, Earl Shilton, 1998, p. 107.
5. The National Archives (TNA): Public Record Office (PRO) HW18/192 *F.O.E.A. to C. in C. Eastern Fleet, 22.2.44.*
6. The National Archives (TNA): Public Record Office (PRO) HW18/192 *Return transport of ores (wolfram, molybdenum, tin, zinc) by U/Bs from the Far East.*
7. *Ibid.*, TNA: PRO HW18/192 *Return transport of ores (wolfram, molybdenum, tin, zinc) by U/Bs from the Far East.*
8. *Ibid.*, TNA: PRO HW18/192 *Return transport of ores (wolfram, molybdenum, tin, zinc) by U/Bs from the Far East.*
9. *Ibid.*, TNA: PRO HW18/192 *Return transport of ores (wolfram, molybdenum, tin, zinc) by U/Bs from the Far East.*
10. *Ibid.*, TNA: PRO HW18/192 *Return transport of ores (wolfram, molybdenum, tin, zinc) by U/Bs from the Far East.*
11. The National Archives (TNA): Public Record Office (PRO) HW18/192 *Résumé of Monsun Boats to 30/10/43.*
12. The National Archives (TNA): Public Record Office (PRO) HW18/192 *Pich to BdU, 13 March 1944.*
13. The National Archives (TNA): Public Record Office (PRO) HW18/376 *Junker to BdU, 12 March 1944.*
14. *Ibid.*, TNA: PRO HW18/376 *Junker to BdU, 12 March 1944.*
15. The National Archives (TNA): Public Record Office (PRO) HW18/376 *Penang to BdU, 25 March 1944.*
16. The National Archives (TNA): Public Record Office (PRO) HW18/376 *BdU to Penang, 10 July 1944.*
17. The National Archives (TNA): Public Record Office (PRO) HW18/376 *Pich to BdU, 18 August 1944.*
18. For more details of this action see: Franks, N., *Search, Find, Kill: The RAF's U-Boat Successes in World War Two*, Grub Street, London, 1995, p. 259.
19. The National Archives (TNA): Public Record Office (PRO) HW18/387 *Offizier Cypher, BdU to Offermann, 6 February 1944.*
20. *Ibid.*, TNA: PRO HW18/387 *Offizier Cypher, BdU to Offermann, 6 February 1944.*
21. Wynn K., *U-Boat Operations of the Second World War, Volume 1: Career Histories, U1–U510*, Chatham Publishing, Chatham, 1997, p. 319.

Chapter 7

Vital
Supplies

Italian Boat, German Commander, Japanese Cargo

The Italian *Luizi*-class submarine *Reginaldo Guiliani* had arrived in Japanese-occupied Singapore in July 1943, having begun its long voyage from German-occupied Bordeaux in May. The *Guiliani* was still in Singapore when the Italian armistice occurred on 8 September 1943, but she was seized by the Imperial Japanese Navy just two days later. The Japanese handed the vessel, along with two other Italian submarines (the *Commandante Cappellini*, which was in Sabang, Dutch East Indies, and the *Luiggi Torelli* in Singapore), over to the German Navy, who commissioned the boat into the *Kriegsmarine* as *UIT-23*.

The Germans placed the Italian submarines under German commanders and attempted the lengthy process of forming German U-boat crews for the boats from the limited pool of manpower available at the U-boat base at Penang. A new commander, *Fregattenkapitän* Heinrich Schäfer, was appointed to *UIT-23* on 6 December 1943. Schäfer was formerly the skipper of *U-183*, a Type IXC40, which had recently arrived in Penang from Europe. Unfortunately Schäfer was not a well man and he became increasingly unwell throughout Christmas 1943, eventually dying of natural causes on 8 January 1944 in Singapore. He was cremated and arrangements were made to return his ashes to Germany aboard *U-804* (*Oberleutnant der Reserve* Herbert Meyer), but the boat was lost on the return journey to Europe. A new commander was appointed, *Kapitänleutnant* Johannes-Werner Striegler (the former First Watch Officer aboard the 'gift boat' *U-511* and commander of *UIT-25*), on Valentines Day, 1944. In the meantime, *UIT-23* was moved to Singapore to take on board a *Yanagi* cargo consisting of rubber, tin, wolfram, quinine and the narcotic opium.

She then returned fully laden to Penang where Striegler assumed command of her.

UIT-23 departed for France that very same day, only to encounter incredibly bad luck. Just twenty-four hours out from Penang she was attacked by the Royal Navy submarine HMS *Tally-Ho*, under the command of Lieutenant L.W.A. Bennington, RN, and sunk. Striegler, along with thirteen of his crew, were rescued from the water by the Japanese and returned to the U-boat base at Penang. The remaining thirty-one crewmen perished in the attack. It must stand as one of the shortest commands in U-boat history, but even though Striegler returned to Penang minus his boat, its valuable cargo and forty-four of his crew, he was again given command of the former Italian submarine, *UIT-25*.

Completed for the Royal Italian Navy on 23 September 1939, the former *Commandante Cappellini* and *Aquila III* was commissioned into the German Navy as *UIT-24* on 6 December 1943, with *Oberleutnant zür See* Heinrich Pahls as commanding officer, another former Watch Officer from the 'gift boat' *U-511*. The boat was assigned initially to 12 *U-Flottille* at Bordeaux, and after being seized by the Japanese was turned over to 33 *U-Flottille* at Penang from September 1944 until 10 May 1945, the crew being a mixture of German and fascist Italian submariners. The Germans added new armaments to the former Italian submarine, a 105mm deck gun and a 20mm flak gun.

On 2 February 1944 *UIT-24* departed from Singapore for Europe, travelling via Penang, with a cargo consisting of the usual *Yanagi* trade goods including 115 tons of rubber, 55 tons of tin and 10 tons of other strategic materials including steel, quinine and opium. On the journey to Bordeaux, *UIT-24* required refuelling, and for this purpose the German Navy had placed the duel oiler and supply ship *Brake* on station in the Indian Ocean. A British destroyer attacked the *Brake* on 12 March, a thousand miles south-east of Mauritius, which forced her to scuttle herself. Fortunately *UIT-24* was able to rendezvous with the provisional tanker *U-532*, which had herself recently fuelled from the *Brake*. The fuel situation forced *UIT-24* to return to the Far East, arriving in Penang on 5 April 1944. A day later she arrived back in Singapore. In common with *UIT-25*, the former Italian submarine was thereafter employed running supply missions between South-East Asia and Japan.

The surrender of Germany found *UIT-24* docked in the Mitsubishi naval yard in Kobe, undergoing repairs. Taken over by the Imperial Japanese Navy as *I-503* on 10 May 1945, she remained in dock for the remainder of the war with no Japanese crew being assigned to her. On 16 April 1946 the US Navy scuttled the *I-503* in the Kii Suido.

The former Royal Italian Navy *Luizi*-class submarine *Alpino Bagnolini* departed for Penang from Bordeaux on 19 January 1944 under the command of *Oberleutnant der Reserve* Karl Wünderlich, who had previously been commissioned from the ranks and served as a Watch Officer aboard *U-29* and *U-628* (where he had been awarded the Iron Cross 1st Class). The Italian boat had been commissioned into the German Navy as *UIT-22* on 11 November 1943 and assigned to 12 *U-Flottille* at Bordeaux. The former Italian submarine *Guiseppe Finzi*, commissioned as *UIT-21* on 14 October 1943, and under the command of Steinfeldt, had been declared unfit for sea because the diesel engines were discovered to be full of faults and defects. The boat was subsequently decommissioned in Bordeaux and scuttled in August 1944. Allied code breakers, who planned to position naval forces to sink the supply submarine en route, instantly tracked *UIT-22*'s departure from Bordeaux. On 12 February a B-24 Liberator bomber of US Navy Squadron VB-107 (based on the British island of Ascension) intercepted and depth charged *UIT-22* in the mid-Atlantic, killing one crewman, wrecking the periscope and rupturing a fuel tank. The German captain reported to U-boat Control that even with the damage inflicted to the fuel supply, resulting in 32 tons of diesel fuel leaking into the sea, the submarine could still sail to Penang without requiring any refuelling along the way.

Because of the problems U-boats were experiencing by this stage of the war in the Bay of Biscay from intense Allied anti-submarine patrols both on the sea and in the air, the Germans attempted to utilize the latest radar detectors to warn them of impending danger. *UIT-22* had on board several spare *Naxos* radar detectors and brand-new Enigma keys. An incoming U-boat for France, *U-178* under *Kapitänleutnant* Wilhelm Spähr (the former commander of the boat, Wilhelm Dommes, remained in the Far East to command U-boat operations), was not equipped with this new technology. U-boat Control decided to transfer *Naxos* technology and Enigma parts over

138

to *U-178* and ordered Wünderlich to rendezvous with Spähr's boat south of the Cape of Good Hope on 11 March. Reading the Enigma decrypts, the Royal Navy thought this rendezvous was an excellent opportunity to destroy both boats together in a combined operation involving both sea and air forces.

At RAF Langebaan in South Africa, No. 262 Squadron provided three Catalina 1B anti-submarine aircraft with orders to carefully search the area of sea identified through Ultra as the likely meeting place for the U-boats. They were further assisted in pinpointing the area by an SAAF aircraft that had reported spotting a U-boat on 8 May. The Catalinas began criss-crossing the ocean, the crews scanning the surface with binoculars, until the aircraft piloted by Flight Lieutenant F.T. Roddick (who was on attachment from the Royal Canadian Air Force – RCAF) came upon the surfaced *UIT-22*. Wünderlich had no time to hand over the *Naxos* technology and the Enigma keys to *U-178*. Roddick descended immediately and set up to begin his attack run, hammering towards the U-boat at a wave-skimming 50 feet. Wünderlich's anti-aircraft gunners opened fire, scoring hits on the Catalina. Roddick began to weave his aircraft about to present a more difficult target while simultaneously, his own gunners returned fire in an attempt to suppress the German flak crews. The U-boat began to turn just as Roddick released a hail of depth charges, which neatly straddled the boat before detonating in gigantic plumes of white water. As the Catalina circled back to observe the results of the attack run, it was clear that *UIT-22* had been struck close in, for the boat had taken on a visible list and not a soul was present on the conning tower. Roddick had one depth charge remaining that had 'hung up' during the first attack. As *UIT-22* attempted to submerge, the Canadian delivered the final bomb close by the U-boat. Following the explosion *UIT-22* was seen to submerge, leaving the water surface thick with oil. Wünderlich's boat must have been severely damaged. As Roddick departed the scene and made for base, a second Catalina arrived to survey the area. The crew were astonished to observe the U-boat surfacing again below them. The pilot attacked immediately, all six of his depth charges forming a neat pattern of destruction around the stricken submarine. *UIT-22* sank into an ever-spreading oil slick, hastened by machine-gun fire from the circling aircraft.

Roddick was later awarded the Distinguished Flying Cross for his successful and ultimately devastating attack that sealed the fate of

Wünderlich and his boat. All forty-three crewmen on board *UIT-22* were killed. *U-178* survived the attack, largely because bad weather hampered further anti-submarine operations, to report the loss of the valuable supply submarine, and limped into Bordeaux on 25 May, never to sail again.

Torpedo Resupply Far East: *U-1062* and *U-1059*

Two factors limited a U-boat's ability to keep fighting at sea. First, and most obviously, fuel was the primary limiting factor on U-boat operations. The second was torpedoes, and what to do if a U-boat expended her supply, but still retained sufficient fuel to continue hunting. The Germans attempted to solve the problem of torpedo resupply by producing a variant of the numerous and highly successful Type VII U-boat, which because of its great numbers and employment as the backbone of the German U-boat offensive in the Atlantic, had been nicknamed the '*Atlantik*' boat.

When a U-boat had expended all of her torpedoes, the commander was left with two options. First, he could return the boat to base and end his war patrol, or second, attempt to obtain spare torpedoes from other U-boats returning home because their fuel situation had terminated their patrol. The new Type VIIF was designed as a specialized torpedo carrier, and the four completed examples (*U-1059*, *U-1060*, *U-1061* and *U-1062*) would provide the U-boat fleet with torpedo resupply at sea, thus enabling patrols to continue until fuel resupply became necessary.

Taking the basic Type VIIC design of the *Atlantik* boat, the Germans modified the submarine by the addition of a large 'plug' located behind the control room. This extra space measured 34.5 feet in length, of which 25.6 feet was used to store twenty-four torpedoes, stacked in four layers of six torpedoes. An additional torpedo hatch was also added to the afterdeck, enabling the resupply torpedoes to be embarked and disembarked with greater ease. The 'plug' also provided the crew with more space for bunks, and refrigerators (vital equipment on long voyages).

Although the design concept was sound, times had changed for the U-boat fleet by the time the first four Type VIIFs were completed in mid-1943. Allied anti-submarine warfare capabilities had increased massively, and it would have proved extremely unwise for two U-boats to sit on the surface of the sea conducting long and laborious torpedo transfers. Therefore, the four Type VIIFs, including *U-1062*, were re-roled as transports.

The German U-boat base at Penang, apart from only possessing enough dockyard facilities to accommodate five U-boats at any one time, was also critically short of torpedoes. The Germans had built up a small supply taken from German armed merchant cruisers and surviving surface blockade-running vessels, but these weapons had deteriorated through being stored for a long time in tropical heat and humidity. For Penang to continue to be a 'going concern' regarding U-boat warfare, fresh torpedoes would have to be delivered to the boats stationed in the Far East, lest their fighting potential be completely eroded, especially after all the problems of actually getting the boats out to Penang in the first place.

On 22 December 1943, Beaufighter TFX aircraft of RAF No. 144 Squadron and No. 404 Squadron, Royal Canadian Air Force, were patrolling the Norwegian coast. They discovered *U-1062*, commanded by *Oberleutnant zür See* Karl Albrecht, sailing from Kiel to Bergen, escorted by a minesweeper. The Beaufighters that were armed with torpedoes and cannon, attacked immediately, blasting the U-boat with cannon shells, but missing with torpedoes. Both the minesweeper and the U-boat replied with accurate anti-aircraft fire, hitting two Canadian Beaufighters that were acting as flak suppressors for the torpedo-armed aircraft. The first aircraft caught fire and crashed into the sea, the second inverted and met the same end. There were no survivors from either aircraft. *U-1062* fared considerably better, suffering only minor damage, although one crewman was killed and two were wounded. She arrived in Bergen without further incident on 23 December to prepare for the voyage to the Far East.[1]

Another torpedo resupply Type VIIF, *U-1059*, departed from Bergen in Norway on 12 February 1944 bound for Penang. Under the command of *Oberleutnant zür See* Günther Leupold, the boat, assigned to 5 *U-Flottille* at Kiel, had been loaded with forty torpedoes for the U-cruisers of the two *Monsun* groups conducting offensive patrols in the Indian Ocean from their base at Penang.

Because of the vast sailing distance to Penang from Norway, U-boat Control had decreed that *U-1059* would rendezvous with the Type XIV U-tanker *U-488*, west of the Cape Verde Islands, allowing *U-1059* to replace the fuel consumed on the journey from Bergen to the coast of West Africa, before proceeding to the Far East. The British had warned the Americans not to attack U-boats while they were refuelling at sea, because such attacks would have alerted the Germans to the fact that the British had broken the modified Enigma code settings. Attacking a U-boat rendezvous was just too obvious to U-boat Control. However, the Americans disregarded the British request and dispatched the USS *Block Island*, a small aircraft carrier, and her escort group from Casablanca, Morocco, on 12 March, with orders to intercept and sink both U-boats. Aircraft from the *Block Island* had already successfully destroyed two Type VIICs, *U-603* (*Oberleutnant zür See* Rudolf Baltz) and *U-709* (*Oberleutnant der Reserve* Rudolf Ites) on 1 March.

On their way to intercept *U-488* and *U-1059*, the American carrier group attacked and damaged the Type IXC40 *U-801* (*Kapitänleutnant* Hans-Joachim Brans), which was heading for its patrol area off the coast of West Africa. *U-801* was caught on the surface, the captain having ordered the boat to be aired, and the crew to undertake some gunnery practice (which would shortly prove extremely fortuitous for some).

U-1059 was discovered on the surface on 19 March by an Avenger–Wildcat team from USS *Block Island*. Incredibly, the American pilots counted eighteen of the U-boat's crew swimming in the sea around the vessel, evidently totally unprepared for the ferocious attack that was immediately launched. The Wildcat conducted a strafing run along the length of the U-boat, while the Avenger dropped two depth charges which caused the immediate destruction of *U-1059*. However, it was a not a totally one-sided affair. The German flak battery had managed to damage the Avenger sufficiently during the attacks to force the pilot to ditch the aircraft in the sea. The Avenger pilot and radio operator were both killed, but the rear gunner, Ensign Fitzgerald, survived, to join eight surviving U-boatmen, including Leupold, in the water. Fitzgerald floated in his rubber survival dinghy amongst his enemies. After pulling one badly wounded German on board his small boat to give the man some emergency medical attention (but pushing him back into the water afterwards), Fitzgerald awaited his rescue with a .38 pistol in one hand and a knife in the other – should any of the U-boatmen attempt to come aboard his lifeboat seeking revenge. The USS *Corry*, a destroyer from the American *Block Island* group, later rescued all of these combatants.

The *Peleus* Massacre: *U-852*

By the end of April 1944 Ultra intercepts had forewarned the British of the approach of a lone U-boat to the coast of Somaliland (now Somalia), which precipitated day and night searches being conducted in the hope of an interception.

The boat the British were looking for was the Type IXD2 *U-852*, which had departed Kiel on 8 January 1944 under the command of *Kapitänleutnant* Heinz Eck, bound for the Far East. Eck was twenty-seven years old and had been in the navy since 1934, latterly in command of a minesweeper until May 1942. Thereafter he had transferred to U-boats, and following training had completed a war patrol aboard *U-124*, under the command of Knights Cross with Oakleaves recipient *Korvettenkapitän* Johann Möhr.

Utilizing Wellington XIII bombers armed with depth charges, at dawn on 1 May 1944 a ferocious battle commenced when a lone aircraft spotted *U-852* running on the surface. As the front gunner pumped rounds into the submarine, the depth charges were released in a low pass, and Eck simultaneously crash-dived his boat. Damage reports and the evidence of his own eyes soon demonstrated the perilous situation the U-boat was in. The concussive underwater explosion of the depth charges had fractured the main inlet valve, and a great jet of icy sea water was rapidly entering the boat. Immediately aborting his dive, Eck ordered the boat to the surface, but as *U-852* completed the manoeuvre the water rapidly accumulating inside the boat was tipped into the engine-room by the angle of the bow. A raging electrical fire broke out as the cold sea water flowed over live electrical components, a damage control party battling to extinguish the conflagration before it spread to the rest of the boat. As men fought the flames inside the narrow confines of the boat, the flak gunners swiftly ascended the conning tower ladder to man the guns. Unable to dive, *U-852*'s only chance of delaying inevitable destruction was to fend off the British aircraft with her anti-aircraft guns and 105mm deck gun.

The Wellington of 621 Squadron, having expended its load of depth charges, now conducted a strafing run over the U-boat, meeting concentrated flak. It was forced to circle out of range of the German guns while the call went out summoning the other search aircraft to join the attack.

The battle to sink *U-852* would last for three days and involve five Wellingtons of 621 Squadron and another of 8 Squadron. By 3 May, having escaped serious damage during the several attacks of the day before, *U-852* was attacked again. The 8 Squadron's Wellington lined up for a depth charge run, but Eck's flak barrage was so intense that the attack was foiled, a 20mm shell hitting the aircraft. For a further three hours, while fuel held out, the Wellington circled the U-boat, staying out of range of the flak guns. A 621 Squadron bomber successfully deposited a string of depth charges across the target, but to little apparent effect. Although the RAF crews attempted to keep the submarine in visual contact as further reinforcements were radioed into position, the Wellingtons were also relying on radar to track the U-boat. A combination of failing light and the U-boat's increasing proximity to the coast of Africa (which caused the radar signal to echo), meant that inevitably contact was lost with *U-852* as night fell.

Eck now decided to head into shore where he could abandon and destroy the wrecked U-boat, instead of being depth charged into oblivion by the steady stream of Wellington bombers hungrily scouring the area for him. At 2.00 am on 4 May British search efforts paid off when an aircraft located *U-852* motionless, sitting in a large oil slick less than 40 yards from the coast of East Africa. The crew was observed to already be ashore. Suddenly there was an almighty explosion as the scuttling charges fired and demolished the stern of the U-boat, the entire submarine slinking beneath the surface forever. Eck had lost six of his crew, killed during the aerial attacks, but himself and the fifty-eight other crew were soon picked up by Royal Navy shore parties and the Somaliland Camel Corps and taken to Aden as prisoners of war. The future for Eck remained in doubt, however, following an investigation into the fate of one of the two ships he had managed to sink during his cruise in the Indian Ocean. During imprisonment in Aden, ordinary members of the crew began to talk to their interrogators about a massacre, which they had witnessed at sea.

On 13 March 1944 *U-852* had intercepted the Greek merchant ship *Peleus* (4,695 tons). The crew were a mixture of Greeks, British, Chinese and Egyptians, along with a Soviet, a Pole, a Chilean neutral and a native of Aden, totalling thirty-five men transporting a cargo of ballast from Freetown to Buenos Aires. Eck tracked the *Peleus* until darkness had fallen, and then, after closing up the range, he fired two torpedoes while surfaced. The *Peleus* exploded, being totally ripped apart by the detonations, which instantly killed perhaps half of the international crew. The ship then abruptly sank. The remainder of the crew clung desperately to wreckage or life-rafts as *U-852* slowly motored into the field of debris.

Eck was concerned to properly record his kill and he required the name and tonnage of the ship in order to do so. Two survivors were hauled aboard the U-boat and the necessary information recorded, before they were returned to the water. Eck then told the survivors to turn off all lights fitted to survival equipment and life-rafts, in order to give *U-852* plenty of time to exit the vicinity before Allied ships arrived. He then went a step further and determined to sink the remaining large pieces of wreckage, including the life-rafts, so that no evidence of the sinking could be discovered. It appears that Eck was obsessively concerned that any lights visible from the sinking, and any seamen who were rescued by the Allies, would betray the presence of his U-boat in the South Atlantic, a fact that he wished to conceal as thoroughly as possible. U-boats would not take survivors on board for the simple reason that space and provisions would not permit such a humanitarian gesture, and Dönitz had issued several orders forbidding displays of humanity lest commanders unnecessarily risk their boats. Survivors were therefore left to fend for themselves, many never to be picked up. On this occasion Eck ordered machine-guns, machine pistols and hand grenades to be brought topside, and for the next five hours Eck mercilessly 'cleaned up' the scene of the sinking, with most of the survivors of the *Peleus* murdered in the water and the lights shot out. Even the 37mm and 20mm anti-aircraft guns fitted to the U-boat were utilized in this grisly business. To add to the disgrace, even the U-boat's medical officer took part in the killing. Eventually Eck lost interest in attempting to sink the life-rafts, which remained remarkably resistant to machine-gun bullets, and *U-852* slinked away into the night.

It was only because three men survived the massacre, being a further forty-nine days adrift before being rescued by a Portuguese neutral, that this heinous crime was discovered. This was the only occasion during the Second World War when a U-boat commander and crew behaved in this manner, and Eck's actions were universally condemned by the U-boat service and personally condemned by Dönitz himself. At his trial in Hamburg in the autumn of 1945, Eck argued in his defence that he had ordered his crew to disperse floating wreckage with machine-gun fire. He claimed that the civilian deaths were accidental or the result of the over zealous following of his orders by the crew. On 17 October 1945 Eck was found guilty of war crimes, along with *U-852*'s Executive Officer (First Watch Officer) *Oberleutnant zür See* August Hoffmann. The Chief Engineer, *Kapitänleutnant* Hans Lenz, the Medical Officer, *Oberleutnant* Dr Walter Weisspfennig and a Leading Seaman, Wolfgang Schwender were also found guilty. Lenz was sentenced to life imprisonment and Schwender to fifteen years (Schwender was released from prison on parole in 1951 and Lenz in 1952). Eck, Hoffmann and Weisspfennig were sentenced to death and executed by firing squad on 30 November 1945.

Eck's only other successful sinking during his patrol was the British ship *Dahomian* for 5,277 tons. On this occasion no survivors were machine-gunned in the water, Eck conducting a submerged attack, and he left the area rapidly. He was given permission to enter the Indian Ocean by U-boat Control, who were unaware of the *Peleus* incident, on 4 April 1944. Judging by Eck's ability to avoid the destruction of *U-852* between 1 and 3 May, during which time he was attacked by six Wellingtons, demonstrates that he must have been a commander of some skill. Unfortunately, however, his callous methods very nearly sullied the reputation of the U-boat Arm. The *Kriegsmarine* was well known as the least 'Nazified' of the German armed forces fighting the Second World War, but Eck's actions were a dark stain upon the honour of the service. Prosecutors at the Nuremberg War Crimes Trials also took up the *Peleus* incident after the Second World War, where they attempted to charge Dönitz with tacitly encouraging the murder of surviving merchant crews by U-boats so that the Allies could not rescue them and employ them to crew other ships. This accusation was proved to be false and the reputation of the U-boat service remains intact.

Continued U-Boat Operations in Southern Waters

The brand new Type IXC40 *U-843* departed from Lorient on 19 February 1944 with orders to patrol the waters off Cape Town. It was commanded by *Kapitänleutnant* Oskar Herwartz, the twenty-nine-year-old former First Watch Officer aboard *U-67* during the latter part of 1942. In common with other boats heading south,

U-843 was detailed to refuel from the Type XIV U-tanker *U-488* that sailed south on 23 February. For security reasons the two U-boats travelled separately to the rendezvous point. Herwartz's brother Wolfgang (a *Kapitänleutnant*) was also a U-boat commander. His boat, *U-1302* (Type VIIC41), sank five ships before being depth charged to destruction by the Royal Canadian Navy frigates HMCS *La Hulloise*, *Strathadam* and *Thetford Mines* north of St David's Head in the Irish Sea with the loss of all forty-eight crew on 7 March 1945.

Oskar Herwartz only encountered neutral merchant ships during the month of March, but was required by U-boat Control rules to stop and search each ship he came upon. By 24 March *U-843* was west of the Cape Verde Islands and here Herwartz refuelled from *U-488*, topping off his tanks preparatory to beginning his patrol around the coast of South Africa. On 4 April, at a prearranged meeting with Spähr, skipper of the France-bound *U-178*, Herwartz gave him new Enigma keys. The exchange almost proved fatal for both boats, as the two surfaced submarines were pounced upon by a lone B-24 Liberator of US Navy Squadron VB-107 – but strangely the Liberator satisfied itself with strafing U-178 with machine-gun fire before disappearing. Presumably the aircraft had already dumped its depth charges on another target and was heading back to base when it came upon the pair of U-boats.

After continuing on alone into the South Atlantic *U-843* scored her first and only success of the patrol, sinking the 8,261-ton British ship *Nebraska* on 8 April.[2] Aircraft continued to plague Herwartz's mission, however, for on 10 April another Liberator (from the same US Navy squadron that attacked *U-178* flying from the British island of Ascension) successfully depth charged the boat, putting *U-843*'s stern torpedo tubes out of action. Herwartz reported both his success in sinking the *Nebraska* and the damage he had sustained, noting on 14 April 'am moving off for repairs'.[3] U-boat Control had originally directed Herwartz to interdict shipping off Cape Town, but they now decided, in the light of the damage to the boat, to redirect him all the way to Batavia. Herwartz reported to Control on 20 April, 'Stern tubes remain defective, 2 "T5" (acoustic torpedoes) unusable.'[4] Herwartz began to proceed towards Batavia and remained silent, causing U-boat Control to speculate on where the boat had gotten to. On 16 May, Control radioed *U-843*: 'Herwartz is reminded of report ordered. Assume boat has been delayed by bad weather.'[5] Two days later *U-843* reported her position and continuing problems as a result of '... permanent damage from A/C bombs [from the attack on 10 April] and defective cooling-water pumps'.[6] Herwartz and Schneewind, who were departing the Far East for the return journey to Europe, were ordered to rendezvous '... for handing over NAXOS, Barkum [*sic*] and Wanze'.[7] It was hoped this exchange would enable Schneewind to negotiate the Bay of Biscay on his return run. Once this had been completed Herwartz was ordered by Control '... do not report execution'[8] of the transfer because of a warning received of an enemy 'battle formation' in the vicinity. This indicated that U-boat Control might be aware that radio traffic *from* U-boats to Control could draw in Allied hunter-killer groups (though the Germans did not yet realize that Enigma had been broken). Herwartz was then ordered to 'proceed to ... hand over a screw [submarine propeller] to Junker (U-???)'.[9] *U-843* refuelled from a Japanese submarine en route, and the exhausted crew arrived safely at the German U-boat base in Batavia on 13 June,[10] after an incredible 116 days at sea. Following this epic voyage, Herwartz made requests to U-boat Control for a mass of decorations to be awarded to his crew. Control was thoroughly in agreement and radioed Herwartz in Batavia: '4 Iron Crosses (1st Class) and 36 Iron Crosses (2nd Class) awarded as requested.'[11] On Herwartz's further recommendation, Chief Boatswain's Mate (2nd Class) Haedke was eventually awarded the German Cross in Gold,[12] despite the fact that he appeared to have been in some trouble since his arrival in Batavia. At the time, however, Herwartz was more concerned with the handing over of the damaged T5 acoustic torpedoes to the Japanese, and whether their condition rendered them useful to the Japanese as model torpedoes.[13]

Hailing from the university city of Heidelberg, *Kapitänleutnant* Hans-Joachim Brans was born on 21 August 1915. Before being assigned to command the Type IXC40 *U-801* in March 1943, Brans served aboard the smaller Type VIIC *U-84* as Second Watch Officer. He was promoted to First Watch Officer for two months in 1943 on another Type IXC40, *U-169*, gaining valuable experience as a commander under training on the type before becoming skipper of *U-801*. A lengthy working-up period followed, with *U-801* assigned to 4th Training Flotilla between March and October 1943. The boat was then declared operational and transferred to 2nd U-boat Flotilla

'*Saltzwedel*' on 1 November. The famous combat flotilla had been operational since September 1939, and had transferred its base from Wilhelmshaven in Germany to the occupied port of Lorient during May–June 1941. Brans and *U-801* came under the command of *Fregattenkapitän* Ernst Kals, a U-boat ace and holder of the Knights Cross who had sunk twenty ships while commanding *U-130* over five war patrols between June 1941 and January 1943. Kals would command 2nd Flotilla until the end of the war, and died in 1979. The additional unit name '*Saltzwedel*' was derived from First World War U-boat ace *Oberleutnant zür See* Reinhold Saltzwedel, who sank an incredible 111 ships over twenty-two patrols and was killed in December 1917 when his boat, *UB-81*, struck a British mine in the English Channel.

Brans left Lorient on 26 February 1944. On 16 March, Avengers of the US Navy Squadron VB-6, flying off the escort carrier USS *Block Island*, intercepted *U-801* in mid-Atlantic, killing one crewman and wounding nine others. Brans's war came to an abrupt end the following day, when the US Navy destroyer USS *Corry* and the frigate USS *Bronstein* pounded the U-boat with depth charges resulting in its loss. Brans was among the ten crewmen killed in the attack, though forty-seven others survived the U-boat's destruction and were rescued by the Americans.

Another brand-new Type IXD2 U-cruiser, *U-851*, was sent out during February 1944. Commanded by thirty-five-year-old Austrian *Korvettenkapitän* Hannes Weingärtner, *U-851*'s cargo was intended to fulfil *Yanagi* trade agreements (for example, *U-851* carried 1,878 bottles of mercury destined for Japanese industry) and supply needs of the Far Eastern U-boat bases (shown on the cargo manifest to include 500 U-boat batteries).

Weingärtner was given a particularly onerous and dangerous task when he sailed from Kiel on 26 February. He was ordered to report weather conditions in the North Atlantic to U-boat Control. Weather reporting by U-boats in various sectors of the Atlantic and Arctic was extremely useful to the Germans, enabling accurate weather forecasts and reports to be compiled for use by the *Luftwaffe*. They were useful to the army in determining the likelihood of an Allied invasion of Europe during 1944. However, unknown to U-boat Control, actually sending radio traffic of any kind was suicidal for a U-boat, enabling the Allies, using Ultra, to pinpoint with some accuracy the position of a particular U-boat. Forces could then be herded into the area in the hope of intercepting and destroying the U-boat. It was unfortunate that the Germans decided to use a U-boat loaded with a massively expensive *Yanagi* cargo to attempt this difficult and hazardous task.

Weingärtner was an experienced peacetime U-boat skipper, having commanded *U-4* in 1935–36, *U-10* in 1936–37, and *U-16* between 1937 and 1939, before taking up a staff appointment. He had never, however, sunk a ship by torpedo or conducted a war patrol. Whatever Weingärtner's experience of peacetime service, *U-851* sank no ships on her first patrol and was last heard from on 27 March 1944, when she reported her position as 380 miles off St Johns, Newfoundland. The boat simply vanished. We can assume Weingärtner and his sixty-nine officers and men went to the bottom of the icy North Atlantic. Perhaps there was an accident or fire arising from an equipment or drill failure, but certainly no Allied forces reported destroying a U-boat in her last reported position or thereabouts during that period. The demise of *U-851* remains an unsolved mystery of the Second World War.

Last to depart Europe for the Far East during February 1944 was *U-537*, another Type IXC40, which left Lorient under the command of *Kapitänleutnant* Peter Schrewe. Schrewe's previous claim to fame was a patrol to the coast of Canada during 1943, *U-537* having sortied from Bergen in Norway. The boat had been ordered to form a landing party of crew and passengers, and drop them ashore in Canada. There they were to set up an unmanned automatic weather station that would transmit data directly back to Europe for dissemination. The German Meteorological Service designed a weather station that was easy to dismantle, and small enough that its constituent parts could pass through the small circular hatches of a U-boat. Two such stations were put aboard U-boats for delivery and establishment in Canada, but only that carried aboard *U-537* made it to North America (the example carried aboard *U-867* was lost with the sinking of the boat on 19 September 1944). When *U-537* arrived off the coast of Labrador, the Germans timed the installation of the station just before the sea froze over for winter, to prevent the Canadians from reaching the spot for several months should they manage to discover its position with direction finding equipment. This proved to be an unnecessary precaution, as the Canadians only took bearings on transmitters at sea. Accompanied by two meteorologists, *U-537* anchored in Martin Bay (Attinaukjuke Bay) on 22 October 1943. The weather station components were all marked with 'Canadian Weather Service', and the U-boatmen also dispersed a specially prepared bag of Canadian litter around the spot to add authenticity should anyone stumble upon the equipment. Twenty-eight hours later the U-boat weighed anchor and headed back out to sea. Incredibly, the automatic weather station landed by the crew of *U-537*, code-named *Kurt*, remained undiscovered in Canada until 1981, when a small Canadian exploration investigated the site at close quarters. The weather station components were scattered about, indicating that the local Inuit inhabitants or others had vandalized it. Some parts were collected up and taken to museums for display.[14]

In February 1944 Schrewe was unlucky and only made it six days into his cruise to the Far East. On 5 March an unidentified Allied aircraft attacked *U-537*, and the resulting depth charge damage meant that there was absolutely no possibility of attempting the remainder of the voyage to the Far East. Reluctantly, Schrewe turned about and headed back to Lorient for repairs. Once safely back at base, a further twenty days passed before the boat was again seaworthy. On 25 March Schrewe once again took *U-537* to sea. This time his journey south was without major incident. After successfully topping off his fuel oil from *U-488* on 17 April, Schrewe was directed away from the U-boat base at Penang, which was in the process of being downgraded to what would eventually become an emergency repair facility owing to the extensive mining of the sea approaches by the British, and the presence of Royal Navy submarines lurking at the entrance to the port. *U-537* was ordered to make for the new U-boat base at Batavia. Schrewe arrived safely on 2 August after 131 days at sea. In his reports back to U-boat Control following the successful completion of his journey, Schrewe was evidently pleased with his crew's performance. Control was especially satisfied with Schrewe, informing Dönitz that, '(Commander) of U537 did not apply for any decoration for himself. Suggest that the commanding officer who has five war cruises to his credit be awarded the Iron Cross (1st Class).'[15]

During March a further four U-boats were readied for their lengthy missions to the Far East. The first to depart was *U-181*, under the steady hand of thirty-eight-year-old *Fregattenkapitän* Kurt Freiwald, taking over from U-boat ace Lüth. On 16 March 1944 the heavily laden boat pulled out of La Pallice harbour to head south. Freiwald attacked and sank the 5,312-ton British ship *Janeta* on 1 May, while in the mid-Atlantic. Cruising into the Indian Ocean, Freiwald was to strike successfully three more times, building up for himself an impressive score of tonnage dispatched to the bottom. On 19 June the 7,118-ton Dutch freighter *Garoet* was sunk, followed on 15 July by the 7,174-ton British ship *Tanda* and finally the 5,265-ton British ship *King Frederick*, before putting into Penang on 8 August after a patrol of 146 days duration. Two days later another boat entered the German base at Penang. This was *U-196*, under the veteran *Korvettenkapitän* Eitel-Friedrich Kentrat. Kentrat's patrol was of a slightly longer duration, having departed from La Pallice 148 days earlier, also on 16 March. He had managed to sink only one ship, however, the 5,454-ton British freighter *Shahzada* on 9 July while in the Arabian Sea. After some rest, Kentrat was ordered to leave *U-196*, handing command to *Kapitänleutnant* Johannes-Werner Striegler, the ill-fated commander of the converted Italian submarine *UIT-23*. Kentrat was ordered to proceed to Japan itself, and there he was instructed by U-boat Control to take command of the small German repair base located at Kobe.

The second gift boat from Hitler to Emperor Hirohito, *U-1224*, was the last boat to sail during March 1944. She was a brand-new Type IXC40. Constructed by Deutsche Werft in Hamburg, she had been placed under the temporary command of *Kapitänleutnant* Georg Preuss, who would go on to command *U-875* until the end of the war.

The Japanese had already provided a crew for *U-1224*, and they had travelled to Germany aboard the Japanese submarine *I-8* the previous year. After extensive training on the unfamiliar U-boat under Preuss, a Japanese officer, Lieutenant Commander Norita, assumed command. *U-1224* then left *Kriegsmarine* service with 31st U-Flotilla, being re-commissioned as *RO-501* of the Imperial Japanese Navy's 8th Submarine Flotilla. On 30 March *RO-501*, code-named 'Marco Polo II' by the Germans, following the voyage of 'Marco Polo I' or *U-511* between May and August 1943, she was to sail into troubled waters. Allied intelligence were aware of her presence, and the Americans determined to hunt down and destroy the *RO-501* long before she had a chance to reach the Far East. Ultra decryptions allowed the Americans to position an interception force consisting of the aircraft carrier USS *Bogue*, and five destroyer escorts, to search the area through which it was known that the former U-boat would sail. The American intelligence estimates proved accurate, for on 13 May 1944 the destroyer escort USS *Francis M. Robinson* caught the *RO-501* on sonar off the Cape Verde Islands, enabling her to launch an immediate and devastating depth charge and Hedgehog attack. The *RO-501* took the entire Japanese crew and several German advisers down with her and was never heard from again.

Hedgehog was an anti-submarine weapon developed by the Royal Navy and was deployed on convoy escort warships such as destroyers to supplement the depth charge. Many small bombs were launched from spike fittings, the bombs only exploding on contact with a U-boat's hull. Over twenty bombs would be launched with a second or two between each barrage, the bombs landing in a pattern over the area of water to be targeted. The Hedgehog had two advantages over the traditional depth charge. When a depth charge explodes it can take up to fifteen minutes before the underwater disturbance can settle down enough to allow a ship's sonar to become effective again. This window of sonar blindness could allow many U-boats to escape the search area. Because the Hedgehog bombs were contact weapons, only exploding when they struck a submarine, the sonar reading was not disrupted unless the U-boat had been hit and probably destroyed. The depth of the U-boat did not have to be calculated before launching a Hedgehog attack – unlike the traditional depth charge. Hedgehog and the *Fido* homing torpedoes were just two new weapons deployed with devastating effect against U-boats, supplementing the concentrated use of depth charges and aerial bombs.

Notes

1. Franks, N. & Zimmerman, E., *U-Boat versus Aircraft*, Grubb Street, London, 1998, p. 100.
2. The National Archive (TNA): Public Record Office (PRO) HW18/394 *Herwartz to BdU, 14 April 1944*.
3. *Ibid.*, TNA: PRO HW18/394 *Herwartz to BdU, 14 April 1944*.
4. The National Archive (TNA): Public Record Office (PRO) HW18/394 *Herwartz to BdU, 20 April 1944*.

5. The National Archive (TNA): Public Record Office (PRO) HW18/394 *BdU to Herwartz, 16 May 1944*.
6. The National Archive (TNA): Public Record Office (PRO) HW18/394 *Herwartz to BdU, 18 May 1944*.
7. The National Archive (TNA): Public Record Office (PRO) HW18/394 *BdU to Herwartz and Schneewind, 24 May 1944*.
8. *Ibid.*, TNA: PRO HW18/394 *BdU to Herwartz and Schneewind, 24 May 1944*.
9. *Ibid.*, TNA: PRO HW18/394 *BdU to Herwartz and Schneewind, 24 May 1944*.
10. The National Archive (TNA): Public Record Office (PRO) HW18/394 *Jakarta to BdU (Ops), 13 June 1944*.
11. The National Archive (TNA): Public Record Office (PRO) HW18/394 *BdU to Herwartz, 8 July 1944*.
12. The National Archive (TNA): Public Record Office (PRO) HW18/394 *BdU to Herwartz, 29 July 1944*.
13. The National Archive (TNA): Public Record Office (PRO) HW18/394 *BdU to Herwartz, 13 July 1944*.
14. Parts can now be viewed in the Canadian War Museum, Vimy House section, Ottowa. For more detailed descriptions of this and other landings by U-boats on enemy coasts see: Mallmann Showell, J., *U-Boats at War: Landings on Hostile Shores*, Naval Institute Press, Annapolis, 2000.
15. The National Archive (TNA): Public Record Office (PRO) HW18/379 *BdU to Dönitz, 22 August 1944*.

Chapter 8

Late War U-Cruiser Operations in the Indian Ocean

U-859 had departed from Marviken, Norway on 8 April 1944 bound for the Indian Ocean. On 26 April the U-boat managed to pick off a straggler from Convoy SC157 south-east of Cape Farewell, the 6,255-ton Panamanian *Colin*. *U-859* arrived in the Indian Ocean in late June and commenced immediate hunting within its designated patrol area. On 5 July 1944, she was sailing some way off the south-east coast of Africa. A Catalina of RAF No. 262 Squadron, based at St Lucia, sighted her 270 miles east-south-east of Durban, South Africa. After a coordinated search, the Catalina reached the limit of its patrol, and was about to return to base when *U-859* obligingly surfaced directly below the aircraft. Simultaneously, U-boatmen manned the anti-aircraft guns and the Catalina attacked. The commanding officer, *Kapitänleutnant* Johann Jebsen, ordered violent evasive manoeuvres in order to disrupt the aircraft's attack, with five depth charges falling only 10 to 15 feet from the pressure hull (depth charges were designed to be effective anywhere up to 25 feet from a submarine's hull). The final depth charge refused to release. During the attack the Catalina had been hit in both the port and starboard wings, and fuselage by anti-aircraft fire. Four times the pilot brought the aircraft in to attack the U-boat, but the sixth depth charge refused to budge, and all the Catalina's crew could do was strafe the U-boat with machine-gun fire until she dived, leaving a trail of oil on the surface caused by a punctured fuel tank. As for *U-859*, her *schnorchel* elevating equipment had been damaged, rendering the *schnorchel* inoperable. The Catalina's strafing runs had also killed one U-boatman and wounded three others.[1]

Between 22 and 23 July Allied aircraft mounted a search for *U-859*, assisted by the sloop HMS *Banff* and the frigate HMS *Tay*, but without success. Jebsen took his boat north into the Gulf of Aden to resume his patrol.

As Allied aircraft searched for Jebsen's *U-859* following her encounter with an RAF Catalina off Durban on 5 July, *U-198* was discovered by No. 23 Squadron, South African Air Force (SAAF) on 6 July. Two land-based Ventura bombers attacked *Oberleutnant zür See* Heusinger von Waldegg's boat, but the U-boat remained surfaced and her anti-aircraft gunners fought back. The first Ventura attack was a failure, the flak gunners scoring hits on both the aircraft's bomb bay and tail, making the release of depth charges impossible. The aircraft returned to base. However, a second Ventura arrived at the scene as the U-boat commenced crash-diving, and released all six depth charges. The crew of the Ventura assumed that they had sunk *U-198*, as the boat disappeared beneath the waves leaving an oil slick on the surface in which life-rafts could be seen floating. In reality, *U-198* had escaped serious damage. The life-rafts had been stowed on deck and had broken free during the attack.[2]

U-859 arrived in the Gulf of Aden by August 1944, having managed to sink two ships, notwithstanding the earlier damage inflicted on the boat. On 28 August Jebsen sank the 7,176-ton American Liberty ship *John Barry* south of Mirbat in Oman, and the 7,422-ton British merchantman *Troilus* on 1 September in the Arabian Sea. Following these convoy attacks, Jebsen set a course for Penang, and his subsequent fate was to provide more compelling evidence to the Germans of the necessity of moving U-boat operations in the Far East from Penang to Batavia or Surabaya. After a patrol of 173 days duration, the exhausted Jebsen and his crew arrived off Penang on 23 September 1944 and prepared to take *U-859* into the base. Unknown to them or the Japanese, lurking at the entrance to the harbour was the British submarine HMS *Trenchant* under Lieutenant Commander Arthur Hezlett, RN. The *Trenchant* released three torpedoes from her stern tubes at *U-859*, one of which impacted the surfaced U-boat squarely amidships, and she sank in moments. Jebsen and forty-six of his crewmen perished as the U-boat made its final disordered plunge to the deep, eight men being rescued from the water by the Japanese, and a further eleven being picked up by the *Trenchant* as prisoners of war. The captured U-boat crewmen were taken to Trincomalee in Ceylon (now Sri Lanka) for interrogation. Commander Hezlett and the *Trenchant* would go on to sink the Japanese heavy cruiser *Ashigara* on 8 June 1945.

It must have been a severe blow to German morale for a U-boat to have made such an epic journey only to be sunk practically inside a safe harbour. The event provided further evidence, if any were needed, of the inadequacy of Japanese anti-submarine patrols around the strategically important base.

The brand-new Type IXD2 *U-860* departed from Kiel on 11 April 1944, also bound for the Far East. Under the command of thirty-six-year-old *Fregattenkapitän* Paul Büchel, who had, prior to a lengthy staff appointment, commanded the Type VIIA *U-32* between 1937 and early 1940, the boat proceeded towards the South Atlantic without encountering any targets. When *U-860* was being thoroughly tested prior to active service in October 1943, several test dives had been accomplished without incident with the Nazi Armaments Minister Albert Speer aboard.

Büchel's progress through the North Atlantic was extremely rough. He encountered storms and massive seas, and in the process of battling through them lost two crewmen overboard. On reporting this fact and his position to U-boat Control on 9 June, while the boat was in the mid-Atlantic, Allied intelligence immediately determined his location and dispatched powerful forces to attempt to destroy *U-860*. A hunter-killer group under the leadership of the American aircraft carrier USS *Solomons* raced north to intercept the U-boat. Aircraft versus U-boat exchanges were in no way a one-sided affair, with the considerable anti-aircraft capability of the U-boat often deciding matters. This was the case on the morning of 15 June, when an Avenger of US Navy Squadron VC-9 discovered *U-860* on the surface, 600 miles south of the British island of St Helena, and attacked. On the fourth attack run over the U-boat, Büchel's flak gunners shot the American aircraft down, the pilot and crew never to be seen again. The aircraft had also failed to report its position before being destroyed, so the Americans had to begin the search for the U-boat over again.

Attacking in numbers was usually the sure-fire way to sink a U-boat, especially when the attacking aircraft were smaller carrier planes rather than larger long-range shore-based bombers. Later, on 15 June, another Avenger, also from Squadron VC-9, located *U-860*, and the pilot's report brought another Avenger and a pair of Wildcats to the scene. These four aircraft took turns hammering the U-boat with rockets, depth charges and machine-gun fire. But the dropping of depth charges from extremely low altitude managed to bring down another Avenger, which was engulfed in the explosion of its own depth charge hitting the submarine's casing, and which resulted in the aircraft crashing into the U-boat, killing the Americans aboard. Damaged beyond repair, Büchel was forced to abandon the U-boat, which promptly sank beneath him. Surface ships from the American hunter-killer groups arrived at the scene of the sinking, rescuing Büchel and nineteen other Germans from the water. The remaining forty-four crewmen died during the attacks and sinking, including one whose body was recovered by the Americans and buried at sea. Büchel and his remaining crew were taken to Recife in Brazil, to the large American naval base that had been established there following Brazil's entry into the war on the Allied side.

U-198 left France on 20 April 1944 with a new commander. Knights Cross with Oakleaves holder *Kapitän zür See* Werner Hartmann had left the boat in January to assume a staff post, command being handed to the very young *Oberleutnant zür See* Burkhard Heusinger von Waldegg. Born on 27 May 1920 in Berlin, von Waldegg's previous U-boat experience had been as First Watch Officer on *U-177* between March and October 1943.

On 10 August *U-198* was sighted by an Avenger of 857 Squadron from the British escort carrier HMS *Shah*, as she was in the process of submerging. A frigate detached herself from the carrier group and conducted a fruitless search of the area. However, the next morning another Avenger from the *Shah* attacked *U-198* with depth charges, and again von Waldegg crash-dived. *U-198* popped up again shortly afterwards, and the flak batteries opened fire on the Fleet Air Arm plane for twenty minutes, before the U-boat submerged for a second time. Some hours later *U-198* was spotted on the surface by a Catalina flying boat, and by dawn on the 12th a Royal Indian Navy sloop, HMIS *Godavari*, under Commander J.N. Jefford, had reached von Waldegg's last reported position. Joined by a British frigate, HMS *Findhorn* under Lieutenant Commander J.C. Dawson, it took the two warships until the afternoon to locate *U-198* on sonar. The feared Hedgehog mortar was used against the submerged U-boat, which resulted in several underwater explosions. Large patches of fuel oil formed on the surface of the sea, confirming *U-198*'s demise. Von Waldegg and his sixty-five men were all killed.

Knights Cross holder *Korvettenkapitän* Jürgen Oesten left Kiel on 20 April 1944, Hitler's fifty-fifth birthday, in command of another U-cruiser, the Type IXD2 *U-861*. His career thus far had been relatively illustrious and he had been awarded the Knights Cross for an accumulation of successes. When in command of *U-61* he had sunk a total of six ships for 20,754 tons and damaged a 4,434-ton freighter during 1939–40. Subsequently, while in command of *U-106*, a Type IXB, during 1941 he had sunk a further eleven merchantmen for 52,702 tons, damaged a further freighter of 8,246-tons and managed to get a torpedo strike on the 31,100-ton battleship HMS *Malaya*. Thereafter, this valuable and experienced officer had been assigned to a desk job at U-boat Control, where he was chief adviser to Dönitz on U-boat operations in the Arctic.

Taken away from staff work, U-boat Control determined to dispatch Oesten to the Indian Ocean via the coast of Brazil in 1944. The 20 July found *U-861* hunting off Rio de Janeiro, where it was rewarded with the sinking of the 1,737-ton Brazilian troopship *Vital de Oliveira* – 101 of the soldiers carried on board perishing in the attack and subsequent sinking. However, Oesten failed to intercept the American transport ship *William A. Mann*, which was carrying the first contingent of the Brazilian Expeditionary Force to Italy. Oesten was a bold skipper, and following the destruction of the troopship he turned his attentions to its small escort vessel, the sub-chaser *Javari*. After firing a single torpedo at the ship, the escort made off and escaped further efforts to sink her. Continuing on his journey south, Oesten intercepted and sank the American Liberty ship *William Gasson* for 7,177 tons on 24 July, which was transporting grain to Europe. On 20 August *U-861* rounded the Cape of Good Hope into the Indian Ocean and came upon a lightly defended convoy, JA12, which was bound for Durban. Oesten pressed home his attack on the convoy, which was only defended by some armed trawlers. He sank the 7,464-ton British ship *Berwickshire* and damaged a British tanker, the 8,139-ton *Daronia*. His final kill before reaching Penang was achieved on 5 September, when the 5,670-ton Greek ship *Ionnis Fafalios* was disposed of east of Mombasa.

After 156 days at sea *U-861* motored into Penang harbour, her patrol being completed on 22 September. *U-861*'s engineering officer, *Kapitänleutnant* Herbert Panknin, was decorated with the Knights Cross for his accumulated service aboard not just his present boat, but *U-57* between 1938 and 1940, and aboard *U-106* between 1940 and 1943. *U-861* remained at Penang until transferring to Singapore, arriving on 2 November, before leaving the following day for the more secure anchorage of Surabaya in Java, which she reached on 5 November. After being loaded with a *Yanagi* cargo that included 100 tons of zinc, *U-861* left Surabaya on 15 January 1945 to attempt the perilous return voyage to Norway. After crossing the equator in mid-March, *U-861* arrived safely in Trondheim on 19 April 1945, after a round-trip lasting a year. Less than a month later the boat was surrendered to the Royal Navy and became one of the U-boats, of a total of 116, disposed of by the British in Operation Deadlight. At the beginning of December 1945 *U-861* was towed out to sea off Malin Head, and then sunk by gunfire from the Polish destroyer *Blyskawica*.

The '*Milchküh*': *U-490*

U-490 was a Type XIV U-tanker, launched on 24 December 1942. Commissioned into service on 27 March 1943, she had been accidentally sunk soon after completion in May 1943, while the boat was conducting working-up in the Baltic. Although salvaged by the Germans, the required repairs were lengthy and included the fitting of a *schnorchel* and some experimental submerged refuelling equipment. This took the U-tanker out of service for seven or eight months. Eventually she was ready to depart for Penang under the command of *Oberleutnant zür See* Wilhelm Gerlach in the summer of 1944.

On the night of 10/11 June, while in the mid-Atlantic, Gerlach instructed the radio operator to send a brief weather report back to U-boat Control, as was standard procedure. The *Kriegsmarine* required U-boats to report on the weather regularly, allowing them to construct detailed reports that could be used in the planning of U-boat operations around the world and to provide additional weather reporting to the army and *Luftwaffe*. However, by the last summer of the war, sending reports by radio (even brief transmissions), had become extremely dangerous for U-boats. Using HF/DF (Huff Duff) tracking, the Allies were able, on the strength of this single short transmission, to plot the position of *U-490* with some accuracy, allowing the dispatch of naval forces to hunt her down and destroy her. Three destroyer escorts from the American carrier group based around the USS *Croatan* were able to further pinpoint the location of *U-490*. By the morning of 11 June, the destroyer escorts discovered the U-boat and began depth-charging operations against her. It would prove to be quite a game of cat and mouse. According to Gerlach, he dived his U-boat deep, to around 1,000 feet and into crush depth territory, to escape the incessant American attacks. His plan was to stay down as long as the air held out on board the U-boat in the hope that the Americans would give up after expending their depth charges or losing contact. The American commanders knew that U-490 had become a difficult target to destroy, but they also knew from their experience that eventually the U-boat would have to surface. If it did not do so the crew would be overcome from carbon dioxide poisoning as the air inside the boat grew thicker as each man exhaled. After pounding U-490 without effect for all morning, afternoon and evening, by 2100 hours the Americans decided upon a strategy of luring Gerlach to the surface. The destroyer escorts retired from the scene noisily and quickly, in order to fool the hydrophone operator on the U-boat into thinking that the Americans had decided to break contact at last. The Americans then slowly, and as quietly as possible, returned to their former positions and sat in silence waiting for the U-boat to break the surface to replenish the air supply.

For forty-seven minutes all was quiet, the gun crews aboard the destroyer escorts USS *Frost* and USS *Snowden* tensely manning the main armament, officers and lookouts scanning the dark water for the tell-tale rush of bubbles as the U-boat blew its tanks and prepared to emerge from the darkness below. The Americans' patience and strategy were rewarded when, at 2147 hours, up popped the big U-boat, and as U-boat officers, lookouts, and gunners raced topside, the horrible truth quickly dawned upon them. From two sides the night air was rent with flashes and explosions, tracing carving through the darkness into the helpless submarine. Gerlach quickly assessed the situation, and realizing that the chances of successfully crash-diving and avoiding the barrage of depth charges that was sure to follow were slim indeed, he frantically signalled to the Americans of his intention to surrender. In the meantime he instructed his officers to scuttle the boat, which was by now being comprehensively riddled with explosive shells and machine-gun bullets, and abandon the craft. The American gunners were ordered to keep firing at the U-boat until it was clear that she was finished. Incredibly, the entire crew of fifty-three men were rescued from the water, not one man having been killed during the final climactic minutes of *U-490's* life. The last German *Milchküh* U-boat had joined her nine sisters at the bottom of the sea, robbing the *Kriegsmarine* of their ability to fuel the boats operating between Europe and the Far East without tasking other fighting boats to perform that duty, and thereby detracting from their missions to sink Allied commerce and warships.

Final Operations of the Italian Boats: *UIT-25*, *UIT-23* and *UIT-21*

Following the surrender of Italy, the submarine *Torelli* languished in Singapore harbour until 10 September 1943, when the Japanese turned the vessel over to the Germans. She was commissioned into the German Navy as *UIT-25*, and assigned to transport duties between the German base in Singapore and the German U-boat repair and parts facility at Kobe, Japan. Following the announcement of the formation of a new Italian Social Republic fascist regime in German-controlled northern Italy in September 1943, some of the former crew of the *Torelli* decided to fight alongside the Germans and partly crewed *UIT-25* alongside German U-boatmen.

Those Italian submariners who chose not to fight for Mussolini were granted safe passage to Europe by the Japanese authorities. Three German merchant surface blockade-runners, the *Burgenland*, *Rio Grande* and *Weserland*, took the Italians on board as passengers and departed from Singapore on 29 October 1943. The great danger faced by German surface blockade-runners, and the high rate of attrition faced by these ships, was amply demonstrated by the fates of the three aforementioned vessels. *Weserland* made it as far as the South Atlantic before being sunk on 3 January 1944 by the American destroyer USS *Somers*. The following day the *Rio Grande* was intercepted by US Navy warships and forced to scuttle. The same fate awaited the *Burgenland*, who was intercepted and scuttled the following day.

Kapitänleutnant Johannes-Werner Striegler assumed command of *UIT-25* on 6 December 1943, but for a short period only, relinquishing command to take over *UIT-23*. This U-boat was the former Italian submarine *Guiliani*, and the German officer originally given command, *Fregattenkapitän* Heinrich Schäfer, had died in Penang from what were presumed to be natural causes on 8 January 1944. However, in February Striegler re-assumed command of *UIT-25*, and the boat was employed for a year on supply missions between the German bases in South-East Asia and Japan, first under Striegler, and from September 1944 under *Kapitänleutnant* Herbert Schrein.

The Royal Italian Navy submarine *Finzi* was in Bordeaux when she was turned over to the *Kriegsmarine* in September 1943 for conversion to a cargo-carrier for work in the Far East. Commissioned as *UIT-21*, she was left behind when the four other former Italian submarines *UIT-22–UIT-25* departed European waters because her general state of seaworthiness was found to be substandard. *UIT-21* remained berthed in Bordeaux under refit until she was deliberately scuttled by German forces on 25 August 1944 as Allied units closed in on the city.

In November 1944 German U-boat operations were redeployed to Batavia, following the increasing damage being caused by Allied bombing attacks on Penang. *Oberleutnant der Reserve* Alfred Meier assumed command of *UIT-25* in February 1945, and later that same month the U-boat sailed to Kobe, Japan, delivering supplies. However, while *UIT-25* was in the Japanese port, American B-29 Superfortress bombers of the US 20th Air Force, based in the Pacific at Tinian, delivered an extensive attack on the port, targeting the Mitsubishi and Kawasaki naval shipyards. The Japanese submarine *I-158* and some merchant ships tied up in Kobe harbour were damaged, and Germany suffered a war casualty in Japan when an enlisted crewman of *UIT-25* was killed during the American attack. *UIT-25* remained in Kobe until the German surrender in May 1945. She was undergoing repairs in the Kawasaki naval shipyard, and was immediately seized by the Imperial Japanese Navy. Commissioned as the *I-504*, the former *Torelli* and *UIT-25* languished in Kobe harbour until the Japanese surrendered in August, with no Japanese submariners assigned to the boat. On 16 April 1946 the US Navy towed *I-504* out to the Kii Suido and scuttled a submarine that had served all three of the Axis partners during the Second World War.

Notes

1. Franks, N. & Zimmerman, E., *U-Boat versus Aircraft*, Grub Street, London, 1998, pp. 165–6.
2. *Ibid.*, p. 166.

Chapter 9

End
Game

The commander of *U-862*, *Korvettenkapitän* Heinrich Timm, held an interesting record when Germany surrendered as the only U-boat commander to have patrolled in the Atlantic, Indian and Pacific Oceans.

Born on 30 April 1910 in Bremen, Timm was formally a merchant marine officer until he entered the Naval Academy in October 1933. A minesweeper commander during the early stages of the war, he had forced the scuttling of the Royal Navy submarine HMS *Starfish* off Heligoland on 9 January 1940, while in command of minesweeper *M-7*. By the time he transferred to U-boats in 1941 Timm had already earned the Iron Cross 1st and 2nd Class. Timm's first command was *U-251*, a Type VIIC, operating in the Arctic Ocean – notably, Timm's successes included attacking Convoy PQ-17 and sailing to Spitzbergen. He completed nine war patrols to the Arctic before taking command of the brand-new *U-862*, a Type IXD2, in September 1943. Timm was respected by his crew, who realized during those nine arduous patrols in the frozen north that Timm was careful with the boat and their lives, but never avoided attacking convoys at every opportunity. He had also managed to bring his boat back from each patrol undamaged.

On 3 June 1944, *U-862* sailed from Norway to the German U-boat base that had by that stage of the war been relocated to Batavia. On the voyage to the Far East, Timm attacked and sank the 6,885-ton *Robin Goodfellow* on 25 July in the South Atlantic. On entering the Indian Ocean, *U-862* sank the 3,614-ton *Radbury* on 13 August while to the south of the island of Madagascar. Timm's successes continued as his boat sailed across the Indian Ocean towards its new Far Eastern base, and on 16 August *U-862* sank the 7,037-ton *Empire Lancer*, then two days later the 5,414-ton

Nairung, followed on 19 August by the destruction of the 5,068-ton British ship *Wayfarer*. This spectacular run of success resulted in Timm being awarded the Knights Cross on *U-862*'s arrival in Batavia on 17 September 1944. However, Timm's success was not without incident. On 20 August 1944, *U-862* was in the northern part of the Mozambique Channel, nosing into the Indian Ocean proper, when a Catalina anti-submarine aircraft of RAF No. 265 Squadron on a transport flight from Mombasa to Durban caught the U-boat running on the surface. Although the Catalina was on a transport flight, carrying an additional four RAF maintenance crew as passengers alongside the normal four aircrew complement, the pilot was conducting anti-submarine surveillance en route. As the aircraft swung in to attack the U-boat, it fired its nose gun. The 37mm flak crew returned fire, scoring hits on the aircraft's starboard engine and wing. As the distance between aircraft and submarine rapidly diminished, the 20mm flak gunners pumped rounds into the cockpit. The Catalina crashed into the sea a mere 30 feet beyond the U-boat, leaving no survivors. *U-862* emerged from the encounter completely unscathed.[1]

On 17 November, Timm sailed *U-862* out of Batavia harbour on a patrol intended to encompass the waters off Australia, which Timm had plied before the war while a merchant navy officer. *U-862* sailed down the west coast of Australia, and then turned east. On 9 December, in broad daylight, the surfaced *U-862* bombarded the 4,724-ton Greek tanker *Ilissos* with her 105mm deck gun, inflicting some damage. However, the tanker returned fire with her 4in gun, and Timm chose to dive to avoid any damage to his boat. Royal Australian Air Force (RAAF) aircraft were ordered to search the area for the German submarine. A naval search was also instituted by the Royal Australian Navy, utilizing three corvettes; HMAS *Lismore*, HMAS *Burnie* and HMAS *Maryborough* throughout the area in which the *Ilissos* was attacked. Christmas Eve 1944 saw Timm sink the 7,180-ton American Liberty ship *Robert J. Walker* off Montague Island, New South Wales, and he ended his cruise by sinking another Liberty ship, the 7,176-ton *Peter Silvester*, which was carrying US Army supplies and 137 unfortunate US Army mules off the Australian west coast, as *U-862* made its way back to Batavia on 6 February 1945. Fifteen survivors were saved from the sea on 9 February. Consolidated Liberator bomber aircraft of No. 25 Squadron, RAAF, located a further group of fifty survivors on rafts on 12 and 13 February. Rations were dropped to these beleaguered survivors. The last survivors of the sinking of the *Peter Silvester* were not located and rescued until 9 March by the American submarine USS *Rock*. On 27 February 1945 *U-862* arrived in Singapore. During the time the submarine was moored in the harbour, it has been reported that the combined 37mm and 20mm flak crews successfully shot down a USAAF *P-38* Lightning fighter-bomber during an air raid on Singapore in May.[2]

On 3 May 1945 after his promotion to *Kapitän zür See*, Kurt Freiwald, commanding officer of *U-181*, addressed all the German crews in Singapore, informing them that Hitler was dead. Shortly afterwards, on 6 May, Vice Admiral Shigeru Fukudome, the commander of the Japanese 13th Area Fleet, accompanied by three other admirals and various staff officers, arrived in Singapore. Fukudome informed the senior German officers present (Freiwald, Dommes and Timm) that all German naval personnel were to be interned – however, they were all invited to a parting dinner where the Japanese officers thanked the Germans for their efforts on the side of the Japanese throughout the war. Later that same afternoon, armed Japanese soldiers arrived by truck at the quayside, and the German naval ensigns were taken down for the last time and replaced by the rising sun flag of the Imperial Japanese Navy on all the U-boats in port.

The war, however, was not over for the German crew of the *U-862*. Although all the German naval personnel in Singapore had been taken off in trucks to the former British plantation at Batu Pahat in southern Malaya, for internment, the Japanese required instruction on how to operate *U-862*, which they had seized and subsequently commissioned as the *I-502*. Accordingly, in July 1945, the former German crew was divided into two thirty-man working parties and reunited with their boat to instruct Japanese submariners on its operation. Not until 15 August did *I-502* leave on her first, and last, trial run with a Japanese crew – Japan surrendering shortly afterwards. Following the Japanese surrender, *U-862/I-502* was turned over to the British, and the German crew was held in the infamous Changi Prison, Singapore. However, in July 1946 the former crew of *U-862* sailed to England, and from there they were repatriated back to Germany in 1947. The Royal Navy disposed of *U-862/I-502* on 15 February 1946, the boat being scuttled in the Strait of Malacca. Released from British captivity in Singapore in

April 1948, one of the last to be sent home, Timm later joined the *Bundesmarine*. Before he retired in 1966 Timm commanded the frigate *Scharnhorst*, and died in 1974 close to his home city of Bremen.

The brand-new Type IXD2 *U-863* was commissioned into the *Kriegsmarine* by *Kapitänleutnant* Dietrich von der Esch on 3 November 1943, and was assigned to 4th Training Flotilla. The 4th Training Flotilla was typical of many U-boat training and working-up establishments, designed to allow a commander to mould his crew into an effective fighting unit, and become familiar with the boat before submitting themselves to the ultimate test for both crew and boat – the war patrol. Based at Stettin in Germany, the flotilla was established in May 1941 and would process nearly 300 U-boats and their crews through training during the unit's history, providing instruction on virtually all types of ocean-going U-boat, including the late-war Electro-boats.

Dietrich von der Esch was typical of many *Junker* officers found throughout the German armed forces. He was born on 31 January 1915 in the upper middle-class neighbourhood of Charlottenburg in Berlin and had previously served as First Watch Officer on *U-98* for two months in 1941, before assuming command of the Type VIIC *U-586*, which he skippered between September 1941 and September 1943, during which time he was promoted to *Kapitänleutnant*. During several arduous patrols in the Arctic, von der Esch sank two ships and damaged two others, as well as undertaking the hazardous task of laying a mine barrage off the Soviet coast and, in October 1942, conducting a reconnaisance of Jan Mayen Island. Soon after assuming command of *U-863* von der Esch's Arctic adventures were recognized by the award of the German Cross in Gold.

On 1 June 1944 *U-863* was assigned to 12th U-boat Flotilla as a 'front boat', which meant that the U-boat had been successfully worked-up in training to operational status. Based at Bordeaux, 12th Flotilla was commanded by *Fregattenkapitän* Klaus Scholtz, holder of the Knights Cross with Oakleaves, and the majority of the long-range U-cruisers assigned to operations in the South Atlantic and Indian Ocean were assigned to Scholtz, including the former Italian UIT-boats operating as dedicated *Yanagi* transports. Following the successful Allied invasion of Normandy in June 1944, U-boat Control decided to evacuate the flotilla to the safety of Norway and

Germany, with the flotilla being officially relocated to Flensburg in northern Germany in August, where it was disbanded. Unfortunately, although the remaining boats, such as *U-863*, relocated (von der Esch going to Bergen in Norway), Scholtz and the 200 or so men of 12th Flotilla not assigned to operational U-boats, such as headquarters staff, engineering and supply personnel, and others, found themselves left in Bordeaux as the Allies continued to advance. Scholtz decided on a bold course of action, leading the remaining personnel of 12th U-boat Flotilla on a foot march towards Germany. However, Scholtz and his command were swept up by advancing American forces on 11 September and made prisoners of war.

Von der Esch, meanwhile, departed from Bergen on 20 July, his boat loaded with *Yanagi* cargo and supplies for the German U-boat bases in Asia, with orders to proceed to Penang to reinforce the remaining boats of *Gruppe Monsun* still operating in the Indian Ocean. It proved to be, as it was for many U-boats during this late-war period, a one-way trip for boat and crew. *U-863* was attacked by a marauding RAF Mosquito N of 333 Squadron on the day of departure, causing enough damage to force von der Esch to make for Trondheim – and repairs. Eventually getting under way on 26 July, *U-863* travelled unmolested south for a little over two months, before, on 29 September she was spotted on the surface east-south-east of Recife in Brazil by a US Navy Liberator of VP-107 flying from Natal in Brazil. The pilot dropped five depth charges, which straddled *U-863*. Some damage was inflicted by this initial attack. The U-boat rapidly lost speed and began trailing a large oil slick behind her. During the attack the U-boat had failed to fire a single anti-aircraft shot at the Liberator. However, on banking around and charging in for a second attack run, the flak guns opened up and the Americans' remaining depth charges failed to release. Soon afterwards a second Liberator appeared at the scene, and the two bombers attempted to suppress the German flak crews with machine-gun fire. The second Liberator fouled up its attack, dropping six depth charges short of the U-boat, and was then struck by flak shells. The American came around again and managed to straddle *U-863* with three depth charges, further damaging von der Esch's boat, but the flak gunners also scored more hits on the big bomber. At this point the Americans observed some of the crew of *U-863* abandoning ship, and the crippled U-boat sank beneath them into the large oil slick on the surface of the water. The first Liberator managed to release its final depth charges directly into the oil slick. Soon afterwards another Liberator arrived, and the three aircraft dropped life-rafts to the approximately twenty German survivors. As was to be the case on so many occasions, the swimmers were never recovered, the death toll amounting to the entire crew of sixty-eight men.

U-180 was no stranger to German–Japanese military cooperation; having previously transported the Indian Nationalist leader Subhas Chandra Bose and his aide Dr Habib Hasan to a rendezvous in the Indian Ocean with the Japanese submarine *I-29* in April 1943, while under the command of *Fregattenkapitän* Werner Müsenberg. Müsenberg had left the boat in January 1944 to join the staff of the Midget Submarine School, and *U-180* had been extensively overhauled. Originally constructed with six diesel engines, the foray into the Indian Ocean had exposed this propulsion system as flawed, and the boat was reconfigured into a traditional two-engine arrangement for further operations.

Müsenberg's replacement as skipper was *Oberleutnant zür See* Rolf Riesen, who was born on 18 December 1919 in Cologne. Between September 1942 and February 1944 he served as a Watch Officer aboard *U-190*, before training as a commander. *U-180* was to be Riesen's first command. Assigned, in common with most other long-range U-boats, to 12th Flotilla at Bordeaux, Riesen took the specially converted cargo-carrying boat south on 20 August 1944. It is believed that while *U-180* was *schnorcheling* on 23 August she struck and detonated a British aerial mine in the Bay of Biscay, approximately 50 miles south-west of the mouth of the Gironde estuary. Riesen and his entire crew of fifty-five stood no chance of escape and all were either killed outright by the explosion, or drowned as the stricken U-boat plunged uncontrollably to the bottom of the sea.

Although *U-195*'s mission was to sail to Penang with cargo for both the Japanese, and the German U-boat base, Penang was not the boat's eventual destination. Allied air attacks had rendered Penang virtually untenable as a base for submarines. The Japanese had assisted the Germans in moving the base to the more secure location of Batavia (now Jakarta, Indonesia). Japanese submarines based in Penang had also withdrawn, to Surabaya, Java. *U-195* was outbound from

Bordeaux loaded with quantities of mercury and lead, steel, optical glass and aluminium for the Japanese, and spare torpedoes and a spare U-boat propeller for the Penang base. On 20 December 1944 *U-195* rendezvoused with *U-843*, which was returning to France, and refuelled her. Continuing on his journey, *Oberleutnant der Reserve* Friedrich Steinfeldt's *U-195* arrived off the coast of Java one week later. In common with arriving Japanese submarines sailing from France, the Japanese sent up an aircraft to provide an escort for the incoming U-boat. Incredibly, the aircraft that met the *U-195* was German, an Arado Ar-196A floatplane, which was formerly housed on the German merchant raider *Michel*, the Arado being flown sporting the red *Hinomaru* roundels of the Japanese, and a German pilot.

U-195 arrived in Batavia harbour to a scene of devastation. The Japanese ammunition ship *Taicho Maru* had blown up, wrecking part of the harbour complex and damaging three *Gruppe Monsun* U-boats that were moored close by. Many military personnel had been killed in the conflagration caused by the *Taicho Maru*'s demise. However, the Japanese and German base commanders and personnel turned out to welcome the new arrival, and *U-195*'s ship's company paraded on deck in tropical uniforms as the boat entered the harbour – on the sides of the grey conning tower the Nazi swastika flag fastened to ease identification for the Japanese. There were plenty of U-boatmen available to welcome *U-195*, as *U-510*, *U-532* and *U-861* were all being prepared for the return run to France.

When *U-195* was ready to depart from Batavia in January 1945, France had already fallen to the Allies, and the U-boat Arm was operating principally from bases in northern Germany and Norway. Steinfeldt sailed for Norway on 19 January 1945, but *U-195* quickly developed a fault with its engines and was forced to return to Batavia. However, the boat was ordered to refuel the departing *U-532* under *Fregattenkapitän* Otto-Heinrich Junker before heading back to harbour. This was achieved on 9 February – the crew passing mail over to the Norway-bound *U-532*, along with diesel fuel. On 2 March *U-195* arrived back in Batavia, but the very next day departed again, bound for the Japanese submarine base at Surabaya, to have her engines repaired preparatory to sailing for Norway.

Events in Europe halted any plans Steinfeldt harboured of returning to Europe, when *Vizeadmiral* Paul Wenneker, the German

Naval Attaché to Japan, cabled Steinfeldt from Tokyo on 7 May announcing the surrender of all German armed forces. Steinfeldt had no choice but to lower *U-195*'s battle ensign and shortly afterwards some Japanese sailors raised their Rising Sun flag on the boat. Steinfeldt and his crew were well-treated by their former allies, the Japanese housing them in an open prison camp run by the Imperial Japanese Navy close to the harbour.

U-195 was officially taken over by the Imperial Japanese Navy as the *I-506* on 15 July 1945. The boat was fully overhauled at the Japanese submarine base at Surabaya, but although the boat was returned to full fighting potential, the Japanese lacked men who were experienced in crewing German U-boats, so she remained idle in port until the Japanese surrender in September. With the Japanese out of effective control, Indonesian rebels overran the port and destroyed the electrical power supply for Surabaya City. When Gurkhas of the British Indian Army arrived to restore order, the previously interned crew of the former *U-195* were released and told to use the U-boat's diesels to run emergency generators thereby providing electricity for the inhabitants of Surabaya. Sadly the U-boat war, now long since over, was to claim one more victim. *Oberleutnant der Reserve* Steinfeldt was never to leave Surabaya, dying of dysentery there on 30 November 1945. As for the former *U-195/I-506*, the Royal Navy took her out into the Bali Sea in February 1946 and sent her to the bottom with scuttling charges.

Commissioned into the German Navy on 12 December 1942, *U-219* was a Type XB U-boat. The Type XB came into existence to fulfil a requirement for a large submarine capable of deploying the *SMA* magnetic mine. The original design for the delivery boat would have led to the Germans constructing U-boats displacing approximately 2,500 tons. However, alterations and design changes recommended by *Grössadmiral* Dönitz were adopted, as he believed the existing Type X and XA U-boat designs to be too large. These changes resulted in the Type XB.

The Type XB minelayer U-boat displaced 2,177 tons and measured 294.6 feet in length. A crew of five officers and forty-seven enlisted men manned a boat carrying sixty-six *SMA* mines, and armed with two stern torpedo tubes with a total of fifteen torpedoes available. Anti-aircraft armament after 1943 was strengthened, resulting in one 37mm and two twin 20mm guns mounted on the superstructure.

U-219 and *U-234* were both selected for conversion into cargo-carriers for use on the Far East run, and the 105mm deck gun was removed from both boats. *U-219* was converted for this role in Brest, the original mine shafts used to store and release the *SMA* magnetic mines being removed or altered. Twenty-four of the lateral mine shafts were removed on both *U-219* and *U-234*, creating four large holds for cargo. The six mine shafts located forward were not removed, but special cargo containers designed to fit into these shafts were designed, each container the same length as three *SMA* mines. Both boats were equipped with a *schnorchel*, enabling them to recharge their batteries without surfacing, and a German Air Force *Hohentwiel* radar. The FuMO 61 *Hohentwiel U* was originally developed for use by *Luftwaffe* aircraft against surface ships. The radar type first appeared in September 1942, and from August 1943 began to be fitted to naval reconnaisance aircraft such as the Heinkel He-177 and Focke-Wulf Fw-200 *Condor*. Later adapted for use on U-boats, small ships, and in-shore installations, it was considered reliable and easy to maintain – ideal for use in U-boats. The *Hohentwiel U* radar range was 10 kilometres against ships and 20 kilometres against aircraft. Resolution (what the radar could see at any one time), was about three degrees, and the operator monitored two oscilloscope screens indicating range and plan position indication.

On 23 August 1944 *U-219* slipped out of Bordeaux harbour under the command of *Korvettenkapitän* Walter Bürghagen (a First World War veteran U-boatman who had served aboard *U-44*, *U-49* and *U-55* until taken prisoner in 1916), and headed for the Far East. Bürghagen was born in Dresden in 1891 and became an officer cadet in 1911.

U-219 was ideally placed to transport cargo to Batavia. Because the Type XB was basically designed as a minelayer, the conversion of the *SMA* mine shafts to accommodate cargo meant that the large U-boat was able to carry quite a considerable load. Although she retained eight torpedoes in the stern compartments and tubes, every other space was taken up with a carefully designed manifest, the cargo taking three or four months to load in stages.

The Germans were still running U-boat operations in the Far East and the Indian Ocean from their bases at Penang, Batavia and Kobe, and spares and new equipment were required by these facilities to keep the remaining U-boats operational. Among the items loaded aboard *U-219* were spare parts for the Arado Ar-196 floatplane that the Germans operated at Penang (which had originally been mounted on a German auxiliary cruiser hunting in the Far East earlier in the war), and new radio equipment for the small U-boat repair and battery manufacturing facility at Kobe. The *Yanagi* cargo for the Japanese consisted of the usual optical glass, mercury and other scarce metals.

U-219 had been loaded to the point of overload, and engineers were required to complete diving tests on the boat before she put to sea proper. They concluded, after struggling to trim the boat and recovering from a dive, that the 105mm deck gun and ammunition were surplus to requirements – both were removed once the U-boat regained her bunker. In May the boat's *schnorchel* was thoroughly tested, in preparation for conducting most of her mission submerged. *U-219* began to *schnorchel* towards the Far East on 26 August. All was well until on 14 September, well out into the Atlantic, the *schnorchel* broke down. Bürghagen had no choice but to return to the former U-boat practice of surfacing the boat at night to charge the batteries, and travelling submerged during the hours of daylight.

U-boat Control directed *U-219* to rendezvous with and refuel the Type VIIF torpedo resupply boat *U-1062* (*Oberleutnant zür See* Karl Albrecht), which was on its return journey from Penang loaded with a valuable *Yanagi* cargo consisting in the main of rubber. Originally *U-1062* would have headed for France, but the U-boat bases were now surrounded by Allied forces and under siege. U-boat Control had diverted the Type VIIF to Norway – a journey that required more fuel than she carried. However, the signals traffic between the boats and Control regarding the rendezvous had been monitored by the Allies, revealing the location and time of the meeting (scheduled to occur on 28 September, south-west of the Cape Verde Islands). The US Navy saturated the location with carrier aircraft, and radar on board the USS *Mission Bay* located *U-219* as she surfaced, the ship immediately launching aircraft against her. *U-219*'s 20mm and 37mm flak gunners successfully shot down the first carrier aircraft that appeared, but the explosive reverberations resulting from the bombs which this aircraft dropped before it was destroyed, although not destined to hit the U-boat directly, caused the engines to stop. Attacked by a second aircraft armed with rockets, which all missed their target, Bürghagen prudently submerged his boat before more serious opposition arrived. U-boat Control still ordered that he must rendezvous with *U-1062*, so Bürghagen was forced to loiter in the area, listening to the hunting and killing of Albrecht and his boat.

U-219 reached the Cape of Good Hope on 11 November without encountering further problems from Allied anti-submarine forces. U-boat Control at this time informed Bürghagen that because of an increase in Allied air operations near the U-boat base at Penang, he was to sail to Batavia. Although *U-219* launched a submerged attack on a supposed merchant vessel sighted on 26 November, when in the Indian Ocean, no kill was achieved. *U-219* successfully reached the relocated German U-boat base at Batavia on 11 December 1944, and remained in port until Germany surrendered in May 1945. Initially, Control had decided to have *U-219* and other boats load up with cargo and depart as soon as possible for the return journey to Europe, but the destruction caused when a Japanese ammunition ship blew up in Batavia harbour, *U-219* being among the U-boats damaged, caused a rethink. While her crew enjoyed Tjikopo rest home in the mountains, the boat was taken into dry dock in January 1945. The boat was ready to attempt the return trip to Germany by March 1945, but then developed faults with her batteries, and other minor defects necessitating moving the ailing U-boat to repair facilities at the Japanese base at Surabaya.

News from Europe demonstrated to the remaining U-boat crews sweating it out in the Far East that Germany was very nearly finished militarily, and clearly the Japanese would take over any U-boats within their sphere of influence following any German surrender. All remaining U-boat crews worked day and night to repair all the boats, and have them ready to leave the Japanese area of operations before the war in Europe ended. None of the officers and crews relished the idea of being imprisoned by the Japanese. Their concern was based upon their observations of the treatment of Italian prisoners of war at the hands of the Japanese after the armistice in 1943, when Italy changed sides. However, U-boat Control decreed in April that all remaining boats in Far Eastern waters, which by now consisted of *U-219* and *U-195* (*Oberleutnant der Reserve* Friedrich Steinfeldt), the former Italian *Merkator* submarines *UIT-24* (*Oberleutnant zür See* Heinrich Pahls) and *UIT-25* (*Oberleutnant der Reserve* Alfred Meier), should remain in the Far East. There no longer existed the refuelling network throughout the Indian and Atlantic Oceans, which would have been required if any of the four boats had seriously contemplated sailing home, as the U-boat campaign had largely shifted focus on to an offensive in the coastal waters around Great Britain. There were no dedicated Type XIV U-tankers remaining, and of the large Type XB class, the only one operating outside of the Indian Ocean was confined for the time being to operations in German coastal waters – this being *U-234* under the command of *Kapitänleutnant* Johann-Heinrich Fehler.

Eventually Germany surrendered. The *U-219* was taken over by the Imperial Japanese Navy and recommissioned as the *I-505*. As with other U-boats commandeered by the Japanese following the demise of Nazi Germany, some members of *U-219*'s crew were allowed to 'volunteer' to remain with their boats in order to train the new Japanese crews in the operation of the boats. Excess U-boatmen were allowed by the Japanese to live at Tjikopo, the special U-boat rest home in the mountains behind Batavia. The former *U-219* was returned to a fully operational state by the combined Japanese–German effort, although the Japanese did not deploy the U-boat against Allied forces. Subsequently surrendered to HMS *Cumberland* on 10 September 1945, along with all the former German U-boats remaining in the port of Batavia, the boat was broken up in 1948. Bürghagen and his crew were released from British captivity as prisoners of war and repatriated to Germany in December 1946.

The Type IXD2 *U-871* was yet another long-range brand-new U-cruiser assigned to reinforce the German effort in the Far East. Commissioned into service on 15 January 1944 by *Kapitänleutnant* Erwin Ganzer, *U-871* completed working-up in the Baltic with 4th Training Flotilla before becoming operational with 12th Flotilla on 1 August.

Ganzer was born on 8 December 1912 in Cologne and entered the naval academy as an officer cadet in 1935. He had previously served on *U-155* as a commander under training between June and August 1943, the boat being skippered at the time by *Korvettenkapitän* Adolf Piening. On 1 August 1944 Ganzer and *U-871* departed from Trondheim in Norway on their first patrol. Many of the boats of 12th Flotilla had been withdrawn from Trondheim following D-Day. On 26 September *U-871* was north-west of the Azores in the Atlantic when a B-17 Flying Fortress of the RAF's 220 Squadron, which was patrolling the area in its role as an airborne escort for Convoy CU40, attacked the U-boat. Massively and fatally depth charged, all sixty-nine crew died as the U-boat was destroyed.

Fighter Jets and Atomic Bombs: *U-864* and *U-234*

Korvettenkapitän Ralf-Reimer Wolfram assumed command of the Type IXD2 *U-864* on her commissioning in December 1943. The U-boat departed from Bergen on her first and only patrol on 7 February 1945. Her departure had been delayed following a British air raid on the U-boat pens at Bergen on 12 January, when she had suffered damage. *U-864*'s mission was to sail undetected to the Far East, using the *schnorchel* technology perfected by the Germans, and deliver another valuable *Yanagi* cargo to the Japanese. Included in the cargo manifest were 1,857 flasks of mercury, parts and plans of the Messerschmitt ME-262 jet fighter-bomber, the Messerschmitt ME-163 *Komet* interceptor, and accompanying these were legal contracts giving Japanese manufacturers permission to construct these aircraft types under licence. The cargo included several other sets of plans for new aircraft and new submarines, as well as plans for Siemens designed and manufactured radar technology. In common with all other underwater trade exchanges, the submarine carried passengers to Japan, as well as German and Japanese aircraft engineers. The Japanese did benefit greatly from the technological advances made by German designers during the war. The Japanese were often able to copy German designs, or alter and improve existing products, in order to produce new 'wonder weapons' for the Imperial forces.

A good example of technological exchange through the *Yanagi* system was the Nakajima *Kikka* ('Orange Blossom') jet fighter-bomber. Throughout 1944 the Japanese military attaché staff at Berlin sent reports full of praise back to Tokyo for the new Messerschmitt ME-262 jet interceptor then coming into service with the battered *Luftwaffe*. In September, the Naval Air Staff instructed Nakajima to design and construct a comparable aircraft capable of being employed as a high-speed bomber that would rely upon speed to evade the attentions of American fighter interceptors. The Japanese Embassy sent plans from Messerschmitt and the company dispatched engineers to Japan to aid the project. Nakajima designers Kazuo Ohno and Kenichi Matsumura scaled the ME-262 down, producing a final design that was two-thirds the size of the original

German aircraft. Essentially, though, the aircraft was a copy of the German jet. When it came to suitable engines to power the bomber, the Japanese initially relied upon Campini-type Tsu-11 engines, but a Japanese Navy designer obtained (through the *Yanagi* exchange programme) detailed photographs of the BMW-003 axial-flow turbojets mounted on the ME-262 airframe. By scaling the engine down and copying the BMW engine configuration and design, the Japanese were able to produce the NE-20 turbojet in early 1945. Importantly, the Japanese never intended the *Kikka* to be employed in a kamikaze role. Japanese military observers in Berlin had reported to Tokyo that only very skilled pilots were able to operate the ME-262, and its early jet engines. For less experienced pilots, taking to the skies in one of these early jet aircraft would have been fatal and extremely expensive to both the German and Japanese war machines. To have devoted so much effort to developing and constructing technically superior machines capable of turning the tide against the Allies, only to have inexperienced teenage pilots crash them, was not an option. Therefore, in common with the *Luftwaffe*, the Imperial Japanese Naval Air Service planed to carefully select the experienced pilots that remained alive, while directing raw recruits with a few hours flying time to the Special Attack (kamikaze) squadrons.

Unfortunately, groundbreaking though the *Kikka* may have been, in common with the Germans extraordinary technological efforts, it was a case of too little too late. The first *Kikka* prototype completed initial ground tests on 30 June 1945, after which it was dismantled and taken to Kisarazu Naval Airfield in July. On 7 August it took to the skies in the hands of Lieutenant Commander Susumu Takaoka for a brief twenty-minute flight. The second test flight on 11 August almost ended in disaster. Due to the large amount of time it took for the aircraft to attain take-off speed, a decision was taken to boost the engine's power by strapping RATOG jet bottles underneath the wings. These were not fitted at the correct angle and the *Kikka* ended up crash landing in the rough beyond the end of the runway. Another prototype was practically ready to fly when the war abruptly ended for Japan on 15 August. Nakajima were also in the process of constructing eighteen other prototypes and pre-production *Kikkas* when Japan surrendered, and none of these were finished. Without the cross-fertilization of ideas and technology occasioned by the *Yanagi* programme, the Nakajima *Kikka* and other forms of weaponry would never have existed.

Equipment manufactured and placed upon U-boats in the latter stages of the war was not necessarily of the finest build quality, often because the Allied bombing campaign had disrupted production and destroyed valuable materials which were difficult to replace or duplicate. Workers who had been 'press-ganged' into working for the Nazi war effort manufactured much of the equipment and parts, and quality control suffered accordingly through anything from sloppy work to outright sabotage. Not surprisingly, U-864's *schnorchel* developed a fault and stopped working, making a journey to the Far East virtual suicide because of the need to surface in order to recharge the batteries. Wisely, Wolfram decided to abort his mission and return to Bergen for repairs before setting out again.

The Royal Navy had successfully deployed its own coastal submarines to shadow the German U-boat ports in Norway, and as luck would have it, the 600-ton HMS *Venturer* under the command of Lieutenant Jimmy Launders RN was watching German naval traffic in and out of Bergen very closely, lying in a submerged position some 35 miles from the Norwegian port. The sonar operator aboard detected sounds in the water on 9 February 1945, and a periscope search revealed a German submarine's periscopes sticking up out of the water as the German commander navigated his boat back to port. Launders knew that the U-boat was not using its *schnorchel* apparatus, as the noise emanating from the German was different, sounding as though the U-boat was running a compressor on board. Wolfram had also raised his HFW/T mast alongside the periscope, enabling him to transmit his position and intention to come in for repairs to the U-boat shore base. Launders was surprised that Wolfram kept his periscope and communications masts up for such a long time, enabling an enemy submarine, warship or aircraft to visually pinpoint the U-boat's position with relative ease. However, Launders was also reliant upon his Asdic sonar, as well as visual observations, in his attempt to manoeuvre his submarine into a position to attack the submerged U-boat. Because both attacker and prey were submerged, Launders was effectively firing blind, and was reliant upon his primitive sonar to plot his target's course and speed before launching his torpedoes.

After nearly an hour of calculations and manoeuvring, and while still submerged, the British submarine fired a pattern of four Mark VIII torpedoes at the submerged U-boat, using passive sonar and a little luck to ascertain the correct attack plot. Two minutes and twelve seconds later the first torpedo found its mark – and *U-864* was hit. Five minutes later HMS *Venturer* was jarred by two further underwater explosions, which indicated that these torpedoes had impacted the seabed. The Asdic operator reported the grisly death-rattle of *U-864*, the noises of metal breaking apart mixed with the sound of rushing water as the U-boat's pressure hull erupted and rapidly filled with the sea, drowning the seventy-three men on board. *U-864* was fitted with bulkheads, which meant that should she have collided with another ship or object when surfaced, the flooding would have been controlled and the boat and men would have survived. Being struck while submerged was more than the bulkheads were designed to cope with, and they failed under the immense pressure of the sea. Launders did not surface to check for survivors. He was lying off an enemy-controlled port and had no wish to attract the attention of German anti-submarine patrol boats. Instead, through his periscope, he scanned the surface of the water for evidence of the demise of *U-864*. Carpeting the surface of the sea was a large diesel oil slick, that was emanating from the U-boat's fuel tanks which had been ruptured as she broke up. Bobbing gently on the top was a flotsam of wood from inside the U-boat and a single large metal canister. The latter was used either as a deck locker for stowing a dinghy or life-jackets or it contained the Focke-Achgelis autogiro reconnaissance aircraft for use in southern waters. No bodies were observed and all went to the bottom, entombed inside their shattered iron coffin. Interestingly, among the dead aboard *U-864* were two prospective U-boat commanders travelling out to the Far East U-boat base, *Kapitänleutnant* Jobst Hahndorff and *Kapitänleutnant* Sven Plass.

In common with *U-864*, the Type XB minelayer *U-234* had been converted on the orders of U-boat Control into a cargo-carrier available for the carriage of *Yanagi* trade goods to Japan. She would have been available for use much earlier in the war, but during construction in Kiel by Krupp she had been severely damaged by an Allied bombing raid in May 1943. She was eventually completed and commissioned into the German Navy on 2 March 1944, and placed under the command of *Kapitänleutnant* Johann-Heinrich Fehler.

Once conversion to a cargo-carrier had been completed, and sea trials and working-up on the *schnorchel* had also been completed, the Germans estimated that *U-234* could carry approximately 250 tons of cargo. The technicians also estimated that *U-234* could carry sufficient fuel and supplies for a six to nine-month voyage. In order to carry all the fuel required to get *U-234* to Japan, two torpedo tubes in the aft torpedo compartment had been converted into fuel bunkers, and a small compartment forward had been flooded with sea water to compensate for this added weight, and balance the boat. At Kiel, a mixture of cargo was embarked on *U-234*, consisting of ten canisters containing 1,235 pounds (560kg) of uranium oxide (U235), which were stored in the six vertical mine shafts located forward. The uranium oxide was not going to be used by the Japanese in the development of atomic weapons technology, but rather as a catalyst for the production of synthetic methanol used for aviation fuel. The entire cargo manifest was a treasure trove of the latest in German technology. Three complete Messerschmitt jet aircraft were disassembled and stowed on board, along with a Henschel HS-293 glider-bomb. Extra Junkers jet engines were crated up for shipment, alongside an incredible 6.5 tons of technical material, including drawings of the Messerschmitt ME-163 and ME-262 jet interceptor aircraft, and plans for the V-1 and V-2 missiles. The Germans provided detailed plans and blueprints for the construction of aircraft production plants in which the Japanese could build, under licence, the jet aircraft and their engines. Blueprints were also provided for the construction of 36C and Z51-class destroyers for the navy, as well as M and S-boats, and all U-boat types (Types II, VII, X, XI, XIII and XXI). Anti-aircraft fire-control computers, FuG 200 *Hohentweil* airborne radars, Lorenz 7H2 bombsights and Lufte 7D bombsight computers were all destined for the Japanese air services. It was almost as if, based on the cargo manifest, the Nazis had decided to send every example of 'war winning' weapons technology they had to hand to their Japanese ally, even though it was plainly obvious that the war was lost for Germany.

The top secret items loaded aboard *U-234* represented the massive advances in military technology made by Germany, and handing it all over to be licence-built in Japan would mean its employment against the Allied juggernaut now bearing down upon the Japanese Home Islands. The Germans were not under any obligation to send the Japanese this equipment, but chose to do so to assist their ally in the fight against the Allies in the final months of the Second World War. Perhaps they realized that with the proper application of this technology their ally still had a chance of inflicting considerable damage upon its enemies.

Twelve passengers were also to travel on *U-234* to Japan. Colonel Genzo Shosi of the Imperial Japanese Army Air Service was an aeronautical engineer. Captain Hideo Tomonaga of the Imperial Japanese Navy was a naval aviator and submarine architect who had originally come to Germany on board the Japanese submarine *I-29* in 1943. The German passengers were being dispatched to Japan in order to assist the Japanese in resisting the American B-29 Superfortress raids on their cities. *Oberst* Fritz von Sandrath of the German Air Force was an expert in anti-aircraft artillery. His job was to enhance Japanese anti-aircraft defence systems over the cities. *Oberst* Erich Menzel, also of the German Air Force was a combat experienced navigator and communications officer. In addition he was an expert in radar, thereby aiding the Japanese in coordinating their anti-aircraft capability with an integrated ground and air radar net providing not only advanced warning of American bombing raids, but also the technology to assist in shooting down the B-29s. Another *Luftwaffe* officer travelling to Japan was *Oberstleutnant* Kai Nieschling, who was a military judge and investigative officer. Nieschling's unusual brief was to rid the German diplomatic community in Japan of the remnants of the Richard Sorge Soviet spy ring.[3]

The German Navy was represented by *Korvettenkapitän* Heinrich Hellendorn, who was an expert in ship-borne anti-aircraft gunnery, and who would serve in Japan as a military observer. *Kapitän zür See* Gerhard Falke was a naval architect, and his job on reaching Japan was to assist the Japanese in the construction of production plants from the blueprints mentioned above. Falke was also sent because he spoke Japanese fluently. *Kapitänleutnant* Richard Bulla, an expert in air-sea cooperation (who had the unique distinction of being an officer in both the *Kriegsmarine* and the *Luftwaffe*), was one of the few German officers also expert in aircraft carrier-based aviation. *Kapitän zür See* Dr Heinz Schlicke, the Director of the Naval Test Fields at Kiel, as well as being a specialist in radar, infrared technology and countermeasures, was being sent to Japan to aid in the development and manufacture of electronic devices and instruments. Willi Messerschmitt's right-hand man, August Bringewald, was the man actually in charge of production of the Messerschmitt ME-262 jet interceptor, and would be on site in Japan to assist in the reassembly and flight testing of the examples of this aircraft travelling with him aboard *U-234* to Japan. Messerschmitt also dispatched Franz Rüf, who was an industrial machinery specialist who designed machines and appliances to actually manufacture aircraft components.

U-234 was heavily laden, and left Kiel on 25 March bound for Horten in Norway. Arriving two days later, *U-234* was involved in an avoidable accident, which spelt disaster for the mission to Japan. Fehler had decided to conduct further *schnorchel* trials before setting out from Norway on the long cruise to the Far East, but the Type VIIC41 *U-1301*, a brand new boat, collided with *U-234* while she was practising her *schnorcheling* off Horten. *U-1301* hit abaft of the conning tower, rupturing a fuel-ballast tank, resulting in the loss of 16 tons of diesel fuel, which spilt into the sea. Urgent repairs were required, but Fehler was unable to dry dock the submarine at Bergen because of the limited dockyard facilities there, so he sailed into a fjord near Kristiansand and the crew effected the repairs themselves. Fehler ordered that the boat be flooded forward to raise the stern out of the water, thereby allowing the repairs to be carried out.

The final passenger to join *U-234* arrived soon after the repairs had been completed. *Luftwaffe General* Ulrich Kessler, who was an expert in anti-aircraft and anti-ship missiles, had been appointed the new German Air Attaché to Japan, and his cover story required him to have transport to take him to his new post in Tokyo. Kessler had originally been a naval officer in the *Reichsmarine*, but in 1933 he had resigned his commission and later became a pilot in the *Luftwaffe*. He commanded *Stuka* dive-bomber squadrons during the invasions of Poland, Norway and France. Kessler's real mission in the dying days of the Third Reich was to go to Japan and assist the Japanese in the development of combat tactics appropriate to the Messerschmitt ME-163 and ME-262 jet aircraft, specifically the employment of jet interceptors against the American B-29s that were currently bombing Japan back to the Stone Age.

When the cargo manifest of *U-234* is matched against the German military and civilian personnel being dispatched to Japan, the Axis strategy becomes clear. The Japanese required a response to the massive American bombing offensive initiated against the Home Islands, and the response was to licence-build German technology. *U-234* carried enough hardware, blueprints and specialist personnel to allow the Japanese to construct jet aircraft factories, construct the aircraft themselves and train their pilots in the effective tactical employment of this new technology. Simultaneously, the Japanese (with direct German assistance) could vastly improve their anti-aircraft defences, especially in the field of radar and radar-assisted gunnery. Had such a programme actually got under way, we can conjecture that the USAAF would have found itself severally tested in the skies over Japan. Even the deployment of the atomic and hydrogen weapons over Hiroshima and Nagasaki could have been delayed or even cancelled were B-29s being routinely and in great numbers knocked out of the sky, probably extending the war into 1946. If these conjectures are put into perspective alongside what we know of Japanese preparations to resist any Allied invasion of the Home Islands (estimates of 3 million well-trained and motivated Japanese troops in the Home Islands, supported by a kamikaze force and other air force units numbering approximately 5,000 piston-engine aircraft), tactically defeating the B-29 over Japan would definitely have greatly extended the war and delayed any contemplated Allied invasion. *U-234*, and other U-boats carrying similar cargoes and passengers, represented for Japan a last hope in the defence of their nation. It must be pointed out, however, that the highly advanced weapons technology Germany was now exporting had failed to make a great impact on the military situation in Europe, largely because Germany did not produce the weapons in sufficient numbers, nor was it able to properly train personnel in their employment. It was a case of too little too late. Historians generally agree that had German leadership taken all the new technology more seriously before meeting terrible reverses on the battlefield after 1943, the war would probably have had a totally different outcome.

On 15 April, as desperate German resistance against the Soviet armies was being worn down in Berlin, *U-234* departed from Kristiansand in German-occupied Norway. For sixteen days, until 1 May 1945, *U-234 schnorcheled* its way towards Japan. A violent Atlantic storm forced Fehler to surface briefly, but *U-234* soon resumed its routine of submerged travel using the *schnorchel*, surfacing for two hours at night only so that the batteries could be recharged and fresh air allowed into the boat. On 8 May 1945 Germany surrendered. *U-234* was by this stage in the mid-Atlantic. Fehler decided that he would surrender his boat to the United States, and accordingly surfaced, raised a black flag (required to show that the boat was surrendering to the Allies) and proceeded west.

Along the way, the crew disposed of all sensitive material and equipment overboard, including the Enigma machine and associated documentation, the *Tunis* radar detector, and the *Kurier* transmitter. Japan was still at war with the United States, and the two Japanese officers on board *U-234*, Colonel Shosi and Captain Tomonaga, found themselves in a difficult situation. They chose suicide rather than capture, and overdosed on sleeping pills. Fehler had both of the Japanese officers quietly buried at sea. He also deposited a samurai sword he had been presented with by the Japanese over the side, along with a large quantity of Swiss francs, before rendezvousing with the American destroyer USS *Sutton*.

The *Sutton* escorted *U-234* into Portsmouth, New Hampshire, where she was tied up alongside the previously surrendered *U-805*, *U-1228* and *U-873*. The Americans were particularly pleased to offload the uranium oxide ore, and opinion seems to suggest that this material was used as part of the Manhattan Project, which produced the atomic bomb that was dropped on Hiroshima. However, it is unlikely that the uranium oxide found its way into the actual bomb dropped on Hiroshima, due to the date *U-234* surrendered. However, if it did, it would be one of the great ironies of the Second World War – that the uranium oxide ore was requested from the Germans by the Japanese, sent when the Third Reich was in its death throes, only to fall into the hands of Japan's enemy, and ultimately to play an important role in forcing Japan into unconditional surrender.

*   *   *

The overall failure of the *Yanagi* underwater trade is extraordinary when the actual tonnage of material transported at such great cost in lives and equipment is compared with that transported between the Germans and Japanese on surface blockade-running ships.

Between 1943 and 1945 Germany received through submarine transport approximately 700 tons of raw materials, along with a few selected Japanese weapons and secret blueprints. The Japanese received in return around 1,800 tons of metals and numerous examples of the latest weapons technology Nazi Germany had to offer. However, this pales into insignificance when compared to what just one surface blockade-running cargo ship could deliver. For example, the *Weserland*, although sunk en route to Germany in January 1944, was packed with 10,000 tons of cargo from Japan. If

184

we restrict an analysis of the relative success or failure of *Yanagi* to tonnage transported, certainly it was insignificant, especially considering the effort expended by the two allies to actually transport the cargo. But that would be to miss the point. The Japanese war machine benefited immeasurably from the delivery to Japan of revolutionary Nazi technologies which were often accompanied by licences to construct copies of this machinery by Japanese companies. Technology such as pulse-jet engines, jet aircraft and flying bombs, and radar detectors and cipher equipment all played a role in Japan's Pacific War. This was the value of the *Yanagi* trade to the Japanese, not least because much of this technology was accompanied by German technicians and military officers keen to demonstrate its usefulness to Japanese industry and the military.

As for traditional U-boat operations – the original reason why Dönitz ordered groups of long-range U-boats to sortie into the region and why later, German U-boat bases and facilities were established in the Far East – U-boats in both the Indian and Pacific Oceans between May 1943 and May 1945 had sunk eighty-nine Allied ships, totalling 454,145 gross registered tons. In return, nine U-boats were lost during this same period. The most successful months for the U-boats in the Indian Ocean and Far East were July 1943 (fourteen ships sunk), February 1944 (eleven ships sunk) and August 1944 (nine ships sunk). By comparison, November 1943, and May and October 1944 witnessed no U-boat successes east of Madagascar, and all operations mounted between January and May 1945 netted only one ship sunk.

In the end, the Indian Ocean became as dangerous for U-boats as the North Atlantic. As the Allies destroyed the refuelling net based on surface tankers, and later U-tanker '*Milchkuh*' boats, operational U-boats were required to spend more time travelling to the Far East and back to Europe than actually conducting offensive war patrols in the region. At the European end, the Germans lost control of France and the important Atlantic U-boat bases, which necessitated a yet more lengthy passage to bases in Norway that lacked the facilities of those in France.

There was general confusion over defining the roles of cargo-carrying submarines employed on the *Yanagi* trade and those submarines intended to extend the U-boat offensive into the Indian Ocean and Far East. The Germans failed to produce any dedicated cargo-carrying submarines before the end of the war, although several designs were suggested. Instead they fell back on using their fighting boats to deliver cargo, for which they were totally unsuitable and ultimately wasted their potential as commerce raiders. The experiment of employing Italian submarines was also a failure. The craft were totally unsuited to operating confidently between Europe and the Far East, especially once the refuelling net had been removed. Valuable German U-boat officers and men were wasted operating these obsolescent submarines, and many died for their efforts.

Relations between the Germans and the Japanese were poor throughout the Second World War, and were based on a mutual distrust of each other's intentions and strategic plans that stretched back to before the war began. Germany and Japan pursued completely different strategic war aims and employed an invisible line across the Indian Ocean as the simplest means of dividing their two spheres of influence.

The Imperial Japanese Navy took virtually no active part in the transportation of *Yanagi* trade goods, with the Germans and Italians moving practically everything on their own. Only four Japanese submarines attempted the passage to occupied Europe, and Japanese naval activity in the Indian Ocean was limited to an attack on the Royal Navy in Madagascar and Ceylon, with virtually no raiding of commerce undertaken by Japanese submarines, which were tied to fleet cooperation.

The *Yanagi* trade highlights what could have been. Had the Germans designed and built dedicated cargo-carrying submarines in large numbers (freeing their U-boats for a concerted anti-commerce campaign in the Indian and Pacific Oceans), this would have greatly strengthened Germany's capacity to prolong the war and damage the Allies' ability to promulgate the war. If such an anti-commerce campaign could have been tied to close cooperation with Japanese submarines also redirected to attack merchant shipping throughout the region, the results could have been alarming for Churchill, Roosevelt and Stalin.

The Germans and Japanese were hampered by the Allies' total penetration of their naval codes, giving the British and Americans a tremendous advantage in defeating especially German attempts to conduct a duel trade and anti-commerce strategy in the Far East. The Germans, however, continued to believe that Enigma was secure until the end of the war.

Finally, had the Germans introduced the Type XXI Electro-boat into service much sooner, and in large numbers, the Allies would have been overwhelmed. Type XXI cargo-carrier, as proposed then rejected by the Germans, could have revolutionized the *Yanagi* trade, and would probably have resulted in a considerably larger delivery of raw materials to the Reich and a greater quantity of revolutionary military technology to the Japanese – with concomitant difficulties resulting from this for the Americans in the Pacific.

As an exercise in making 'what could have been' historical assertions, the intermittent *Yanagi* trade and German Far East U-boat operations provides us with a wealth of possibilities. As a practical exercise in the delivery of much-needed war materials between two geographically and emotionally distant allies, it is an example of 'too little, too late' – but it is also a tribute to the submariners who undertook epic voyages and who often paid the ultimate price, and a tribute to the code breakers, destroyer crews and pilots who determined to stop Germany and Japan from prolonging the war.

Notes

1. Franks, N. & Zimmerman, E., *U-Boat versus Aircraft*, Grub Street, London, 1998, p. 167.
2. *Ibid.*, p. 184.
3. This is one of the most famous spy incidents. During the Second World War, Richard Sorge, a handsome and debonair member of the Nazi Party, and employee at the German Embassy in Tokyo, passed on top secret information and files concerning Japan's government and military to the Soviet Union. Sorge was arrested and executed in November 1944, but felt he had done such a successful and thorough job that he stated shortly before his death: 'There are no more secrets in Japan left to steal!'

Appendix I

Japanese Seaplane Attack
on the United States

The states of the Pacific Northwest, such as Oregon and Washington, are covered with thick forest that stretches for hundreds of miles. These forests provided the Japanese with a plan to divert American men and resources away from other theatres of war, and to demoralize the American people by striking directly at mainland America. The Japanese attacks aimed to start huge forest fires throughout the Pacific Northwest, and the Japanese developed two methods to achieve this aim. First, seaplanes would be launched from Japanese submarines, the submarines surfacing undetected close to the Oregon coast. These seaplanes would deliver a small amount of incendiary bombs in an attempt to start a conflagration. Second, large balloons were designed and launched from mainland Japan, complex devices designed to cross the Pacific and release incendiary and anti-personnel bombs on America, code-named '*Fugo*' by the Japanese or 'windship weapons'.

The *I-25* was one of eleven Japanese submarines that had been modified to carry, launch and recover the two-seater Yokosuka E14Y1 floatplane (code-named 'Glen' by the Allies). A large submarine, with a crew numbering ninety-seven and a cruising range of 14,000 miles, the *I-25* had been constructed by Mitsubishi at Kobe, Japan, and completed in October 1941. Although she was positioned off Hawaii during the attack on Pearl Harbor on 7 December 1941, damage precluded her from launching her aircraft to conduct reconnaissance for the attack fleet. In order to carry an aircraft, the submarine had been modified with a waterproof hangar positioned in front of the conning tower. To fit the Glen, its wings and horizontal stabilizer were folded up, and the floats removed. The aircraft was launched by means of a compressed air catapult positioned on two rails running along the submarine. After completing a sortie, the pilot landed the Glen in the sea, taxied up to the submarine, and the aircraft and crew were recovered.

189

Lieutenant Nobuo Fujita of the Imperial Japanese Navy came up with the idea of utilizing the reconnaissance aircraft carried aboard the B-1 I-15 type submarines, of which the *I-25* was the sixth boat commissioned, to launch incendiary attacks upon mainland United States and the subsidiary target of the Panama Canal. The *I-25* was given the first mission, and Fujita would pilot the Glen. However, the *I-25* had already visited the shores of America once before and conducted attacks. On 27 May 1942 her Glen was launched on a reconnaissance flight over Kodiak Island, Alaska, preparatory to the Japanese invasion of the Aleutian Islands. So important was the photo-reconnaissance data derived from this sortie that another I-15 class submarine, the *I-26*, was on station with an empty hangar, ready to recover the *I-25*'s Glen should a problem arise. The *I-25* continued her mission, travelling down the American coast, attacking the freighter *Fort Camosun* with her deck gun off Washington on 20 June. On the night of 21 June, the *I-25* launched the first attack on mainland United States since the British in 1814, when she fired seventeen shells from her deck gun at Fort Stevens, a US Navy coastal defence installation on the north coast of Oregon. Some damage was inflicted on the baseball backstop and a major security alert was started. Fears grew that a Japanese invasion of Oregon was about to commence.

Having completed its patrol, the *I-25* then turned for Japan, arriving back in Yokosuka by 27 July. On 15 August 1942, the *I-25* departed Japan again and headed back to the United States, this time to initiate Lieutenant Fujita's audacious plan to bomb America. By early September the Japanese submarine had arrived in foul weather off the Port Orford Heads in Oregon. The seas were too heavy to launch the Glen until 9 September. Surfacing just before dawn, the crew of the *I-25* hastily assembled the aircraft and loaded incendiary bombs. Using the Cape Blanco lighthouse as a navigational beacon, Fujita and his crewman took off at sunrise and headed north-east until they reached the lighthouse, then turned south-east and covered a further 50 miles, releasing an incendiary bomb onto Mount Emily, in Siskiyou National Forest. Flying east for several miles, Fujita dropped his second bomb, and then headed back to the *I-25*. Unfortunately for Fujita, the bad weather, which had delayed the launch of his Glen on the submarine's arrival off the coast of America, had also saturated the forests – his two incendiary bombs proved ineffective. Fujita headed back towards the submarine at low-level, but as the aircraft and crew were being recovered from the Pacific, a lone US Army Air Corps A-29 bomber, on patrol from McChord Field at Tacoma, spotted the surfaced Japanese submarine and attacked. Completing recovery of the Glen as the American aircraft released its bombs, the *I-25*, with minor damage, dived to the bottom of the sea west of Port Orford.

A second sortie was planned and executed on the night of 29 September, the submarine surfacing just after midnight approximately 50 miles west of Cape Blanco. The American authorities along the Pacific coast enforced a strict blackout, but lighthouses remained in operation. Fujita took off and used the Cape Blanco lighthouse again as a navigation marker. He flew east for ninety minutes, released his two bombs, and then returned to the submarine. Fujita reported seeing flames on the ground, but the American authorities found no trace of the attack, although an unidentified aircraft was reported flying east of Port Orford.

The final two incendiary bombs were to remain on board the *I-25*, which reverted to attacking shipping along the American coast. On 4 October the *I-25* sank the freighter *Camden* off Coos Bay in southern Oregon, killing one sailor. She struck again on 6 October, sinking the tanker *Larry Doheny* off Cape Sebastian. This success cost the lives of two sailors and four US Navy crewmen manning deck guns on the merchant ship. A few days later the *I-25* departed the American coast for Japan, and on the way home sank the Soviet submarine *L-16* off Alaska, the Soviet Union not being at war with Japan until 1945. The captain of the *I-25* mistook the *L-16* for an American boat.

Appendix II

Commissioned Ranks of the *Kriegsmarine*

Kriegsmarine Rank	Royal Navy Equivalent
Grössadmiral	Admiral of the Fleet
Generaladmiral	Admiral (commanding a fleet)
Admiral	Admiral
Vizeadmiral	Vice Admiral
Konteradmiral	Rear Admiral
Kommodore	Commodore
Kapitän zür See	Captain
Fregattenkapitän	Commander
Korvettenkapitän	Lieutenant Commander
Kapitänleutnant	Lieutenant
Oberleutnant	Lieutenant
Leutnant zür See	Sub Lieutenant
Fahnrich	Midshipman

Commissioned ranks ending in '*der Reserve*' indicate a Naval Reserve commissioned officer.

Appendix III

Command Structure of the Southern Area U-Boats and Bases, March 1944 to May 1945

> **Admiral Paul Wennecker**
> Special Naval Attaché Tokyo
> (Responsible for U-boat supply)

> **Fregattenkapitän Wilhelm Dommes**
> Chief of Southern Area
> Headquarters: Penang, Malaya

Fregattenkapitän	*Kapitänleutnant*	*Korvettenkapitän*	*Kapitänleutnant*	*Korvettenkapitän*
W. Erhardt	**W. Grützmacher**	**Dr H. Kandeler**	**K. Hoppe**	**E-F Kentrat**
CO: Singapore	CO: Penang	CO: Djakarta	CO: Surabaya	CO: Kobe

'CO' is Commanding Officer

Appendix IV

Decorations and Awards available to the U-Boat Arm

The Iron Cross 2nd Class
The most commonly awarded German military decoration of the Second World War. The insignia consisted of a black and silver enamel iron cross, suspended from a red, white and black riband. Only the riband was worn – visible through the second button of the tunic.

The Iron Cross 1st Class
In the form of a black and enamel iron cross, the insignia was worn on the left breast pocket of the tunic. Normally awarded to U-boat

193

officers and senior non-commissioned officers (NCOs) on the successful completion of several war patrols, or for gallantry or meritorious service.

1939 Bar to the Iron Cross 1st and 2nd Class 1914
For those men who had served in the First World War, and been decorated with the Iron Cross 1st and/or 2nd Class, and who were subsequently awarded the Second World War versions of these decorations, a special bar in the form of a silver Nazi eagle was worn. The eagle was attached to the buttonhole black and white riband of the Iron Cross 2nd Class 1914, or worn directly above the Iron Cross 1st Class 1914 on the breast pocket of the tunic.

The Spanish Cross
A silver cross worn on the right breast pocket of the tunic. Awarded for outstanding service during the German intervention in the Spanish Civil War between 1936 and 1939. Only a few U-boatmen were awarded this decoration, with only a handful of U-boats conducting operations off the Spanish coast. Most recipients were *Kriegsmarine* officers and senior NCOs who served in cruisers or destroyers, and only later transferred to U-boats.

The German Cross
Awarded in two classes, Gold or Silver, the insignia was a large enamel cross with a central swastika motif. Instituted in 1940 as an intermediate award between the Iron Cross 1st Class and the Knights Cross of the Iron Cross, both classes were awarded sparingly for gallantry, meritorious or similarly noteworthy service or achievements. A total of 550 Gold awards were made to U-boatmen.

The War Merit Cross
A silver cross with swords passing through the centre of the insignia, this decoration was awarded in two classes. The lower class was worn on the left breast pocket, the higher class worn around the neck of the recipient in the same manner as the Knights Cross of the Iron Cross.

The Knights Cross of the Iron Cross
The pre-eminent German gallantry and meritorious service award of the Second World War, the insignia was an iron cross worn

around the neck from a red, white and black riband. Awarded only sparingly, U-boat recipients were either decorated personally by Hitler or by Dönitz. A total of 144 awards of the Knights Cross were made to officers and men of the U-boat service. There also existed three further insignia awarded to holders of the Knights Cross, denoting further awards of the medal:

- *Knights Cross of the Iron Cross with Oakleaves* – a small silver oakleaf cluster was worn attached above the iron cross element of the Knights Cross, denoting the award of a second Knights Cross: twenty-nine U-boat officers were so honoured.

- *Knights Cross of the Iron Cross with Oakleaves and Swords* – two small silver swords were fixed to the Oakleaves insignia denoting the award of three Knights Crosses: five U-boat officers attained this decoration.

- *Knights Cross of the Iron Cross with Oakleaves, Swords and Diamonds* – known as 'brilliants', a small cluster of diamonds was added to the Oakleaves cluster denoting the award of four Knights Crosses. Only two U-boat commanders ever attained this supreme decoration.

As well as decorations for gallantry and meritorious service, all ranks of U-boatmen could be awarded decorations concerning service, wounds received and other forms of merit:

U-boat War Badge 1939
Instituted in 1939, this oval shaped silver badge depicting a U-boat in the centre surmounted by a Nazi eagle, was awarded throughout the war to all U-boatmen who successfully completed two war patrols. It was worn on the left of the tunic, below the breast pocket.

U-boat Badge with Diamonds
This special award was awarded only twenty-nine times to U-boat officers, usually after they had received the Oakleaves to the Knights Cross of the Iron Cross. It was the same design as the U-boat War Badge 1939 with a studding of diamonds added to the insignia, and was worn in the same manner.

U-boat Front Clasp
Available in either Bronze or Silver, this decoration was awarded for distinguished or meritorious service, with many NCOs being awarded it from May 1944. The insignia was worn above the left breast pocket.

Merit Badge for Midget Forces
Awarded in a total of seven different grades depending on the number of midget submarine missions completed by the individual, this late war decoration was introduced to recognize meritorious service among the brave U-boatmen manning *Biber* and *Molch* midget submarines.

The Wound Badge
Identical to the Wound Badge 1914, the insignia took the form of an oval badge, with two crossed swords passing behind a German infantryman's helmet in profile. The Second World War version contained a Nazi swastika on the side of the helmet. It was awarded in three classes:

- *The Wound Badge in Black* – awarded for one or two injuries.

- *The Wound Badge in Silver* – awarded for three or four separate injuries.

- *The Wound Badge in Gold* – for five or six separate injuries.

Not all the badges were worn at once. If a man already had the Wound Badge in Black and was wounded for a third time, he would replace the insignia below his left breast pocket with the Wound Badge in Silver and so on.

Sources and Bibliography

Archives
National Archives, Public Record Office, Kew, London

ADM1/14955

FO10/7837

HW1/3168
HW1/3177
HW1/3651

HW12/615
HW12/646
HW12/653
HW12/748

HW18/192
HW18/371
HW18/375
HW18/376
HW18/379
HW18/387
HW18/394

Published Sources

Allan, I, *U-Boats under the Swastika*, Arco, New York, 1973.
Bagnasco, E., *Submarines of World War Two*, Naval Institute Press, Annapolis, 1977.

Blair, C., *Hitler's U-Boat War: The Hunted, 1942–1945*, Cassell & Co., London, 1998.

Boyd, C., *The Extraordinary Envoy: General Hiroshi Oshima and Diplomacy in the Third Reich, 1934–1939*, University Press of America,Washington DC, 1980.

Boyd, C., *Hitler's Japanese Confidant*, University of Kansas Press, Lawrence, 1993.

Boyd, C. & Yoshida, A., *The Japanese Submarine Force and World War II*, Naval Institute Press, Annapolis, 1995.

David, S., *Military Blunders*, Robinson Publishing Ltd, London, 1997.

Dönitz, K., *Memoirs: Ten Years and Twenty Days*, Greenhill Books, London, 1990.

Edwards, B., *Dönitz and the Wolf Packs*, Arms and Armour Press, London, 1996.

Elliot, P., *Allied Escort Ships of World War II*, Naval Institute Press, Annapolis, 1977.

Fahey, J., *The Ships and Aircraft of the U.S. Fleet*, Naval Institute Press, Annapolis, 1976.

Franks, N., *Search, Find and Kill: The RAF's U-Boat Successes in World War Two*, Grub Street, London, 1995.

Franks, N. & Zimmerman, E., *U-Boat versus Aircraft*, Grub Street, London, 1998.

Gannon, M., *Operation Drumbeat*, Harper & Row, New York, 1990.

Griffin, G., *An Operational Necessity*, G.P. Puttnam's Sons, New York, 1967.

Hashimoto, M., *Sunk: The Story of the Japanese Submarine Fleet, 1941–1945*, Henry Holt & Co., New York, 1954.

Kemp, P., *U-Boats Destroyed*, Arms and Armour Press, London, 1997.

Mallmann Showell, J., *The German Navy in World War Two*, Arms and Armour Press, London, 1979.

Mallmann Showell, J., *German Navy Handbook 1939–1945*, Sutton Publishing, Stroud, 1999.

Mallmann Showell, J., *U-Boats at War: Landings on Hostile Shores*, Naval Institute Press, Annapolis, 2000.

Martiessen, A. (Ed), *Führer Conferences on Naval Affairs*, The MacMillan Company, New York, 1948.

Miller, D., *U-Boats: History, Development and Equipment, 1914–1945*, Conway Maritime Press, London, 2000.

Mollo, A., *The Armed Forces of World War II*, MacDonald and Co. (Publishers) Ltd, London, 1981.

Niestle, A., *German U-boat Losses during World War II*, Greenhill, London, 1998.

Poolman, K., *Allied Escort Carriers of World War Two in Action*, Blandford Press, London, 1988.

Preston, A., *U-Boats*, Arms and Armour Press, London, 1978.

Rohwer, J., *Axis Submarine Successes, 1939–1945*, Naval Institute Press, Annapolis, 1983.

Sharpe, P., *U-Boat Fact File*, Midland Publishing, Earl Shilton, 1998.

Spector, R., *Eagle Against the Sun*, Free Press/Macmillan, New York, 1985.

Stern, R., *Battle Beneath the Waves: U-Boats at War*, Cassell & Co., London, 1999.

Stern, R., *Type VII U-Boats*, Arms and Armour Press, London, 1991.

Tarrant, V., *The Last Year of the Kriegsmarine: May '44–May '45*, Arms and Armour Press, London, 1994.

Vause, J., *U-Boat Ace: The Story of Wolfgang Lüth*, Naval Institute Press, Annapolis, 1990.

Vause, J., *Wolf: U-Boat Commanders in World War II*, Naval Institute Press, Annapolis, 1997.

Warren, A., *Singapore 1942: Britain's Greatest Defeat*, Hambledon and London, London, 2002.

Wynn, K., *U-Boat Operations of the Second World War: Volume 1: Career Histories, U1–U510*, Chatham, London, 1997.

Wynn, K., *U-Boat Operations of the Second World War: Volume 2: Career Histories, U511–UIT25*, Chatham, London, 1998.

Ugaki, M., *Fading Victory: The Diary of Admiral Matome Ugaki, 1941–1945*, University of Pittsburgh Press, Pittsburgh, 1991.

Ultra in the Atlantic: U-Boat Operations, National Security Agency, Washington DC, 1945.

Newspapers and Journals

Cryptology
New York Times
World War II
Proceedings
Navy Review

Index

205

207

Yamamoto, Admiral Isoroku, 57
Yanagi:
    Allied assessments of, 33–4
    blockade-runner routes, 36–9
    cessation of blockade-runner sailings
        1942, 34–5
    cessation of blockade-runner sailings
        1943, 43
    cessation of blockade-runner sailings
        1944, 47

Japanese lack confidence in, 33
    operation proposed, 21
    rubber importation to Germany, 30–1
    ships used, 31–2
Yokohama (Japan), 40, 42
Yokoi, Rear Admiral Tadao, 24, 66

Z-23, 130
Zenshiro, Admiral Hoshina, 59
ZH-1, 130